P9-DMC-055

*Attitude Psychology
and the Study of Public Opinion*

Attitude Psychology and the Study of Public Opinion

Forrest P. Chisman

The Pennsylvania State University Press
University Park and London

Library of Congress Cataloging in Publication Data

Chisman, Forrest P   1944–
    Attitude psychology and the study of public opinion.

    Bibliography: p. 241
    Includes index.
    1. Public opinion. 2. Public opinion polls.
3. Attitude (Psychology) 4. Public opinion—United
States. I. Title.
HM261.C524   301.15'4   76–10345
ISBN 0–271–01227–7

For My Parents

Contents

Acknowledgments

Anyone who is presenting his first book to the public has far more people to thank than he can remember, let alone cite. There are, however, some people who contributed more or less directly to the preparation of this book and whose help I would like to acknowledge. Thanks go first to my parents for their faith, inspiration, and support of all sorts over the years. Then I would like to thank Mrs. Marion Bressler and Mrs. Eleanor Coble, who stimulated in me an interest in scholarship and made much of my subsequent education possible. Thanks are also due to Sanford Lakoff and John Rodman, who showed me the fascination and value of the field of political theory and worked patiently with me to explore some of its elements. I owe special thanks to Donald Brown, who taught me how to deal with the challenge of developing an extended argument and who persevered with me through many difficult months. I also want to thank Sir D.N. Chester for having enough faith in me to make my graduate education possible and Brian Barry, who had enough understanding and patience to bear with my tentative efforts over many years. Special thanks are also due to my D.Phil. examiners, Marie Jahoda and the late John Plamenatz, who gave me invaluable guidance. In addition I would like to acknowledge the contributions of Lloyd Morrisett, who more than any other single individual helped make this book possible, and of Paul Lazarsfeld, John M. Russell, and Lou Cowan for their encouragement. Finally, my greatest thanks go to my loving wife, Anna, who supported and believed in me when this project seemed hopeless and who sacrificed greatly to make it a success. She is the heroine of this book.

Introduction

My purpose in this book is to criticize some of the basic assumptions that underlie certain influential modern studies of public opinion, principally *The American Voter* and other related work carried out at the University of Michigan's Survey Research Center, as well as V.O. Key's work, including *Public Opinion and American Democracy*. Such a critique is much needed and will be of value to all students of public opinion—from the college freshman to the advanced scholar. Over the past 30 years or so public opinion research has enjoyed a remarkable boom, and it has gained great importance in the fields of scholarship, commerce, and political affairs. The opinion researcher has become a distinctive breed of academic animal, and every university must have one. Large research centers have been established, societies have been formed, and specialized journals have been created. In short, public opinion research has taken on all the trappings of a well-developed intellectual discipline, and it now constitutes a large portion of the social sciences. Moreover, academic studies, with which I am primarily concerned, are only the tip of the iceberg. In American business, market research—by applying the insights of academicians—has become a large industry; also the public opinion researcher is playing an important and growing role in politics. Today, few candidates are willing to venture into the political wilds without having the way charted by pollsters, who draw on the insights of academic studies of public opinion, and these same pollsters find a market for their wares in the television and newspaper industries.

The studies I examine have played a seminal role in the booming field of public opinion research. Their techniques and major findings constitute the foundation upon which much subsequent work has been built. Because these studies are over 15 years old, at the very least their age and the magnitude of the discipline which they have helped establish suggest that it is time for a stocktaking. Has public opinion research been proceeding along the proper lines or has it been off target from the beginning? Are the classical studies in this field an adequate basis for public opinion research, and have they ever been? These are the questions I discuss. I confine myself, however, to the studies of political opinions conducted by major academic researchers; as a result, my answers will only be partial. Nevertheless, if I can show shortcomings in these seminal studies, I think I will have rendered a service to all forms of public opinion studies as well as to our everyday understanding of public opinion.

I approach the studies with which I am concerned by considering them a combination of two intellectual traditions: that of discussing public opinion, which has flourished in political theory since the late eighteenth century, and that of analyzing attitudes, which has been central to social psychology since the late nineteenth century.

The way students of politics generally discuss public opinion has its origin in the work of such nineteenth-century liberal democratic theorists as Tocqueville, J.S. Mill, and Bryce. These theorists understood public opinion as the views that private citizens hold about politics, and they usually described those views by saying that members of the general public like or dislike, approve or disapprove of, particular political objects, such as candidates for office or government policies. Nineteenth-century liberals considered public opinion important for two major reasons. First, they claimed that the political opinions held by each member of the general public motivate his voting choices and, as a result, public opinion determines the outcomes of elections. Second, they believed that the distribution of opinions about a given issue in the general public affects the decisions which members of government make regarding that issue. Although they did not believe that all political opinions perform these functions, empirically minded theorists in the nineteenth century suggested that it would be valuable to record and analyze those opinions which do motivate votes and to use information about public opinion to investigate how some opinions influence government decisions. Unfortunately, they lacked any reliable way of determining the opinions of large numbers of people, and their ability to draw conclusions about public opinion was therefore severely limited.

The authors of the contemporary studies with which I am concerned believe they can remedy this defect in nineteenth-century discussions of public opinion by making use of certain aspects of attitude psychology. Psychologists generally define attitudes as evaluative tendencies and often describe an individual's attitudes by saying that he or she tends to like or dislike, approve or disapprove of, certain objects. In addition, they have developed techniques for assigning attitudes to large numbers of people. The authors of the studies with which I am concerned believe that popular attitudes toward political objects are similar to the likes and dislikes which traditional public opinion theorists discussed in that they perform the same functions in the political process. They do not believe that all political attitudes perform these functions, just as traditional theorists did not believe that all political opinions do. Nevertheless, the authors claim that by using techniques borrowed from attitude psychologists to record public attitudes toward a variety of political objects, and by using theories and findings about politics and the psychological characteristics of attitudes to discriminate between different attitudes, they can determine which popular views motivate voting choices and explain how some attitudes affect government decisions.

These claims are the basis for many kinds of analysis found in attitude studies of public opinion. The authors of these studies use information about political attitudes to investigate such political institutions as parties and pressure groups, to explain the outcomes of particular elections, and to examine such recurrent political phenomena as nonvoting. In most of these analyses, they assume that the attitudes they record perform the functions which traditional theorists attributed to public opinion, and generally the validity of their conclusions depends on this assumption.

In short, the authors of the studies with which I am concerned combine attitude psychology with ideas about public opinion by attempting to use techniques, concepts, theories, and findings borrowed from attitude psychologists to record and analyze attitudes that perform the two major functions which traditional theorists attributed to public opinion. The chapters that follow are devoted mostly to examining whether the authors of attitude studies can, in fact, claim to record motives for votes and to explain how popular views influence government decisions. I believe it is important to examine these particular claims as opposed to other claims of attitude studies for three reasons. First, although many political scientists have examined the specific methods and findings of attitude studies of public opinion, there has been little consideration of the fundamental assumptions on which those methods and findings are based. By discussing the assumptions that attitude studies can identify motives for votes and explain the influence of public opinion on government decisions, I hope to illuminate an important and neglected aspect of those studies. Second, although all the analyses found in attitude studies of public opinion are not based on the claims that I consider, the authors of attitude studies regard the analyses based on those claims to be among their most important contributions to political science. For example, the authors of *The American Voter* believe that the conclusions they draw from evidence about motives for voting choices are their major accomplishments. Third, I think that the claims I examine are the most problematic parts of attitude studies of public opinion and thus deserve closer scrutiny than other parts of those studies.

This book is not, therefore, a comprehensive examination of attitude studies of public opinion. It focuses on a limited number of their basic assumptions. Because these assumptions are important and have not been discussed widely, however, I hope to perform a valuable service simply by explaining them. I also hope that my criticisms will contribute to a better general understanding of an important area of empirical political science.

Part I of this book is devoted to outlining the two intellectual traditions that the authors of attitude studies of public opinion attempt to combine. In Chapter 1 the ways in which traditional political theorists discussed public opinion are explained; in Chapter 2 certain ideas developed by attitude psychologists that have an important bearing on the studies with which I am concerned are reviewed; and in Chapter 3 the ways that authors of attitude studies of public opinion attempt to combine attitude psychology with traditional ideas about public opinion are detailed. These first three chapters set the background for a discussion of whether the authors of attitude studies can claim to both identify motives for votes and explain how popular views influence government decisions.

Part II is a discussion of the first of the two major claims made by the authors of attitude studies of public opinion: that they can identify motives for votes. I feel that at least one major effort in this direction, the analysis found in *The American Voter,* has not been successful, and the reasons for its failure are examined. In Chapter 4 the methods that the authors of *The American Voter* use to identify motives for votes and the reasons they believe those methods are successful are discussed. Their claim that they can identify motives for votes has two components: an argument that they can show that issue attitudes have no influence on voting choices and an argument that they can show that party preference is the major determinant of votes. Each of these arguments is assessed in separate chapters.

The first argument is criticized in Chapter 5. The authors of *The American Voter* do not examine all the attitudes that might influence partisan choices, and they fail to analyze issue attitudes as carefully as they should. They claim that issue attitudes cannot be motives for votes because those attitudes are not widely held, are not linked to perceptions of candidates and parties, and are influenced strongly by party preference. While I think there is some justification for these claims, in the end none of them is sufficient to foreclose the possibility that issue attitudes determine voting choices. The authors of *The American Voter* are derelict in not applying to issue attitudes the same techniques of analysis that they apply to other kinds of attitudes; they might have done this, and certain other studies which do apply those techniques suggest that issue attitudes do, in fact, influence votes. In addition, if studies of public opinion gave more attention to the salience of issue attitudes they might give those attitudes their rightful place among the major influences on voting choices.

Chapter 6 is addressed to the argument that the authors of *The American Voter* have shown that party preference has a stronger influence on voting choices than any other attitude and that it, in fact, determines most other attitudes related to voting. As I point out, there is other evidence that, when taken together with the evidence presented by *The American Voter,* can explain the durability of party preference and its relationship to other attitudes without compelling us to conclude that party preference is the major motive for votes. Almost every person receives information year after year which suggests that one party is more effective than the other in taking stands which are consistent with his or her issue attitudes, and this may be the reason party preference is such a durable attitude and why it is so closely linked to other attitudes.

Chapter 7 discusses the consequences, for an understanding of the American political system, of the fact that the authors of *The American Voter* are unable to identify motives for votes. In particular, there is ample ground for thinking of the average voter as more rational than portrayed by those authors; also, it may be that the political system is being stabilized by factors other than those considered by the authors. Chapter 7 also points out some of the positive contributions the authors of *The American Voter* have made to our understanding of politics, and a balanced assessment of their work is attempted.

In Chapter 8 some reasons for the shortcomings found in *The American Voter* are considered. These shortcomings arise from three mistaken assumptions: that (1) enduring attitudes must have a stronger influence on votes than other attitudes, (2) only widely held attitudes can have a major influence on the outcomes of elections, and (3) answers to free-response questions are expressions of a few broad policy attitudes. Why these assumptions are mistaken and how certain influences on the authors of *The American Voter,* as well as on the authors of other attitude studies, may have led them to adopt these assumptions are explained. In addition, it is shown that in their work the authors of *The American Voter* are perpetuating a serious shortcoming of traditional studies of public opinion: the assumption that a few widely held attitudes determine votes. The significance of this assumption for traditional studies of public opinion is discussed.

Part III investigates the second major claim made by the authors of attitude studies: that they can show how public opinion influences government decision making. In Chapter 9 the model of the influence of public opinion on government found in V.O. Key's work and accepted by most contemporary students of public opinion is outlined. Key believed that members of the public influence government by transmitting their views to members of government and by selecting members of government who have views similar to their own. Key's theory is contrasted with other theories of the influence of public opinion on government.

In Chapter 10 attitude studies of the influence of public opinion on government that follow Key's model are criticized. I try to show that they focus on the influence of the public on government to the neglect of the influence of government on the public; they neglect the role of political and social elites in bringing about correspondences between governmental and public views; and they do not consider adequately the processes by which limited sectors of the public influence public opinion. Key's attempts to show that his model of the influence of public opinion on government describes the processes by which public and governmental views become similar are examined. Also, a more ambitious attempt by Miller and Stokes to operationalize the same model is considered at greater length. In both cases, as I demonstrate, the evidence presented is inadequate to show that correspondences between views of the public and of government members are the result of the influence of the public on government, as opposed to the influence of government on the public. In addition, alternative ways in which the relationship between public opinion and government decision making might be assessed are suggested.

Chapter 11 considers the claims that the authors of attitude studies can identify the factors which lead to correspondences between government and public views and that their findings lead to a better general understanding of the American political system. In both cases, my criticisms in Chapter 10 force us to conclude that the authors of attitude studies have not been successful in their attempts and, in particular, they have adopted a model of the American political system which is far too restrictive. Alternative models of the relationship between public opinion and government that they might adopt are explored. Finally, the relationship of these shortcomings to traditional theories of the influence of public opinion on government is examined. I point out that contemporary researchers have perpetuated a shortcoming of traditional theories by focusing mainly on the influence of public opinion on government to the exclusion of other relationships between government and the public, and reasons why both traditional and contemporary studies may have adopted this point of view are examined.

In Part IV I summarize my argument and draw some general conclusions about attitude studies of public opinion.

Before beginning my discussion, it is important to note one more point about the form the discussion will take. This book is primarily a critique of public opinion research rather than an attempt to discover and interpret new evidence about public opinion. With only a few exceptions, I have no quarrel with the data collected by the authors of attitude studies of politics or with the methods used to gather them. Rather, I criticize the conclusions that are drawn from the data once they have been gathered. Consequently I base my critique almost entirely on the findings of the social scientists who conducted the research.

I. The Background

This section explores the constituents of attitude studies of public opinion and how they are combined. In Chapter 1 traditional definitions of "public opinion" are presented, and the importance of this concept to political theorists is considered. In Chapter 2 some of the fundamental assumptions of attitude psychology and their relevance to investigations of public opinion are discussed. Finally, Chapter 3 demonstrates how traditional ideas about public opinion are combined with ideas drawn from attitude psychology to form attitude studies of public opinion. This discussion is the background against which specific attitude studies are criticized in succeeding sections.

1. Public Opinion

In this chapter, what political theorists have traditionally meant by "public opinion" and why they have considered it important are explained. This task is not as difficult as it might seem because most theorists have agreed on these points. Therefore attention is focused on one "core" notion of public opinion that synthesizes the ideas found in many different studies of politics. My task in this chapter is also simplified because it is not necessary to delve into the remote past of political theory. Although there have been attempts to show that concepts equivalent to "public opinion" can be found in Greek, Roman, medieval, and Renaissance thought, the examples cited are few and the connotations of the concepts mentioned are usually uncertain.[1] Only since the late eighteenth century has "public opinion" become part of the working vocabulary of political theorists, so I am concerned almost exclusively with theorists who have written since that time.

I devote particular attention to liberal democratic theorists because the concept of "public opinion," throughout its brief history, has been closely associated with their work. Such liberal thinkers as Bentham, James Mill, and John Stuart Mill were the first political theorists to refer commonly to public opinion, and most extensive discussions of the concept have been conducted by such other liberals as Tocqueville, Bryce, and Lippmann. The core notion of public opinion I discuss is not theirs alone, however, although most of my references will be to their work. It is also the notion adopted by most conservative thinkers, such as Hegel and Burke.

The core notion of public opinion most theorists have adopted is, simply stated, that public opinion consists of the views held by members of the general public about subjects of widespread concern. These simple ideas of political theorists conceal a complex body of thought, however. To explain more precisely what political theorists over the last 200 years have meant by "public opinion," what they have meant by a "public" is considered. Then, what they have meant by "opinion" and what kinds of opinion they have generally been concerned with are discussed. Next, why political theorists have considered public opinion important and why late eighteenth- and early nineteenth-century liberal democratic theorists were the first to develop an interest in it are explained. Finally, how political theorists have investigated public opinion is outlined briefly.

A Public

There are three important characteristics of a "public" in discussions of public opinion: a public consists of people who do not hold government office; it consists of people who are all citizens of the same nation-state; and it consists of all or a large part of those citizens.

As to the first characteristic, all political theorists refer to a public as a group of individuals who do not hold government office. Public opinion is said to be the opinions of "the people" or "the citizens," as opposed to the opinions of "the government" or "the rulers." In recent years, students of politics have made this explicit in definitions of public opinion. For example, Leiserson writes of it as "the distribution of personal opinions on public objects in the population outside government." Earlier theorists generally imply, rather than explicitly state, that public opinion is held by people who do not hold government office. They write that public opinion is conveyed to, influences, or is critical of government. Bentham, for example, refers to public opinion as a "tribunal" that "judges" government. Presumably, if public opinion were the same as government opinion, theorists would not say that government was on the receiving end of it. Regardless of how they express themselves, however, most theorists seem to agree that public opinion is held by "outsiders," as Lippmann calls members of the public.[2]

As to the second characteristic, most discussions of public opinion focus on the opinions of "outsiders" who all live in the same nation-state. For example, Tocqueville, Bryce, and Lippmann write about American public opinion.[3] In fact, for reasons mentioned later, most nineteenth- and early twentieth-century discussions of public opinion deal with the United States, and the American public can in many ways be regarded as *the* public of public opinion theory. Nevertheless, Dicey and Bagehot are concerned primarily with English public opinion, and Tocqueville occasionally refers to French public opinion.[4] Sometimes, however, political theorists discuss public opinion more broadly. For example, J.S. Mill outlines certain characteristics he believes public opinion has in most democratic countries. Even when they do not focus on the public of a particular country, however, theorists generally refer to people who live in different countries as members of different publics. Thus Mill writes of "the English public" and "the American public."[5] For the most part, therefore, a public is defined in terms of nationality.

As to the third characteristic, when they discuss public opinion political theorists are generally concerned with the opinions of all or a large part of the people who live in a particular country. The word "mass" is frequently used to refer to the holders of public opinion. For instance, when discussing American public opinion, Tocqueville refers to the opinions of "the mass of the nation," and Bryce refers to the public as "the whole mass of the citizens." Thus public opinion does not consist of the opinions of only a few politically active people in a particular society. It consists, rather, of the opinions of what many theorists refer to as "the average man" or what Bryce refers to as "the man in the cars."[6]

When they discuss public opinion in England, however, Mill and Bagehot define the public in a slightly more restricted sense than most theorists define it. Mill writes that "those whose opinions go by the name of public opinion [are] in England, chiefly the middle class," and Bagehot writes that the working classes "contribute almost nothing to our corporate public opinion." Apparently what Mill and Bagehot mean is that the public consists of people who have the right to vote and play an active role in the political life of the country in other ways. In the passage quoted, Bagehot is discussing the facts that in his time members of the working classes could not vote and there were no working-class members of Parliament. Mill also seems to imply that the public consists of the politically enfranchised classes when he writes that whereas public opinion in England consists of middle-class opinion, in America it consists of the opinions of "the whole white population."[7] Regardless of exactly why they restrict the meaning of "the public," however, it is clear that Mill and Bagehot, like other theorists, think of it as a large group of people.[8] Moreover, it is clear that with regard to modern democratic states, their definition of public opinion is synonymous with the broader definitions offered by most political theorists. This is because in those states everyone outside government has the right to vote and participate in the political process in other ways.

Probably the best synonym for "the public" is, therefore, "the citizens." This is a good synonym if we believe that "the citizens" can mean either the politically enfranchised sector of a society or, simply, everyone in a society who does not hold government office. Political theorists have, of course, always been concerned with citizens in both of these senses; but it was not until the late eighteenth century that they began to discuss what "opinions" citizens held. To understand what novel contribution public opinion theorists have made to political thought, therefore, it is necessary to understand what they mean by "opinion."

Opinion

In discussions of public opinion, many words and phrases are used as synonyms for "opinion." Theorists often refer to opinions as "what the people think" about some matter or as their "views," "beliefs," "principles," "judgments," or "likes and dislikes." As this profusion of terms suggests, the word "opinion" has several connotations. Three of these are particularly important to political theorists.

First, when political theorists say that someone has an opinion, they sometimes mean that he regards something favorably or unfavorably. Thus Mill refers to opinions as "likes and dislikes," and Bryce refers to them as "sentiments of approval and disapproval."[9] Theorists generally understand opinions in this way when they discuss opinions about persons, certain kinds of private behavior (e.g., drinking or gambling), or political issues. In all three cases "likes and dislikes" or "approval and disapproval" can take many different forms. For example, Mill discusses Athenian public opinion toward Socrates.[10] In this case liking or disliking is believing that Socrates should be spared or put to death. In contrast, Bryce discusses public opinion about political candidates.[11] Here liking or disliking consists of believing that a candidate should or should not be elected. In the case of opinions about particular kinds of private behavior, saying that an individual dislikes a certain kind of behavior may mean that he resolves not to engage in it himself or thinks that some actions should be taken to prevent other people from engaging in it. Thus Mill refers to opinions that excessive drinking is bad and that people should be prevented from becoming alcoholics.[12] Finally, in the case of opinions about political issues, liking or disliking consists of adopting a particular point of view on an issue. It is the point of view that can be said to be liked or disliked. For example, theorists refer to opinions that government should pass a particular law or should simply pay attention to a particular problem.

Second, political theorists sometimes refer to an individual's political or religious principles as his "opinions." For example, Bryce writes of opinions about "what principles ought to be applied in governing" a country, and Mill refers to religious beliefs as "religious opinion."[13] These kinds of opinion might, of course, be referred to as likes or dislikes or sentiments of approval or disapproval, but this would generally sound odd. For example, we could say that a devout Christian "likes" or "approves of" the doctrine of the Holy Trinity, but we would probably say that he "accepts" or "believes" it. Likewise, we could say that someone "likes" or "approves of" justice or equality, but we would generally say that he "believes in" them. These distinctions may be due to the fact that we think of principles as more considered and more serious than likes or dislikes. Alternatively, we may think that principles generally are parts of broad belief systems, whereas likes and dislikes often are not. Whatever the reason for our distinctions between principles and likes or dislikes, however, traditional public opinion theorists often use the concept of "opinion" to bridge those distinctions.

Third, public opinion theorists occasionally refer to opinions as beliefs about matters of fact. For example, Lippmann defines opinions as "the pictures in our heads." As an illustration of these "pictures," he cites public beliefs that a certain government official issued orders which caused a particular international incident.[14] Here again, it does not make sense to refer to opinions as likes or dislikes or sentiments of approval or disapproval, although we may say that beliefs about matters of fact are often the basis for other kinds of opinion.

These are not the only ways in which public opinion theorists refer to opinions, but they are by far the most common. Generally, therefore, public opinion consists of the likes or dislikes, principles, or beliefs about matters of fact held by the citizens of a particular country. Strictly speaking, most political theorists would consider any public likes or dislikes, principles, or beliefs to be parts of public opinion. Usually, however, they focus on only certain sorts of opinion, and it is important to point out what such opinions are. For the purposes of convenience in this and other discussions that follow, opinions are referred to only as likes and dislikes, except where indicated. Most of what I say about likes and dislikes is true of principles and beliefs as well. I confine myself to likes and dislikes, however, because I am concerned primarily with them in future chapters and because it often requires awkward expressions to refer to all three sorts of opinion at once.

Political theorists are interested in public opinion primarily when all or most members of the public have an opinion about a particular subject, that is, they usually discuss opinions about subjects of widespread public concern. For example, Bryce writes that the opinions which interest him are formed when a few public leaders transmit their views to all or most members of the mass public. To take another example, Tocqueville is concerned primarily with opinions about what he calls "matters of state," and he writes that in America these opinions are held by "everyone, more or less." And Dicey writes that public opinion consists of opinions "held by the whole mass of the people."[15] Usually political theorists discuss public opinion about national political leaders or issues. They seem to believe that these are the subjects which most often arouse widespread concern. As mentioned earlier, however, they sometimes refer to public opinion about controversial private individuals or controversial kinds of private behavior.

Sometimes theorists refer to the opinions of only a small part of the general public. For example, Tocqueville refers to an anti-British riot in Baltimore as an example of public opinion in action, and Burke, when running for re-election, refers to the opinions of his constituents as "public opinion." Even in such cases, however, theorists are usually interested only in opinions about subjects of widespread national concern. Thus Tocqueville is interested in the anti-British riot because he believes it reflects widespread opinions about England, and Burke refers primarily to opinions that his constituents hold about national issues, such as foreign policy (although, admittedly, he is also interested in their opinions about himself). One of the few important discussions of local public opinion is Tocqueville's description of New England town meetings.[16] He does not, however, use the term "public opinion" to refer to the views expressed in those meetings. Like most theorists, he uses it to refer only to opinions about subjects of concern to all or most members of a national public.

One way to describe the interest of public opinion theorists in opinions about subjects of widespread concern is to say they are interested in the opinions of what has often been called "a public." The notion of a public was first articulated by certain late nineteenth-century sociologists, most notably Tarde and Christiansen, and it was adopted by some students of politics, most notably Lowell, Bentley, and Truman.[17] "A public" is simply any large group of people who do not interact with each other on a face-to-face basis, but who do have some common concerns. Thus a public can consist of everyone who opposes capital punishment or everyone who is worried about the state of the economy. Sociologists often say that groups of people share common concerns because they have the same socioeconomic characteristics, are exposed to the same media of mass communications, or hold the same values. Thus a public may sometimes be synonymous with a social class, the readers of a particular newspaper, or a religious group. Generally, however, publics are defined in terms of their concerns, rather than other characteristics. "A public," in Albig's words, is "an attention group."[18]

We can say, therefore, that political theorists who discuss public opinion are generally interested in the opinions that members of "*the* public" (the citizens of a state) hold when they form "*a* public" about some matter. In addition, there is a second important characteristic of the opinions they discuss. Most political theorists believe that public opinion is often fairly uniform; that is, they believe that only a few points of view on any given subject can be found in the public and, as a result, when a subject is of widespread concern each point of view is held by large numbers of people. For example, Bryce writes that public opinion consists of "two or three prejudices or aversions, two or three prepossessions for the leader of a party."[19] He admits that public opinion is sometimes more diverse, but Bryce and other theorists are generally interested in cases consisting of only a few widely held points of view. In particular, they devote most of their attention to cases in which a majority of the members of the public hold the same point of view about some matter.

In summary, therefore, most political theorists understand public opinion as the likes and dislikes, principles, and beliefs held by the citizens of a particular state, and they are interested particularly in opinions about subjects of concern to all or most citizens.

Why Bother about Public Opinion?

Most political theorists have been interested in public opinion because they have believed that widely held opinions and, in particular, majority opinions have powerful effects on the political and social systems of some countries and that those effects may often be harmful. The social effects of majority opinion are often called "the tyranny of the majority," and its political effects are often called "rule by public opinion." To understand why political theorists have been interested in public opinion, then, it is necessary to understand what they mean by "the tyranny of the majority" and "rule by public opinion" and why they consider these phenomena problematic.

The tyranny of the majority is a notion of greater interest to Tocqueville and J.S. Mill than to the other theorists mentioned.[20] By "the tyranny of the majority" they mean that whenever the majority of people in a society adopt the same opinions about some matter, deviant individuals are forced to adopt those opinions or at least act in accordance with them. Strictly speaking, Tocqueville and Mill believe that the tyranny of the majority occurs only in societies in which there are political institutions allowing for widespread popular participation in government; in which there is a fairly high degree of social and economic equality; in which most people have, for some reason, adopted the notion that everyone is more or less equally endowed with intellectual abilities; and in which most people have adopted the ethical principle that no one person's wishes are, in principle, more entitled to satisfaction by the state or society than any other person's wishes. Tocqueville and Mill believed that all these conditions generally develop at the same time in a society, that they are part of its overall "democratization." Tocqueville and Mill believed that the America of their time was fully democratic in this sense and that England and France were fast becoming democratic. Thus their conclusions about the tyranny of the majority apply mainly to these three countries. They believed, however, that there was a tendency for all countries to become democratic and that, as a result, the tyranny of the majority would become a factor in political and social life throughout the world.

In a democratic society, according to Tocqueville and Mill, the majority has four ways of forcing deviant individuals to adopt or act in accordance with its opinions:

1. It has a certain moral force. This is particularly true when the opinions held by members of the majority are about political or social issues, such as whether government should take a certain course of action or whether a certain sort of behavior should be permissible. In such cases a deviant individual may think that because everyone's

wishes should be considered equally valid, the wishes which should prevail should be those of the greatest number of people. Tocqueville and Mill conclude, perhaps wrongly, that because the individual believes that the majority's wishes should prevail, he is adopting them as his own.[21]

2. Believing that everyone is equal in intellect, the deviant individual may believe that the best test of whether a proposition is correct is whether most people agree with it. Thus he may believe that the opinions of the majority are bound to be wiser than his own and that he should therefore adopt them.

3. The majority has the power to compel obedience to its wishes by social sanctions and, at times, by physical force because, being more numerous than the deviants, the majority can always win a test of physical or social strength. Strictly speaking, this would only cause a deviant to behave in accordance with the wishes of the majority rather than adopt those wishes as his own; but Tocqueville and Mill suggest that when he becomes accustomed to acting in accordance with the wishes of the majority, an individual is likely to adopt those wishes sooner or later.

4. The majority can command the power of the state. As a result, members of the majority can always have their way in politics, and this may lead other people to adopt their opinions simply because there is no point in resisting them.

Tocqueville and Mill are troubled by the tyranny of the majority for several reasons. For one, they are troubled because it is an absolute power. The majority can compel deviants to do anything and, as a result, it can and does violate individual liberties. Second, Tocqueville and Mill believe that the opinions of the majority may not be superior in wisdom to the opinions of deviant individuals. Thus society may be steered down the wrong path. Third, they believe that by enforcing uniformity of opinion, the tyranny of the majority deadens the intellectual and moral faculties of all members of society, whether deviants or members of the majority. There is no longer discussion or debate, and people either lose the ability to make judgments for themselves or never develop it at all.

Tocqueville and Mill are, therefore, interested in the tyranny of the majority because they believe it is a new (in their day) and possibly harmful political phenomenon that may one day be widespread. While most other public opinion theorists also discuss the "tyranny of the majority," on the whole they are more interested in "rule by public opinion." Tocqueville and Mill share this interest, although it is more important in Tocqueville's than in Mill's work.

When they refer to "rule by public opinion," theorists mean that the decisions of government are often influenced strongly by the opinions of the general public; they believe this occurs in the same sort of society in which Tocqueville and Mill believe the tyranny of the majority occurs. Theorists write that in such societies governments act "in accordance with" public opinion. By this they mean that members of government do whatever the majority, or at least a large sector, of the public wants. Most nineteenth-century theorists believe that, like the tyranny of the majority, rule by public opinion occurs primarily in the United States and to a lesser extent in England and France. They also believe that, like the tyranny of the majority, it will accompany the worldwide growth of democracy.

It requires only a few examples to show how emphatically political theorists state that public opinion is a political force. Tocqueville writes (speaking of the United States) that "although the form of government is representative, it is evident that the opinions, the prejudices, the interests, and even the passions of the people are hindered by no permanent obstacle from exercising a permanent influence on the daily conduct of affairs." When he refers to the opinions of the people in this passage, Tocqueville means the opinions of the majority; he concludes, in the same section, "In the United States the majority governs."[22]

In "On Liberty," Mill also writes of rule by public opinion. He refers to "the ascendancy of public opinion in the state" and observes that in modern states, "the idea of resisting the will of the people . . . disappears from the minds of practical politicians." In addition, Mill refers to Tocqueville's analysis of the influence of majority opinion on government with approval.[23] In "On Liberty," however, Mill is more interested in the tyranny of the majority than in rule by public opinion.

Probably the most extensive discussion of the influence of public opinion on government is found in Bryce's work. Bryce writes that in the United States, "the will of the people acts directly and constantly on its key agents" and that "the rulers look constantly at the manifestations of current popular opinion . . . to shape their course in accordance with those manifestations." As a result, he says, the United States has "a form of government different from the representative system."[24] This is because "public opinion is constantly felt by these agents [the government] to be legally as well as practically the controlling authority" in the state.[25] Although he considers the tyranny of the majority briefly, almost all of Bryce's analysis of public opinion is taken up with discussion of the influence of majority opinion on government.

In explaining how rule by public opinion comes about, most theorists place great emphasis on the importance of elections. Tocqueville and Bryce say that rule by public opinion occurs in the United States because members of the public elect almost all their public officials and the terms of those officials are short. For example, Tocqueville writes that Americans decided that their officials should be elected *"directly* and for *very short* terms in order to subject them not only to the general convictions, but even to the daily passions of their constituents," and Bryce writes that "public opinion declares itself through elections."[26]

Elections, according to Bryce and Tocqueville, make government responsive to public opinion in two ways. For one, Bryce says that people "vote their opinions." In other words, they vote for candidates whose policies they favor and, as a result, they install officials who are likely to act in ways approved by public opinion. Bryce realizes, however, that in the United States, where there are only two parties, "voting for a man is an inadequate way of expressing one's views of policy because the candidate is sure to differ on one or more questions from those who belong to the party [the people who vote for him]." A more important way in which elections make government responsive to public opinion, according to Tocqueville and Bryce, is that members of government try to please members of the public to insure that they will be returned to office at the next election. Thus Bryce writes that "fear of popular displeasure to manifest itself at the next election is the most powerful of restraining influences" on government.[27]

Assuming that members of government have some motivation to act in accordance with public opinion, how do they know what members of the public want them to do? Tocqueville and Bryce explain that public opinion can be conveyed to government in many ways. For instance, American society contains a number of organized groups, ranging from trade associations to affinity groups to religious sects. Tocqueville and Bryce believe that the leaders of these groups often express the views of their members to government through public statements or direct contacts with political leaders. In addition, they say that Americans who share a particular point of view on a given issue often form special lobbying groups to express that point of view to government. Also, some citizens who are not members of organized groups may influence government officeholders through personal conversations, letter writing, or petition signing. Finally, they say that newspapers generally reflect popular views and that political parties may, in some cases, be mechanisms for large numbers of people to convey their opinions to government. On the whole, Tocqueville and Bryce believe that these sources of information keep government well apprised of public opinion about most issues.[28]

When they refer to rule by public opinion, therefore, traditional public opinion theorists have in mind two different but related processes. First, they believe that public opinion "rules" in the sense that the opinions held by members of the public influence their votes and, as a result, determine the selection of government personnel. Second, they believe that public opinion influences government decisions because members of government realize that they will be judged by their actions at election time, and this leads them to act in accordance with public wishes. These two processes are not always distinguished clearly in traditional theories. To identify them more clearly in the remainder of this chapter and in the chapters that follow, the first process is referred to as "the influence of public opinion on the outcomes of elections" and the second process is referred to as "rule by public opinion." This is in the spirit of traditional public opinion theorists because they usually refer to the influence of public opinion on government decisions when they write of "rule by public opinion."

Most political theorists have mixed feelings about rule by public opinion in the second sense just discussed. On the one hand, almost all theorists have something bad to say about it. Generally, they point out that members of the public are often ill informed about political issues, they have poor standards of judgment, their inclinations may be erratic, and majority factions may force government to further their own interests at the expense of the rights and the well-being of minorities. On the other hand, most theorists also see some good in rule by public opinion. Bryce and Tocqueville believe that it creates political stability, encourages respect for the law, exposes corruption, moderates the influence of many special interests, and effectively controls bureaucracy.[29]

Many theorists clearly think that the disadvantages of rule by public opinion outweigh its advantages. This is Mill's position in "On Liberty." Other theorists, such as Tocqueville and Lippmann, are more equivocal. They believe that rule by public opinion has serious flaws; but they also believe that it is inevitable in modern states and that, as a result, there is no point in wringing our hands about it. They see their task as pointing out both the strong and weak points of rule by public opinion, rather than drawing overall conclusions. Only Bryce, of all the theorists discussed, is an enthusiast for rule by public opinion. He writes that "the strongest point of the American system, the dominant fact of the situation, is the healthiness of public opinion and the control which it exerts."[30]

The major reason Bryce's conclusions about rule by public opinion differ from the conclusions of other theorists appears to be that he holds a somewhat higher estimate of the average citizen's ability to make wise choices about public policy. He writes that "the opinion of the whole nation . . . is the most competent authority to determine the ends of national policy."[31] In context, it is apparent that by "the ends of national policy" he means not only the broad directions of policy, but also decisions on particular issues. Bryce believes that members of the public are competent to make these decisions for several reasons. To begin with, they are constantly observing and discussing public affairs. In addition, because their numbers are great, their cumulative wisdom is also great. Finally, they are naturally more aware of their own needs and thus the needs of the nation than any small ruling group could be. For all these reasons Bryce concludes that despite its defects, rule by public opinion is an admirable system.

Bryce does have one serious concern about rule by public opinion, however. He observes, "The obvious weakness of government by opinion is the difficulty of ascertaining it."[32] He believes that although the mechanisms which transmit information about public opinion to government may be adequate for most purposes, the American political system could be improved if there were a more reliable way of determining what the people think about particular issues. Bryce does not suggest, however, what better mechanisms than the existing ones there might be.

Nineteenth- and early twentieth-century political theorists were, therefore, interested in the influence of public opinion on elections and in rule by public opinion because they believed that these were novel political phenomena having powerful and problematic effects on the political systems of some countries. Discussions of the effects of public opinion on government together with discussions of the tyranny of the majority constitute a large part of the literature on public opinion. Therefore it is fair to say that political theorists have been interested in public opinion primarily because they have been concerned (or, in Bryce's case, hopeful) about the effects of majority opinion on politics and society.

A Dream and a Nightmare

The preceding discussion explains the general reasons why public opinion has been of interest to political theorists, but it also raises two difficult questions about the history of the concept. First, if public opinion has such important effects on politics and society, why was it not a subject of interest to political theorists before the late eighteenth and early nineteenth centuries? Second, why should public opinion have been of greater interest to liberal democratic theorists than to other political theorists? Students of public opinion have generally answered the first question by citing major events in the political and social history of the late eighteenth and early nineteenth centuries. Lazarsfeld summarizes the views expressed in most discussions of the subject as follows: "It is generally agreed that it was the rise of the middle class, the spread of democratic institutions, the expansion of literacy, and the growth of mass media of communications which gave rise to the concern which was loosely called public opinion.''[33] Lazarsfeld's comments apply mainly to the development of interest in the influence of public opinion on elections and in rule by public opinion, rather than to the development of interest in the tyranny of the majority; but this is not problematic for my purposes here. For reasons explained in Chapter 3, the focus in most of this book is on the influence of public opinion on elections and rule by public opinion; as a result, attention in this section is devoted to the development of interest in these subjects.

According to the theory formulated by Lazarsfeld and others, there was no reason for political theorists to develop an interest in public opinion before the late eighteenth century because the mass public simply did not play a large role in the affairs of government. Ordinary citizens could not vote, and other channels of political influence were not open to them. Moreover, the means of mass communications were so primitive that members of the general public were not usually aware of the affairs of government; thus the formation of mass opinion about politics was impossible. Finally, great disparities of wealth and social conditions and deferential social customs reinforced the other factors that kept members of the public politically uninformed and inactive. In short, many of the conditions that traditional theorists believed necessary for the development of the influence of public opinion on elections and of rule by public opinion simply did not exist before the late eighteenth century.

Lazarsfeld and others believe that these conditions were created by a number of events, including the French and American revolutions, the full flowering of the industrial revolution, public agitation and political reforms in England, the development of better means of mass communications, and more widespread literacy. Lazarsfeld sees the growth of interest in public opinion among political theorists largely as a reaction to these events. Political theorists began discussing public opinion because they wished to explain the increasing influence of the general public on government. They first began discussing it in the late eighteenth and early nineteenth centuries because this was the first period in history during which the mass public exerted such an influence.

Although one can question some of the details of this theory, its general conclusions can be supported by a large body of evidence. Several authors have pointed out that it was, in fact, during the French Revolution that the concept of public opinion was first commonly used in discussions of politics.[34] Revolutionary pamphleteers referred to public opinion as the spirit of widespread popular support that had made the dramatic events in France possible, and subsequent discussions of the concept often focused on the Revolution. In addition, interest in public opinion first developed in Great Britain during the period of popular agitation surrounding the Reform Bill of 1832, and the concept was used primarily by those who believed that British political institutions should allow more popular participation. Moreover, as pointed out previously, most nineteenth-century discussions of public opinion were studies of its influence on government in America. The authors of these studies often mentioned that they were interested in this subject because they believed that America had novel political, social, and economic conditions which were highly democratic and would eventually spread to the rest of the world. Finally, in reading early discussions of public opinion, one cannot help being struck by the feeling of excitement and discovery expressed by the authors. This is an intangible quality in their work that cannot be reproduced by citing a few sentences. Nevertheless, one gets the impression that these authors felt that in public opinion they had discovered a new political and social phenomenon which was demanding their attention.

There are, therefore, good reasons for thinking that interest in public opinion first developed during the late eighteenth and early nineteenth centuries because the mass public first became an active force in politics then. This does not, however, explain why public opinion should have been a subject of greater interest to liberal democrats than to other political theorists of the time. Liberal democrats did take the lead in developing public opinion theory; as already pointed out, extensive discussions of public opinion were first conducted by Bentham, J.S. Mill, Tocqueville, and Bryce. Although definitions of liberalism may differ, certainly any viable definition must include the ideas of these theorists. Why was it that the men who were leaders of liberal democratic thought in the late eighteenth and early nineteenth centuries were also the first theorists to devote a great deal of attention to public opinion?

Students of public opinion have not attempted to answer this question. But an examination of some of the major characteristics of late eighteenth- and early nineteenth-century liberal democratic theory, particularly the way in which liberal democrats discussed popular participation in government, provides one possible answer: that public opinion was both a liberal dream and a liberal nightmare. Most commentators would probably agree that among the principles characteristic of liberal theory are a belief that the state should be an instrument by which citizens can further their private interests, a belief in elections and a broad popular franchise as means of achieving this, a belief in political equality, an atomistic view of society, and a belief in the dignity and worth of the individual and in the necessity of limiting the kinds of authority government and society can exert over him or her.[35] These beliefs are found in many parts of the work of liberal theorists and, taken together, account for much of the appeal of their thought.

Many of these principles are reflected in the distinctive way in which many late eighteenth- and nineteenth-century liberal theorists discussed popular participation in government. Their views about popular participation can be characterized by saying that they advocated popular sovereignty and were sometimes attracted by direct democracy. Generally, however, they advocated representative government; but they were uncertain about whether a representative should be a delegate of his constituents or whether he should exercise a substantial prerogative in decision making.

Within late eighteenth- and nineteenth-century liberal democratic thought about popular participation there were, therefore, several potentially conflicting strands. These strands are exemplified by the theory of popular participation that J.S. Mill advances in "Representative Government." Mill writes that "the ideally best form of government is that in which sovereignty or supreme controlling power is vested in the entire aggregate of the community."[36] From this he deduces that the best form of government would be one in which there is a great deal of popular participation, and at several points he seems to suggest that this would ideally be a government in which all citizens are members of a popular assembly.[37] Mill thinks that popular participation is important because he believes that the object of government is to serve the interests of members of the public and that each man is the best judge of his own interests. As a result, unless each man can defend the measures he considers best, his interests are likely to be damaged. Thus Mill writes that "the rights and interests of every or any person are only secure from being disregarded when the person is himself able, and habitually disposed, to stand up for them."[38]

Although he expresses some support for direct democracy, Mill believes that it would have several serious defects if applied in his time.[39] First, it is obviously impossible for the entire population of a modern nation-state to meet together in an assembly. Second, although each individual may be the best judge of his own interests, he is not necessarily the best judge of how those interests can be forwarded or reconciled with the interests of other people. Third, ordinary citizens may be insensitive to certain higher pleasures that Mill believes government should advance (such as studying philosophy or enjoying the fine arts) or certain fundamental human rights which he believes government should protect. For all those reasons, Mill rejects direct democracy and concludes that the representative system is the best feasible form of government.

Referring to his idea that government should be an instrument for the satisfaction of private interests, Mill states that the purpose of a representative assembly should be "to indicate wants, to be an organ for popular demands.'' Referring to his idea that each individual is the best judge of his own interests, he writes that members of the public should make every effort to "keep alive and active in [the mind of the representative] the influence of their sentiments."[40] Nevertheless, Mill also stipulates that representatives should be persons of above average wisdom and experience and should not be bound to act in accordance with the expressed wishes of their constituents.[41] Indeed, he suggests that their role is at least in part to educate the public and that constituents should not be too hasty to judge their representatives.[42] Rather, constituents should presume in favor of their representatives' views if there is any doubt and should review their overall performance rather than their actions on any particular issues at election time.

Thus, in his discussion of popular government, Mill attempts to balance several potentially conflicting principles. On the one hand, he believes that good government is possible only when each citizen can have a voice in the decisions of government. On the other hand, he believes that government decision makers should possess above average wisdom and political experience and should not be obliged to act in accordance with day-to-day popular wishes. In effect, Mill believes that members of the public should be both inside and outside government. In the sense that he expresses some support for the notion of popular assemblies and believes that the average citizen's expressions of his own interests should direct government affairs, Mill believes the public should be inside government. In the sense that he does not, in the end, believe that members of the public should exercise the formal decision-making power of government and in the sense that he believes members of government should not be subjected to overly strong public pressures, Mill believes the public should be outside government. Mill attempts to resolve these conflicts by devising a system of representative government. In this system members of the general public are outside government in that formal decisions are made by a group of men having unusual wisdom and experience who do not have to heed day-to-day public wishes. Members of the public are inside government in that they elect members of government and, generally, members of government are expected to try to satisfy public interests as expressed by members of the public.

It is beyond the scope of this book to pass judgment on whether Mill succeeded in resolving the conflicts mentioned. However, the problem of how to resolve them was not his alone. In their discussions of popular participation, many late eighteenth- and nineteenth-century liberal theorists attempted to devise political systems in which the public was at the same time inside and outside government. Moreover, most of these theorists ended up favoring some form of representative government.

If Mill's ideas about representative government have been characterized correctly and if these ideas, in their broad outlines, are typical of
the ideas that other late eighteenth- and nineteenth-century liberal democratic theorists held about popular participation in government, then it
should not be surprising that those theorists took such a strong interest
in public opinion. The influence of public opinion on government was
simultaneously a liberal dream and a liberal nightmare.

It was a dream for several reasons. To begin with, liberal democrats
could see public opinion as an expression of the interests of members of
the general public. Liberal democrats regarded public opinion as a collection of views on government policy held by all or most citizens of a
state. Each individual's political views supposedly reflect his perceptions of his own interests, and public opinion therefore reflects the public interest in the sense that many liberal democrats understood it. Moreover, liberal democrats referred to public opinion as the views of people
who do not hold government office. As a result, the influence of public
opinion on elections and rule by public opinion could be regarded as
processes by which members of the public, while outside government,
exercise a powerful control over its decisions. In addition, liberal democrats observed that these processes were facilitated by many of the
political and social conditions, such as a broad popular franchise and
social equality, which they advocated. Finally, they believed that the
influence of public opinion on government was strongest in a country
having a representative political system: the United States. In short, the
influence of public opinion on elections and rule by public opinion were
liberal dreams in that liberal democratic theorists could regard them as
processes by which actual operating political systems of the sort they
advocated were made responsive to the public interest as they understood it.

The influence of public opinion on government can be considered a
nightmare for liberal democrats in that it realized some of their greatest
fears about popular government. Liberals observed that in practice, rule
by public opinion created many of the problems they had warned overly
strong popular influence on government would create. Members of the
public often favored unwise measures and often disregarded fundamental human rights. As a result, majority opinion often did not reflect the
best interests of the public, and governments that acted in accordance
with majority opinion were not acting as instruments for furthering those
interests. Moreover, liberal theorists believed that rule by public opinion
and the influence of public opinion on elections were accompanied by
the tyranny of the majority. They saw in that phenomenon a new form of
political and social absolutism which could destroy civil liberties and
trample the dignity of the individual.

In short, the influence of public opinion on government touched some
of the major concerns of liberal democrats, and this is possibly one
reason they took such a great interest in it. On the one hand, they could
see the influence of public opinion on government and rule by public
opinion as processes that enabled representative government to function
as they believed it should function; they could also see countries in
which those processes operated as real-life examples of how political
systems should be constructed. On the other hand, liberals observed
that the influence of public opinion on elections and rule by public opinion had many of the effects which they feared most in popular government and which they hoped representative systems would mitigate. Liberal democratic theorists may have taken such a great interest in public
opinion and its effects, therefore, because they believed that those effects demonstrated both the strengths and possible weaknesses of the
kinds of political systems they advocated. By carefully studying public
opinion they could show the good effects of liberal ideals in operation
and come to understand ways of institutionalizing those ideals. Moreover, by criticizing rule by public opinion they could defend themselves
against any attacks on their theories that democratic excesses might
cause.

Support can be provided for this theory about why late eighteenth-
and nineteenth-century liberals had a strong interest in public opinion if
we contrast their attitude toward public opinion with that of conservative theorists and earlier liberals. Conservative theorists did not, of
course, advocate widespread popular participation in government. They
believed that members of the public should be outside government, not
that systems should be devised by which they could be both outside and
inside government. Thus conservatives would not be attracted strongly
by the influence of public opinion on elections and rule by public opinion
or greatly interested in their effects. They could simply show that these
processes are contrary to their principles without entering into pro-
longed discussions of how they operate. In fact, most discussions of
public opinion by conservative theorists are brief. Finding little attrac-
tion or intellectual interest in it, Burke and Hegel, for example, dismiss
public opinion with a few paragraphs, and many conservative theorists
barely mention it at all.[43] The conservative attitude toward public opinion is well summarized in Hamilton's brief riposte to Jefferson: "Your
people, sir, are a great beast."

Liberals before the late eighteenth century could also easily dismiss
public opinion because their theories did not include the particular elements found in the liberal theories I discussed earlier. Rousseau, for
example, brushes over public opinion and does not appear to consider it
important.[44] He believes that the purpose of government should be to

arrive at and implement "the general will."[45] Although ideas about what Rousseau means by "the general will" differ, he clearly believes that it was something different from what he called "the will of all."[46] According to Rousseau, "the will of all" is formed when each member of society considers his individual interest in isolation from the interests of other members of society and concludes that government should act in accordance with his interest. "The will of all" is a collection of all these individual perceptions of interest. It is similar to public opinion. Rousseau rejects the notion that "the will of all" should determine public policy, and he also rejects representative government.[47] According to him, "the general will" can be embodied in legislation only if all members of the public meet together and decide public affairs in an assembly.[48] In short, Rousseau believes that members of the public should be inside government (in the sense that he believes in direct democracy) rather than that systems should be devised by which they could be both outside and inside government. He says that representative government, in which members of the public attempt to influence affairs of state from outside government, can only lead to rule by "the will of all." Given Rousseau's ideas about the principles on which governments should be constructed, there was no reason for him to dwell on public opinion at length. Although he does not identify public opinion with "the will of all," it can be said that in his discussion of that concept he dismisses public opinion and devotes most of his attention to matters he considers more important.

All in all, there are reasons to believe that late eighteenth- and nineteenth-century liberals took a great interest in public opinion because, unlike conservative theorists or earlier liberals, they advocated representative systems in which members of the public would be at the same time inside and outside government. One can, of course, argue that it is wrong to explain the development of interest in public opinion solely in terms of certain characteristics of liberal democratic thought. Perhaps liberal democrats would not have paid much attention to public opinion and perhaps their theories would have taken different forms if the public had not exerted an increasingly greater influence on government during the late eighteenth and nineteenth centuries. Perhaps, too, if earlier liberals had lived during this period they would have taken an interest in public opinion. One can also argue, however, that liberal democratic thought may have been at least one factor that stimulated the growth of popular influence on government. All these points of view may have some validity, and it is unnecessary to insist that any one of them is correct. On balance, therefore, the fact that public opinion was first discussed extensively by Bentham, J.S. Mill, Tocqueville, and other contemporaneous theorists can probably be best explained as the result

of an interplay of historical events and certain characteristics of a particular school of liberal democratic thought.

How Public Opinion Was Analyzed

For purposes of discussion, traditional studies of public opinion can be
said to have three major components. First, those studies contain a
strong empirical component. It should be apparent from the discussion
in the section titled "Opinion" that traditional theorists believed it
important to find out what characteristics public opinion has and how it
influences government by observing the course of public affairs. Indeed, many of their books are travelers' reports of observations in
foreign lands. Admittedly this is empirical political science in the
crudest sense. The empirical component was based on some fairly
primitive research techniques, such as talking to a variety of citizens
about politics, reading newspapers, and observing such political phenomena as elections, public assemblies, and riots. Moreover, some
traditional discussions of public opinion have little or no empirical content. Nevertheless, many of the leading public opinion theorists of the
nineteenth century, such as Tocqueville and Bryce, were among the
most renowned students of politics in their time because they placed so
much emphasis on simply going out and observing how political systems operate and then reporting their findings. If empiricism is defined
in these broad terms, it can be said that traditional studies of public
opinion had a strong empirical component.

The second major component of traditional studies of public opinion is
what would today be called "empirical theory building." Traditional
public opinion theorists clearly considered it important to structure their
observations in terms of descriptive models of how certain parts of the
political process operate and what factors cause them to operate as they
do. Their observations on how rule by public opinion comes about are a
good example of this. Here we have a well-developed model of how a
variety of political, social, and economic conditions combine to create a
process in which public views are transmitted by certain elite elements
in society (journalists, party leaders, etc.) to members of government,
who are obliged to act in accordance with them.

The third major component of traditional public opinion theory is a
strong interest in how the observed or possible effects of public opinion
on government measure up to political ideals. As already pointed out,
traditional theorists were primarily interested in public opinion because
they were concerned about whether its effects on government were
beneficial. The standards of judgment they applied to public opinion
differed somewhat, and they did not all reach the same conclusions

about its effects. Nevertheless, evaluating those effects was one of their major endeavors.

Admittedly, the distinctions between these three components are somewhat artificial, and they are offered in no particular order of priority. The political values of traditional public opinion theorists may well have affected their empirical theory building and their observations, or the components may have affected each other in other ways. As a result, it is hard to say which component exercised the most influence over the directions of public opinion theory. Therefore, it is best to simply characterize traditional public opinion theory as a field of political studies that was remarkable in its own time because of its strong components of empirical observation and empirical theory building and because it combined these components with a strong interest in evaluating the effects of public opinion in terms of normative theories of politics.

Summary and a Forward Look

In this chapter I have explained what political theorists meant by public opinion, why they considered it important, and how they discussed it. My primary interest has been in the ideas of theorists who wrote before the twentieth century. This is not because twentieth-century students of politics have neglected public opinion. On the contrary, there has probably been more written on the subject each year over the past few decades than in the entire nineteenth century. My reason for focusing on the ideas of early theorists has been, rather, to set the background for a discussion of their influence on contemporary students of politics.

Contemporary studies of public opinion are also influenced by the ideas of attitude psychologists, however. Thus before discussing the influence of public opinion theory on contemporary studies, it is necessary to first discuss attitude psychology.

2. Attitude Psychology

In this chapter some of the major ideas of a school of psychology I call "attitude psychology" are outlined briefly. Attitude psychology is a difficult field to define because the study of attitudes can be seen simply as an interest of many different psychologists or as a unique discipline. On the one hand, behaviorists, cognitive theorists, and disciples of other major schools of psychology all have an interest in attitudes, and each of them approaches the subject differently. On the other hand, during this century there has been an increasing interest in the study of attitudes per se; theories, techniques, and findings that to a large extent can be discussed without reference to the ideas of other schools of psychology have been developed. Most studies of attitudes fall somewhere between these two poles. They are produced by psychologists whose primary interest is in the study of attitudes per se and who share certain ideas about attitudes. These psychologists generally approach the study of attitudes from the perspectives of other schools of psychology, however, and in many cases they use ideas from those schools to supplement the ideas they have in common. It is the body of ideas they have in common that I call "attitude psychology."

My purpose is not to conduct a comprehensive analysis of attitude psychology. My concern is only with those ideas about attitudes that play an important part in contemporary studies of public opinion. In the following section of this chapter the way psychologists define "attitudes" is considered. In the next section it is shown that they believe an individual's attitudes tend to be consistent with each other. The final section discusses how they record attitudes.

Attitudes

The concept of "attitude" is highly complex, and its meaning has varied over the years. Since the history of these different meanings has been traced thoroughly elsewhere, an explanation of what contemporary psychologists mean by "attitudes" is focused on here.[1] Psychologists generally define an attitude as an "enduring evaluative disposition" toward some object or class of objects and often say that attitudes are comprised of "cognitive, affective, and behavioral components" which are "consistent" with each other.[2] Many of these ideas are found in the brief definitions of attitudes listed in Figure 2.1, but others are found only in more extended discussions of attitude psychology. The best way to unravel these ideas is, first, to consider what psychologists mean when they refer to "consistent cognitive, affective, and behavioral components" of attitudes and, second, to consider what they mean when they say that attitudes are "enduring evaluative dispositions."

Donald Campbell: acquired behavioral dispositions.
Irving Sarnoff: a disposition to react favourably or unfavourably.
Arthur Cohen: evaluative predispositions.
E.S. Bogardus: a tendency to act toward or against some environmental factor.
Osgood, Suci, and Tannenbaum: a disposition toward certain classes of behavior.
Sherif and Cantril: a functional state of readiness.
Gordon W. Allport: a mental and neural state of readiness.
Isidor Chein: a disposition to evaluate certain objects, actions and situations in certain
    ways.
M. Brewster Smith: inferred dispositions of an individual around which his thoughts,
    feelings and action tendencies are organized to an object.
Theodore Newcomb: viewing with some degree of favour or disfavour.
Milton Rokeach: a relatively enduring organization of beliefs around an object or situation
    predisposing one to respond in some preferential manner.
Katz and Stotland: tendency or predisposition to evaluate.
E.E. Davis: an inferred factor within the individual which involves a tendency to perceive
    and react in a particular manner toward some aspect of his environment.
Smith, Bruner, and White: a predisposition to experience, to be motivated with respect to
    and to respond to a class of objects in a certain way.
Krech, Crutchfield, and Ballachey: a system of feelings, cognitions, and beliefs.
Secord and Backman: certain regularities of an individual's feelings, thoughts, and predis-
    positions to act toward some aspect of his environment.
Jahoda, Deutsch, and Cook: a more or less enduring predisposition to respond affectively
    toward a specified entity.
L.L. Thurstone: the sum total of a man's inclinations and feelings, prejudice or bias,
    preconceived notions, ideas, fears, threats, and convictions about a specified topic.
Thomas and Znanecki: a tendency to action.

Figure 2.1. Definitions of "Attitude"

Building an Attitude. Each of the three components of an attitude consists of a different way an individual can react to some object. Thus Sherif and Cantril write, "Attitudes always imply a subject-object relationship." The full range of attitude objects will be defined shortly, but for the moment it is sufficient to say that these objects may be people, inanimate objects, occurrences, or what Sherif and Cantril call "concepts," such as government policies or religious principles.[4]

When psychologists write of the "affective" component of an individual's attitude, they often mean his or her "feelings" toward an object. Feeling is a vague word, however, and the best way to understand what psychologists mean by the affective component is to consider what kinds of behavior they believe indicate an individual's feelings. Psychologists mention two behavioral manifestations of feelings. First, they sometimes mention physiological manifestations of emotion, such as rises in blood pressure and galvanic skin reflexes.[5] If an individual experiences these when he encounters an object, psychologists say he is displaying some feeling toward it. Second, psychologists sometimes refer to certain verbal expressions about an object as indications of an individual's feelings.[6] Roughly, psychologists would probably say that an individual expresses his feelings if he says that he evaluates the object in some way. For example, he might say that he likes, dislikes, approves, disapproves, or prefers the object. Thus, when they refer to the affective component of an individual's attitude, psychologists mean his feelings of liking or disliking and what might be called his "emotional" reactions to an object (as indicated by physiological measures).

By the "cognitive" component of an individual's attitude, most psychologists mean his knowledge or beliefs about a particular object. Here again, the kind of behavior they refer to is the best indication of what they mean. Psychologists generally say that an individual expresses his knowledge or beliefs about an object if he makes statements about the object which describe it in some way.[7] For example, an individual might say that an object has certain physical characteristics. If the object is a person, the individual holding the attitudes might say that the person took certain actions or that he has certain good or bad qualities, such as wisdom or dishonesty. A statement of belief may also be a statement about the future. For example, an individual might say he believes that a certain political candidate will be elected or that the candidate's policies would benefit the nation. Of course, many statements of knowledge or belief may indicate an individual's feelings in the sense of his likes and dislikes. This is particularly true when an individual attributes good or bad qualities to some object. Some psychologists say that beliefs of this sort are part of the affective component of attitudes; other psychologists say verbal expressions of evaluation are part of the cognitive component.[8] For the purposes of analysis, however, psychologists generally distinguish in some way between statements of belief, understood as an individual's statements attributing some characteristic to the attitude object or predicting something about it, and statements of feelings, understood as an individual's statements that he likes or dislikes the object. For my purposes, the precise rationale for this distinction, its philosophical validity, and the proper way to divide the three components are unimportant. It is important to realize, however, that psychologists make a distinction roughly along these lines.

The behavioral component of an individual's attitude consists of his overt, nonverbal actions toward an object. More precisely, psychologists generally say that it consists of his "action tendencies" toward an object.[9] We will be in a better position to see why psychologists refer to the behavioral component in this way after we have considered what, in general, they mean by "tendencies," or "dispositions." It is often awkward to refer to behavioral components as action tendencies, however. So for the time being the behavioral components of attitudes will be referred to as "actions" and "action tendencies" interchangeably, with the understanding that "action tendencies" is the proper term.

Holding an Attitude. The three components of attitudes are, therefore, an individual's feelings, beliefs, and action tendencies toward an object. Before we can see in what sense these are "components" of attitudes, we must consider what psychologists mean when they say that feelings, beliefs, and action tendencies are "consistent" with each other. Generally, they say that the three components of an individual's attitude are consistent if his beliefs and action tendencies toward an object reflect his feelings toward it in some way.[10] They say that an individual's beliefs reflect his feelings about an object if, assuming he has favorable feelings about the object, he also has favorable beliefs about it. For example, he may believe that a person he likes is wise, virtuous, or has good ideas about something. He may also hold certain beliefs about the object that are not, strictly speaking, favorable or unfavorable to it, but which support his favorable or unfavorable beliefs. For example, he may believe that a political candidate took an action he regards as wise, whereas other people may consider the action unwise. Psychologists say that an individual's actions can be considered consistent with his feelings if, again assuming that he has favorable feelings toward an object, he takes actions favorable to it. For example, he may kiss a girl, vote for a political candidate, or buy a particular brand of soap.

When psychologists say that an individual has an attitude they mean, in part, that his feelings, beliefs, and action tendencies are consistent in the sense just discussed.[11] Feelings, beliefs, and action tendencies are, therefore, components of attitudes in the sense that an individual's attitudes are comprised of these three different sorts of reaction to objects. When all three components reflect the same feelings about an object, we can think of them as three aspects of a single evaluative posture that an individual has toward the object. When psychologists say *that* an individual has an attitude, they mean that he or she has a posture of this sort toward some object; when they say *what* attitude he has, they describe the posture. I shall say that descriptions of evaluative postures are "assignments" of attitudes. Because the common characteristic of a group of feelings, beliefs, and action tendencies which leads psychologists to consider them components of an attitude is that they all display the same evaluation, psychologist generally assign attitudes by indicating what evaluation all three components display;[12] that is, they generally assign attitudes by saying what the affective component of an individual's attitude is.[13] They say, for example, that he has a "favorable" attitude toward a politician or that he "likes French cooking." As a result, psychologists generally do not describe all three components when they assign attitudes. Nevertheless, they regard attitudes as evaluative postures that include beliefs and action tendencies as well as feelings.

We can now see what the full range of attitude objects is. Anything toward which an individual has a consistent evaluative posture can be considered the object of an attitude. Thus we can say that individuals have attitudes toward the president of the United States, seventeenth-century music, winter sports, or abortion, as long as in some sense they have consistent feelings, beliefs, and action tendencies toward those objects.

This is not all that psychologists mean when they say an individual has an attitude, however. They also say, as already mentioned, that attitudes are "enduring dispositions," or "tendencies." By this they mean three things. First, when psychologists say that an individual has an attitude, they mean not only that all three components of his evaluative posture are consistent with each other at one point in time, but also that they are consistent with each other and display the same evaluative posture over a period of time; that is, if we can say that an individual likes something today, we will be able to say that he or she likes it next week or next month. Psychologists do not put a specific time limit on how long an individual's attitudes last. They simply say that attitudes are "relatively enduring" feelings, beliefs, and action tendencies;[14] that is, attitudes are not simply momentary responses toward some object. Psychologists also generally distinguish between an individual's attitudes and his expressions of those attitudes. When they say that an individual has an attitude they mean he will have the same feelings and beliefs about an object and tend to perform the same sorts of actions toward it over a period of time. When they say that he expresses his attitude, they mean that he expresses his feelings or beliefs about the object or that he takes actions toward it on particular occasions.

The second thing psychologists mean when they say that attitudes are enduring dispositions is that although an individual's expressions of evaluation are generally consistent with his attitudes, when they assign an attitude to an individual they are not simply describing the evaluations of an object which he has expressed over a period of time. All psychologists would probably agree that when they assign an attitude to an individual they are at least predicting from observations of his behavior that he will display certain sorts of behavior in the future.[15] In addition some psychologists, following Allport, define attitudes as "states of readiness" to respond, or they refer to attitudes as tendencies "underlying" an individual's expressions of evaluative behavior.[16] In these cases, psychologists seem to be imputing a psychological continuum of some sort to the person to whom they assign the attitude.

What psychologists mean when they refer to continuous psychological "states" and whether they are well advised to refer to them are, of course, some of the most troublesome questions about the philosophy of science. Although it is beyond the scope of this work to discuss these questions fully, it is important to know that there are two major views about the sense in which attitudes are psychological states.[17] First, when some behavioral psychologists say an individual has an attitude, they are making a prediction about his behavior and nothing more.[18] When these psychologists say an individual is in a "state of readiness," they mean only that there is a statistical probability that he will engage in certain sorts of behavior over a certain period of time.

The second point of view about the sense in which attitudes are psychological states is held by certain other psychologists, such as Sherif and Cantril, and Smith, Bruner, and White, who are not members of the behaviorist school.[19] They say that when an individual has an attitude, various aspects of his personality, such as his goals, values, and wants, are organized together with his beliefs, feelings, and action tendencies in some stable configuration. They often suggest that this configuration "causes" or "determines" behavior. Thus they regard goals, values, and so on, as in some sense psychological "entities" that have motivational power. Psychologists who adopt this point of view generally say that when they assign attitudes they are not only describing and predicting behavior, but are also identifying stable configurations of psychological entities.

Campbell gives two reasons these two points of view are not really conflicting: (1) behaviorists generally explain certain characteristics of an individual's attitudes (e.g., how they are formed and why they change) in terms of certain of his other psychological traits, and (2) other psychologists generally accept evidence that an individual's evaluative behavior can be predicted as necessary and sufficient grounds for assigning attitudes to him.[20] Campbell says that all psychologists think of attitudes as analogous to "templates" that people carry around in their heads. Through these templates an individual's drives are channeled in certain object-specific directions. It is not necessary to decide here whether Campbell's reconciliation is successful or whether one point of view or the other is more correct. Both points of view are accepted in the discussion that follows.

The third thing psychologists mean when they refer to attitudes as tendencies or dispositions is that the cognitive and behavioral components "tend" to be consistent with the affective component, not that they are always consistent. It is easiest to understand what they mean when they say these components tend to be consistent by considering the cognitive and behavioral components separately.

Psychologists often find that individuals to whom they assign attitudes have beliefs inconsistent with their feelings, but they also find that these individuals generally have more beliefs that are consistent rather than inconsistent with their feelings. Moreover, they think the latter is true because the individuals to whom they assign attitudes often "select" beliefs that are consistent with their feelings about attitude objects.[21] In other words, psychologists frequently find that if, for example, an individual has a favorable attitude toward an object, he will expose himself to favorable information about it more often than to unfavorable information ("selective exposure"); he will also notice ("selective perception") and remember ("selective retention") its good qualities and the favorable things other people say about it more often than its bad qualities and the unfavorable things people say. In addition, psychologists expect that an individual who has an attitude will often be more likely to believe information about an object that is consistent with his feelings toward it than information which is inconsistent with those feelings; also, he will sometimes invent rationalizations to support his feelings. Finally, psychologists have observed that individuals who accept beliefs inconsistent with their feelings will often, after a period of time, change or forget those beliefs. If, however, an individual maintains a number of beliefs inconsistent with his feelings, psychologists expect that his feelings will change and he will form a new attitude in which his beliefs and feelings are consistent.[22]

Psychologists do not expect that individuals to whom they assign attitudes will always maintain consistent beliefs and feelings in the ways discussed here, but they believe that consistency will be maintained frequently enough for them to say that the cognitive and affective components of attitudes "tend" to be consistent. By this they mean either that there is a high statistical probability that an individual to whom they assign an attitude will have consistent beliefs and feelings, or that some "force" which maintains consistency in some, but not all, beliefs and feelings is part of the psychological makeup of that individual.

Psychologists have found that the behavioral components of attitudes are more often inconsistent with the cognitive and affective components than the cognitive and affective components are with each other.[23] In fact, this inconsistency has been observed so frequently that it has been suggested that action tendencies should not be regarded as components of attitudes at all. Psychologists have observed, however, that in the case of some kinds of attitudes (e.g., attitudes toward commercial products and some political attitudes) all three components are frequently consistent.[24] Moreover, they have found that sometimes when an individual is forced to take actions inconsistent with his beliefs and feelings, those beliefs and feelings will change to become consistent with his actions.[25] They believe, therefore, that all three components of certain kinds of attitudes in certain situations "tend" to be consistent. Psychologists refer to a "tendency" for all three components to be consistent in the same sense that they refer to a tendency for beliefs and feelings to be consistent. In other words, they either mean that for certain attitudes in certain situations there is a statistical probability that all three components will be consistent, or they mean that if an individual holds an attitude, some psychological "force" makes the beliefs, feelings, and action tendencies of all or most of his attitudes consistent.

Implications. Psychologists refer to attitudes as evaluative dispositions, or tendencies, therefore, because they wish to indicate that they are concerned with beliefs, feelings, and action tendencies which persist over time and that the three components of attitudes are frequently, but not always, consistent. The notion that attitudes are dispositions or tendencies in this sense has two important implications.

The first implication is that because psychologists believe that individuals to whom they assign attitudes have the same evaluative tendencies over a period of time, they also believe that those individuals have the same evaluative tendencies in many different situations.[26] "Situation" means any characteristics of an attitude object, objects related to it, or circumstances in which it is encountered that may vary over time. Psychologists have found that many situational factors may affect an individual's evaluative behavior. The expectations of other people, their status, and the way they present different points of view about an object have all been found to be important in this respect. Over a period of time an individual will probably encounter most objects in different situations, and if he is influenced strongly by situational factors, his behavior will vary over time. When they say an individual has an attitude, however, psychologists mean that his behavior will generally be consistent. This means that characteristics of the situations in which he encounters the attitude object generally do not determine his behavior. We might say that psychologists believe that the behavior of an individual who has an attitude is determined by some psychological factor which he "brings to" different situations, rather than by some characteristic of those situations.

Situational factors do, however, play an important role in several respects in discussions of attitudes. To begin with, psychologists generally regard attitudes as acquired dispositions, and they believe that an individual who holds an attitude must have been influenced to adopt it by situational as well as psychological factors at some point in time.[27] In addition, situational factors may influence the way an individual expresses an attitude.[28] For example, in a situation in which most people approve of an object, an individual with an unfavorable attitude toward it may not voice his disapproval as strongly as he would in other situations. The behavior of individuals who hold attitudes is, therefore, often considered a resultant of both situational and psychological factors. Finally, psychologists believe that situational factors often cause people to whom they have assigned attitudes to behave inconsistently and that situational factors also cause inconsistencies between attitude components. In particular, many psychologists believe that the major reason the behavioral components of attitudes are often inconsistent with the cognitive and affective components may be that actions are more strongly influenced by situational factors than beliefs and feelings are.[29] Nevertheless, most psychologists believe that once an individual has acquired an attitude, situational factors alone generally will not determine his behavior.

The second important implication of the notion that attitudes are dispositions or tendencies is that we can now see why psychologists refer to the behavioral components of attitudes as "action tendencies," whereas they refer to the cognitive and affective components as "beliefs" and "feelings" rather than "belief tendencies" and "feeling tendencies." This is probably easiest to understand if we regard attitudes and their components as persistent psychological states or entities. Thus when psychologists say that an individual has certain beliefs, feelings, or action tendencies they mean that some psychological entities or states corresponding to each component are parts of his psychological makeup over a period of time. These entities or states determine his expressions of belief and feeling and his actions; but, unlike those expressions and actions, they are in some sense continuous characteristics of the individual. For example, we can say that an individual is in a state of readiness to express a belief all of the time, but he actually expresses that belief only on certain occasions. In ordinary language we often say that an individual "has" or "holds" beliefs or feelings over a period of time, and we often distinguish his beliefs and feelings from his expressions of belief and feeling. For example, we might say that an individual disliked the Democratic party for many years but that he expressed his dislike to his friends only on certain occasions. It would, therefore, be superfluous for psychologists to refer to the cognitive and affective components of attitudes as "belief tendencies" or "feeling tendencies" because the words "beliefs" and "feelings" convey adequately the notion of continuous psychological states. However, there is no one word, such as "belief" or "feeling," that conveys the notion of a continuous tendency to act. Certainly, the word "action" does not convey that notion. We usually use it to refer to discrete instances of behavior rather than behavioral tendencies. As a result, psychologists generally refer to the behavioral component of an individual's attitude as his "action tendency" because no one word, such as "action," conveys the notion of a readiness to act. In contrast, they refer to the cognitive and affective components of his attitudes as "beliefs" and "feelings" rather than "belief tendencies" or "feeling tendencies" because the words "belief" and "feeling" are commonly used to denote continuous psychological states.

If we think of assignments of attitudes and their components (by which I mean statements that an individual has a certain attitude or component) as predictions of behavior, the reasons for referring to the behavioral components of attitudes as "action tendencies" rather than "actions" are somewhat similar. Psychologists who adopt this point of view, like other attitude psychologists, regard all three attitude components as tendencies. When they say that an individual has a tendency (whether a belief, feeling, or action tendency), they are predicting that his behavior toward an object will be consistent over a period of time. When they say that he expresses a belief or feeling or takes certain actions, however, they are describing discrete instances of his behavior. As a result, they refer to the behavioral components of attitudes as "action tendencies" rather than "actions" to suggest that when they say someone has an attitude they are, in part, predicting that his overt, nonverbal behavior will be consistent; they are not simply describing discrete instances of that behavior.

Moreover, psychologists who think of assignments of attitudes as predictions of behavior refer to the cognitive and affective components of attitudes as "beliefs" and "feelings" rather than "tendencies to express beliefs" or "tendencies to express feelings," because, ordinarily, when it is said that an individual has a belief or certain feelings about some matter, the implication often is that his expression of belief and feelings about that matter will be consistent in the future. For example, if someone says that an individual "believes that the population of China is 800,000,000 people," it would normally be expected that whenever he cites the population of China, he will say that it is 800,000,000 people. When we say that someone has a belief or feeling we may not only be making a prediction about his behavior, but in some cases we are doing so in part; this is seemingly sufficient reason for psychologists to refer to the cognitive and affective components of attitudes as beliefs and feelings. There is, however, no one word, such as "belief" or "feeling," that conveys the notion that individuals will tend to take consistent actions in the future; psychologists therefore refer to the behavioral components of attitudes as "action tendencies."

Another Kind of Attitude.   An individual's attitude toward an object is, therefore, his tendency to have the same evaluative posture, comprised of consistent beliefs, feelings, and action tendencies, toward the object over a period of time. The way in which psychologists believe these components of attitudes are related to each other after an individual has formed an attitude toward an object has been discussed. It is also important to realize, however, that psychologists believe individuals do not always acquire beliefs, feelings, or action tendencies toward an object at the same time. They have found that sometimes an individual acquires certain beliefs and only subsequently acquires feelings or action tendencies consistent with them. Sometimes he develops feelings of liking or disliking for an object without knowing much about it, and it is only later that he adopts a number of beliefs to support his feelings. Finally, psychologists have found that when an individual is forced to take favorable or unfavorable actions toward an object, he may later develop beliefs and feelings consistent with those actions.[30]

Because they believe that the three components of attitudes may be acquired separately, psychologists say that an individual may hold "partially formed attitudes," meaning attitudes consisting of only two components. The partially formed attitudes that psychologists most frequently encounter are those having cognitive and affective components, but no behavioral component;[31] that is, individuals may have consistent beliefs and feelings but inconsistent action tendencies toward an object. Psychologists rarely, however, find that individuals have consistent beliefs and action tendencies but inconsistent feelings, or consistent feelings and action tendencies but inconsistent beliefs, toward an object. Partially formed attitudes may endure for a long time and may never develop into full three-component attitudes. They have many of the characteristics of fully developed attitudes, but they also have special characteristics of their own. These special characteristics are not of importance here, however, so it will be assumed that all attitudes have the characteristics discussed in this section.

Consistency of Attitudes

The preceding section showed how psychologists define attitudes. This is the first aspect of attitude psychology that has an influence on contemporary studies of public opinion. The second aspect is the notion that an individual's attitudes toward different objects tend to be consistent with each other. This notion, often called the "homeostatic principle," is accepted by many attitude psychologists, such as Festinger, Heider, Osgood, Cohen, and Sherif. It is the basis for many of the theories they have developed about how attitudes are formed and how they change.[32] Obviously the homeostatic principle complements the ideas about how the components of attitudes are related to each other. Just as psychologists believe that the components of any one attitude tend to be consistent, they believe that different attitudes also tend to be consistent. Although most psychologists would probably agree on what they mean by consistency among attitude components, however, they disagree on what they mean by consistency among different attitudes. Two examples will illustrate different points of view on this subject.

Festinger refers to consistency and inconsistency among attitudes as "assonance" and "dissonance" among different "cognitions."[33] By cognitions Festinger means, primarily, beliefs; but he often refers to cognitions as feelings as well, and he sometimes refers to an individual's "cognition" that he has taken or should take some action. For my purposes, it is acceptable to regard "cognitions" as a blanket term covering all three attitude components. Festinger writes that two cognitions are dissonant if "one follows from the obverse of the other."[34] He says that dissonance can be "logical," "cultural," or "learned."[35] By logically dissonant cognitions, he means beliefs that are the direct opposite of each other. For example, beliefs that an event occurred and did not occur are logically dissonant.

By culturally dissonant cognitions, Festinger means at least two things. First, he means beliefs, feelings, and actions that are in some sense inconsistent because of the way society operates. For example, it would be inconsistent for me to believe that I have only $200 in the bank and that I can buy a Cadillac. Second, Festinger believes that in any society there are values and norms that lead most people to regard some beliefs, feelings, and actions as inconsistent. For example, most people would regard it as inconsistent for me to dislike a presidential candidate and still vote for him because they believe that the purpose of voting is to elect the best candidate. Festinger regards cognitions that are inconsistent in terms of the values and norms of a society as well as cognitions that are inconsistent because of the way society functions as "culturally dissonant."

By learned dissonance, Festinger means inconsistencies among everyday beliefs, feelings, and actions that are unrelated to widely shared values and norms or other kinds of rules which govern the operation of a particular society. For example, the belief that I can run my car and the belief that its gasoline tank is empty are dissonant in this sense.

Festinger believes that both the components of a given attitude and the components of different attitudes can be regarded as assonant or dissonant with each other. He states that in either case people tend to avoid or reduce dissonance between their feelings, belief, and actions.[36] There are a number of ways they can do this. For example, they may simply refrain from adopting beliefs, developing feelings, or taking actions that are inconsistent with the components of the attitudes they already hold. Alternatively, if they realize that some of the components of their existing attitudes are inconsistent, they may change the inconsistent components in some way. In either case, their desire to avoid or reduce dissonance will have an effect on the kinds of attitudes they hold. If one component of my attitude toward a presidential candidate is a belief that his economic policy is wise, I will probably not adopt a favorable attitude toward an economist who opposes that policy. Alternatively, if for some reason I adopt a favorable attitude toward the economist, I may change my belief about the candidate's policy and subsequently change my attitude toward the candidate.

Festinger believes that dissonance within a particular attitude is most likely to be reduced if the attitude contains a number of dissonant cognitions and if the individual attaches great "importance" to those cognitions.[37] Similarly, he believes that individuals will be most likely to reduce dissonance between attitudes if each attitude contains a number of cognitions that are dissonant with the cognitions in other attitudes and if the individual considers those cognitions important. Festinger has worked out complex rules for predicting how dissonance will be reduced, but these are not important here. It is important only to realize what he means by logical, cultural, and learned dissonance and to understand that he believes individuals will tend to reduce dissonance of all three sorts.

Heider refers to consistent and inconsistent attitudes as "balanced" and "unbalanced" rather than "assonant" and "dissonant."[38] Unlike Festinger, he is concerned primarily with the way an individual's attitudes toward people are related to his attitudes toward other objects that in some way are associated with those people. He conceptualizes the relationship between these two sorts of attitude by saying that they can be thought of as triangular structures (see Figure 2.2). The corners of the triangles are occupied by the person who holds the attitude, o, another person, p, and an object, x. All three elements are linked by evaluative bonds. These can be bonds of liking (which Heider indicates by a + sign) or bonds of disliking (which Heider indicates by a − sign). The person, o, can either like or dislike p and x, and p can either like or dislike x. Heider believes that an individual will tend to arrange relationships of this sort so that all the evaluative bonds have the same sign (i.e., they are all relationships of liking or of disliking), or so that two of the signs are negative and one is positive. Heider says that in these cases an individual's attitudes will be in a "balanced state," which he defines as "a harmonious state, one in which the entities comprising the state and the feelings about them fit together without stress."[39]

BALANCED

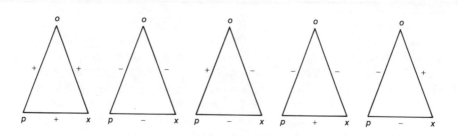

UNBALANCED

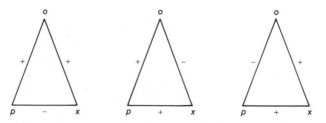

Figure 2.2. Heider's theory of psychological balance. (Compiled from Fritz Heider, *The Psychology of Interpersonal Relations* [New York: Wiley, 1967], pp. 174–217.)

More simply, Heider believes that individuals tend to adjust their attitudes in light of their beliefs about how people and other objects toward which they hold attitudes are related to each other. An individual may achieve balance between his attitudes by adopting only attitudes and beliefs that are balanced with his existing attitudes. An individual may also achieve balance by changing his attitudes and beliefs about some objects or persons if they are unbalanced with his other attitudes and beliefs. In either case, attempts to maintain balanced attitudes will affect what attitudes an individual holds.

Heider's theory is both more specific and more rigid than Festinger's. Heider considers inconsistencies between only two attitudes at a time, and it is unclear how his ideas can be generalized to more attitudes. Festinger, on the other hand, can discuss dissonance among any number of attitudes that contain dissonant cognitions. In addition, Heider does not consider, as Festinger does, that cultural norms often determine what cognitions individuals consider inconsistent, or that the relative number and importance of inconsistent cognitions may have a bearing on whether and how individuals reduce dissonance. On the other hand, because his theory is more specific and mechanistic than Festinger's, Heider can make firmer predictions about what attitudes an individual will adopt in a given case and how his attitudes will change.

Both Festinger and Heider, however, accept the homeostatic principle. Although that principle has been criticized, it continues to be widely applied in discussions of attitudes. How it plays a role in discussions of political attitudes will be explained shortly. But for the present it is sufficient to realize that in one way or another, many psychologists believe an individual's attitudes tend to be consistent with each other.

Measurement of Attitudes

The third aspect of attitude psychology that has an important bearing on contemporary studies of public opinion is the way psychologists determine what attitudes individuals hold.[40] Because attitudes are defined as tendencies to like or dislike objects and because psychologists believe that an individual's expressions of evaluation are generally consistent with his attitudes, the simplest way to determine what attitude an individual has toward an object would seemingly be to ask him to express his feelings about it. This is, in effect, what psychologists do. Thurstone explains their approach to assigning attitudes when he writes, "We shall use opinions as a way of assigning attitudes."[41] By "opinions" Thurstone and many other psychologists mean verbal expressions of evaluation; so in this discussion expressions of evaluation will be referred to as "opinions."

There are several difficulties with assigning attitudes by simply asking individuals to express their feelings about a given object, however. First, as already pointed out, psychologists do not believe an individual will always express evaluations consistent with his attitudes. As a result, any one of his opinions about an object may not reflect his evaluative posture toward it. Second, attitudes are defined as tendencies to evaluate an object consistently over a period of time, and the fact that an individual expresses an opinion at one point in time does not necessarily mean he will continue to express similar opinions. Third, psychologists are often interested in comparing the attitudes of different individuals. They wish to be able to determine whether individuals have the same or different attitudes toward an object and whether their attitudes are favorable or unfavorable to it to different degrees. If they simply ask individuals to express their feelings about an object, the individuals may express themselves in different terms; as a result, their expressions may be difficult to compare.

Psychologists generally solve the first problem by recording several opinions expressed by an individual about a given object. They assume that most, if not all, of these will be expressions of his attitude. They might solve the second problem by recording an individual's opinions at different points in time, and some psychologists do this. Interviewing people repeatedly is expensive, however, and poses certain logistic problems. Psychologists generally avoid these difficulties by assuming that if an individual expresses a number of opinions which are, in some sense, consistent evaluations of an object over a short period of time (e.g., during an interview), he will probably express consistent opinions for some time thereafter. They believe, as Thurstone says, that "some mechanism" must be responsible for making an individual's responses consistent during the course of an interview and that a psychological mechanism of this strength must be "relatively enduring."[42]

Assuming that psychologists can solve the first two problems of assigning attitudes, they are still faced with the problem of how to record attitudes in a way which will enable them to compare the attitudes of different individuals. Psychologists generally solve this problem by presenting each individual whose attitudes they wish to measure with a number of statements that are favorable or unfavorable to an object to different degrees. They ask the individual to indicate which of these statements he "agrees with most" or which is "closest" to his personal attitude. They regard his endorsements of statements as expressions of his opinions. If an individual endorses statements that are, in some sense, consistent evaluations of the object, he is assumed to have an attitude toward it; if several individuals endorse the same consistent statements, they are said to have the same attitude. Finally, psychologists believe they can determine how favorable or unfavorable each group of consistent statements about an object is. As a result, they can say that individuals who endorse consistent statements which are favorable or unfavorable to an object to the same degree hold an attitude toward the object which is favorable or unfavorable to that degree.

Most psychologists assign attitudes by using some variation on the method just outlined, although there are exceptions. To assign attitudes in this way, however, psychologists must be able to identify groups of statements about a given object that are consistent evaluations of it, and they must be able to determine how favorable or unfavorable to the object each of these groups of statements is. Psychologists have developed a number of techniques that, they believe, enable them to accomplish these tasks. These are often called "scaling techniques" because they are used to assign opinions (and subsequently individuals) to different points on scales of favorableness or unfavorableness to objects. Three scaling techniques—Thurstone scaling, Guttman scaling, and content analysis—are of particular importance in attitude studies of public opinion.[43]

All these techniques for attitude assignment have been accepted for many years, and recently more sophisticated techniques have been developed by students of public opinion. The techniques to be discussed here, however, were those primarily used by students of public opinion at the time when the studies that are reviewed in future chapters were carried out; thus this discussion is limited to them.

Thurstone Scaling.   This was the first highly sophisticated technique developed for recording attitudes, and its basic assumptions underlie many other techniques.[44] Thurstone assumes that individuals express consistent evaluations of an object if they express only opinions which are favorable or unfavorable to the object to the same degree. Opinions of this sort will be called "equivalent opinions." Thurstone identifies equivalent opinions and ranks them according to favorableness and unfavorableness in the following way.

First, he collects a number of evaluative statements about an object. He might do this by asking several people to write out their opinions about the object, by scanning the newspapers for references to it, or by consulting some other source. These statements are then submitted to a panel of ordinary people, whom Thurstone calls "judges." The judges are asked to indicate how favorable or unfavorable they think each statement about the object is by placing it on a 7- or 11-point scale, the ends of which are marked, respectively, "very favorable" and "very unfavorable." For example, if point 11 is "very unfavorable," and if a judge places a statement at point 9, he is indicating that he thinks it is a fairly unfavorable evaluation of the object, but not as unfavorable as a statement that would be placed at point 10 or 11. Thurstone says that statements which are placed at the same point by a large number of judges are equivalent evaluations of the object. He then constructs a series of questionnaires, each of which is comprised of evaluations ranked at different points by the judges. Each individual whose attitude is to be determined is asked to indicate which statements on the questionnaires he "most agrees with" or which statements are "closest" to his feelings. If an individual agrees with a group of statements, all of which the judges have placed at the same point on one of Thurstone's scales, he is assumed to have an attitude toward the object which is favorable or unfavorable to the degree indicated by that point. For example, if all his responses fall at point 9 on an 11-point scale, he is said to have a fairly unfavorable attitude.

Thurstone also has a double check on his work. If there are some opinions that his judges assign to, for example, point 9 on a scale, and those opinions are endorsed by people who endorse most other opinions at point 9 and also by people who endorse most other opinions at point 5, Thurstone discards those opinions from his questionnaires. He is assuming that if individuals hold different attitudes they will consider different opinions "closest" to their attitudes. He believes, therefore, that the way to distinguish between people with different attitudes is to construct scales in such a way that the opinions of individuals whose attitudes are to be measured "cluster" around different points on the scales. The "clustering" of opinions means that each individual will endorse only opinions which the judges have ranked at the same degree of favorableness or unfavorableness. If most of the opinions assigned to a particular point by his judges produce this clustering effect, Thurstone assumes that they indicate differences between attitudes; he also assumes that any opinions which are endorsed by individuals whose opinions otherwise cluster around different points are not useful for assigning attitudes. Of course, Thurstone must rely on the decisions of his judges to indicate how favorable or unfavorable each group of opinions is. But if the assignments made by the judges produce a clustering effect, he believes he can at least assume that they distinguish between individuals who hold different attitudes.

Guttman Scaling.   This is a complex technique, and it is impossible to explain it fully here.[45] It is possible, however, to explain the basic logic of Guttman scaling by considering an imaginary example. Suppose we conducted an experiment in the following way:

We are interested in attitudes toward a certain person, and we have a list of statements about that person that are all favorable, but to different degrees. For example, one statement might be "She is tolerable," and another might be "She is superb." We wish to determine the attitudes of ten individuals toward the person, and each of these individuals has an attitude toward her that is favorable to a different degree. We ask each individual to tell us whether he agrees or disagrees with each of the statements about the person; we present the statements to the individuals beginning with the least favorable statement, going on in order of favorableness to the most favorable. Everyone agrees with the first two statements; but on the third statement everyone agrees except one individual, and that individual never agrees with another statement. On the fourth statement, everyone agrees except one other individual, and he never agrees with another statement. Our experiment continues like this until everyone has "dropped out" except one individual, or until our statements are exhausted.

If we conducted an experiment of this sort, Guttman would say that the last individual to drop out has the most favorable attitude toward the person, that the first individual to drop out has the least favorable attitude, and that the other individuals have attitudes which are favorable to a degree indicated by the order in which they dropped out. Guttman assumes that if an individual has an attitude which is favorable to an object to a certain degree, he will endorse any opinions which are favorable to that degree and any opinions which are less favorable; but he will not endorse opinions that are more favorable. According to Guttman, therefore, there is a range of opinions that are consistent with an individual's attitude. This range consists of the most favorable opinion he will endorse plus all less favorable opinions. Guttman believes the way to determine whether an individual has an attitude is to determine whether he will endorse all opinions that are favorable to an object up to a certain point; and the way to determine what attitude he has is to determine the most favorable opinion he will endorse. Guttman's notion of consistent opinions differs, therefore, from Thurstone's notion. Thurstone considers consistent opinions to be only those opinions that are favorable or unfavorable to an object to the same degree.

Guttman's problem, therefore, is to devise some way of ranking all the statements he presents to individuals according to their favorableness or unfavorableness to an object. We can see how he does this by varying our imaginary experiment somewhat. Suppose that in our attempt to assign attitudes toward a person, we did not know how favorable to that person each of a group of statements was, and that we simply presented the statements to the individuals whose attitudes we wished to measure without knowing whether we were presenting them in order of favorableness. Suppose, however, that the individuals still dropped out, as described above. Guttman believes that we could assume that the statements had been presented in order of favorableness because he believes this pattern of behavior will occur only if statements are presented in that order. If our experiment proceeded in this way, therefore, Guttman would say that it enabled us to rank both the statements and the attitudes of the individuals responding to them according to their favorableness.

Of course, Guttman cannot assume that he will always offer statements to individuals in the order of their favorableness by chance. He does assume, however, that each individual will always agree or disagree with any given statement regardless of when it is offered to him (i.e., whether it is offered first, second, third, etc.). Guttman proceeds, therefore, by asking the individuals whose attitudes he wishes to measure to agree or disagree with a number of statements about an object, which he does not attempt to present in any particular order. Using a mechanical device, he then experiments with different orders in which the statements might have been offered. He does this until he finds an order such that, if the statements had been offered in that order, the individuals to whom they were offered would have behaved in the way the individuals in our imaginary experiment did. Guttman then uses this ordering of statements and individuals to assign attitudes in the way just described. Often Guttman cannot discover an order of presenting all his statements which would enable him to infer that individuals would have behaved in the same way the individuals in our imaginary experiment did. As a result, he often ranks only a subgroup of statements and uses that subgroup to assign attitudes. Guttman's technique can be applied to unfavorable as well as favorable statements; but he does not believe that statements of both sorts should be presented to individuals at the same time. Thus he must make a preliminary decision about whether particular statements are favorable or unfavorable before using them to assign attitudes.

Content Analysis.   The third technique for assigning attitudes which is of concern here is content analysis. This is one of the few techniques in which individuals whose attitudes are to be measured are not generally offered a series of statements which they are asked to agree or disagree with. Content analysis was developed fully by Berelson in the early 1950s as a technique for investigating popular culture, particularly the mass media.[46] This is still the primary use of the technique, but it is sometimes used to assign attitudes. In the study of popular culture, content analysis is used to determine how frequently statements of various sorts occur in newspapers, speeches, movies, and so on. For example, we might count the number of favorable and unfavorable references to the Vietnam War that appeared in newspapers each year from 1960 to 1970. If the ratio of unfavorable to favorable references increased each year, we might regard this as an index of increasing public (or journalistic) opposition to the war.

   Content analysis can be used as a method of assigning attitudes in a similar way. We can begin by asking subjects what is often called a "free response," "open ended," or "unstructured" question about an object: for example, "What do you like or dislike about mushroom soup?" We can then record everything they say in response and count the number of favorable and unfavorable statements they make. If an individual makes more favorable than unfavorable statements, we can assume he has a favorable attitude toward the object. We can go further by assuming that the higher the ratio of his favorable to his unfavorable statements, the more favorable his attitude is. We can make similar assumptions if the individual makes more unfavorable than favorable statements. "Coding," as the counting of favorable and unfavorable statements is called, is usually carried out by several people. Each of them decides whether each statement is favorable or unfavorable to the attitude object, and their decisions are checked to see whether they agree with each other. Statements the coders do not agree about are not used for assigning attitudes.

Content analysis can be refined in many ways. For example, coders might be asked to count statements that are favorable or unfavorable to different degrees or to count statements they identify with a particular point of view (e.g., "conservative" responses to a question about the national economy). Whatever its variations, however, the basic assumption underlying content analysis is that if an individual has a favorable attitude toward an object, he will express more favorable than unfavorable opinions about it, and if he has an unfavorable attitude toward the object, he will express more unfavorable than favorable opinions about it. Unlike Thurstone and Guttman, therefore, psychologists who use content analysis to assign attitudes do not distinguish a particular group of consistent opinions which they believe any individual who holds a particular attitude will express. We can say that psychologists who use content analysis consider all the opinions an individual expresses about an object to be consistent with his attitude; or we can say that they regard only the majority of those opinions which are favorable or unfavorable to be consistent. Regardless of how we interpret their procedures, the important point is that psychologists who use content analysis use different groups of opinions to assign attitudes to each individual. Individuals are said to hold different attitudes because they express different numbers of favorable and unfavorable opinions, not because they express favorable or unfavorable opinions that have a different content.

There are many variations on the scaling techniques outlined here. Psychologists often go through all the steps I have said are involved in applying each technique, but they also often skip steps or introduce others. The basic theories of Thurstone scaling, Guttman scaling, and content analysis are, however, fundamental to most methods of assigning attitudes. Furthermore, many of the findings of attitude psychology are based on the assumption that those theories are correct.

Scaling techniques of the sort just discussed are not the only methods psychologists use to assign attitudes, however. Many psychologists, including the authors of *Opinions and Personality* and *The Authoritarian Personality,* use more lengthy procedures; examples are in-depth interviews and batteries of psychological tests aimed at exploring many aspects of subjects' personalities.[47] They use these procedures because, like many other psychologists, they believe that many aspects of an individual's personality, such as his values, goals, and anxieties, are among the factors which determine what attitudes he adopts.[48] They also believe that these personality traits are often affected by the individual's attitudes. Thus, by studying many aspects of an individual's personality, psychologists hope to identify the psychological factors that determine his attitudes and to describe those attitudes more fully than they could by the use of scaling techniques. In-depth interviews and personality tests are not used widely in attitude studies of public opinion; for this reason they are not discussed further here. In Chapters 3 and 4, however, it is shown that the authors of those studies believe that an individual's attitudes are strongly affected by many of his personality traits.

Attitude Intensity.   Before ending this discussion of attitude measurement, a word should be said about the measurement of attitude intensity. Most psychologists believe that intensity is an important characteristic of attitudes, but they rarely define it precisely. Key comes as close as most writers to a satisfactory definition when he says that intensity is the "strength or depth of feeling" of an individual's attitude.[49] The core idea about intensity seemingly shared by most psychologists is that even though a group of individuals may all like or dislike a particular object to the same degree, they may differ in the strength of their feelings toward it. For example, one individual who is moderately favorable toward a political candidate may feel that the candidate and his chances of success are of tremendous importance for the country, whereas another individual who is moderately favorable toward the candidate may feel that the candidate and his chances of success are not of great significance.

Thus psychologists often distinguish between what they call the "content" of an attitude, its "direction," or an individual's "position" toward an object (his favorableness or unfavorableness toward it) and the "intensity" of an attitude or how strongly an individual "feels" about an object (how strongly he holds his position or how much he cares about the object). Content and intensity are sometimes called "components" of attitudes, and it is difficult to say whether or how they should be distinguished from the three components (cognitive, affective, and behavioral) discussed earlier.[50] Because this point is not important for my purposes in the following chapters, it will not be discussed here. I shall regard content and intensity as characteristics of all three components, rather than identify each with any one of the components, because this is the most common practice among attitude psychologists.

Because psychologists generally believe that the intensity of attitudes differs from the content of attitudes, they often measure it differently. The scaling techniques discussed earlier are usually regarded as techniques for determining attitude content. Generally, having assigned an individual to a certain position on an attitude scale using one of these techniques, psychologists then ask him such questions as "How strongly do you feel about this? Not at all strongly? Fairly strongly? Very strongly?"[51] The individual is asked to check one of these categories, and the category he checks is considered an indication of the intensity of his attitude. Unfortunately, the measurement of intensity is not always this simple because psychologists sometimes use the same questions to measure both content and intensity. In those cases, they score the answers to the questions one way when they wish to determine content and another way when they wish to determine intensity. An example of this procedure is discussed in Chapter 4 ("Six partisan attitudes").

However they record intensity, psychologists have found that individuals who hold the same position toward an object do not always have the same intensity of feeling about it. This reinforces psychologists' belief that intensity is in fact a characteristic of attitudes which should be separated from content. On the other hand, psychologists often find that individuals with extreme positions (people who dislike or like an object very much) have more intense attitudes than people with less extreme views (people who are fairly indifferent to an object).[52] Thus, if intensity is plotted against position on a graph, a U- or J-shaped curve often will be formed. These findings lead psychologists to believe there is some sort of functional relationship between intensity and position. Thus they sometimes use information about the relationship between these two characteristics of attitudes as part of their techniques of scale construction.[53]

Summary and a Look Forward

Some of the more important ideas about attitudes found in the literature of contemporary social psychology have been outlined in this chapter. To understand these ideas fully, it is necessary to see how they are applied in particular studies. Because I am concerned only with studies of political attitudes, however, the variety of uses of attitude psychology will not be discussed. Rather, how ideas drawn from attitude psychology are applied in investigations of public opinion will be explained in the next chapter.

3. Attitudes and Opinions

This chapter discusses how the authors of certain contemporary studies of politics combine ideas drawn from attitude psychology with traditional ideas about public opinion. There are numerous studies in which these two sorts of ideas are combined, but, for convenience, this chapter focuses on only four: *The American Voter,* by Campbell, Converse, Miller, and Stokes; *Voting,* by Berelson, Lazarsfeld, and McPhee; *Public Opinion and American Democracy,* by Key; and *Public Opinion,* by Lane and Sears.[1] These books were chosen because they are among the best-known contemporary works on public opinion and because, taken together, they contain most of the major ideas about how attitude psychology can be applied to the investigation of public opinion.

All four books are based primarily on data gathered by administering questionnaires to large representative samples of the American public. Through their questionnaires, the authors collected different kinds of information about the individuals they interviewed. For example, they recorded the age, occupation, and income of each individual. They also asked each subject whether he voted in the last election, which newspapers he reads, and whether he had recently made a contribution to a political party. Most of the items on these questionnaires, however, ask the individuals interviewed to express their evaluations of such political objects as parties, issues, or candidates. I shall show that the authors of these books combine attitude psychology with traditional ideas about public opinion by claiming that the questionnaire items enable them to assign attitudes, as understood by attitude psychologists, and by claiming that these attitudes have the characteristics which traditional theorists attributed to public opinion. In other words, they identify public attitudes with public opinion as it has been understood traditionally. I also point out that many of the most important conclusions drawn by the authors of the books discussed are based on these claims.

The next section of this chapter demonstrates that the authors of attitude studies of public opinion claim they are investigating political attitudes and that they use a number of ideas borrowed from attitude psychologists in their work. The section after that demonstrates that they believe they are studying public opinion as it has traditionally been understood. The final section demonstrates that they are interested in political attitudes for many of the same reasons that traditional theorists were interested in public opinion, and some of the findings about political attitudes they consider most important are reviewed.

Attitudes and Attitude Studies

What They Say.   The authors of the studies under discussion believe
that they are recording and analyzing attitudes as understood by attitude psychologists because they frequently say they are investigating
attitudes, because they discuss attitudes in many of the ways that psychologists do, and because they frequently refer to the work of attitude
psychologists. The relationship of these studies to attitude psychology
is most apparent in *The American Voter*. In Chapter 2 of that work
Campbell et al. clearly define their objective as the study of attitudes.
They describe their approach to political science by saying that they
are cutting across the "funnel of causality" (the causal background of
an individual's political actions) at the level of individual psychology.
They characterize this as the "attitudinal approach."[2] In Chapter 4
they say they are investigating "individual attitudes," which they identify as "the public's cognitive and affective map."[3] "Cognitive and affective map" sounds much like the two most consistent components in
the three-component notion of attitudes. The authors select these two
allied components as the subject of their study and treat them as a unit.
Like attitude psychologists, they refer to the cognitive component as
an individual's "beliefs," "information," or "perceptions," and they
frequently refer to the affective component as his "feelings." We
would expect that if they understand attitudes in the way psychologists
do, Campbell et al. would discuss whether individuals maintain beliefs
and information consistent with their feelings. In fact, at several points
they discuss the kinds of political information which individuals hold,
and they note consistencies and inconsistencies between that information and the general evaluative postures of individuals.[4] On the whole,
they conclude that beliefs and feelings tend to be consistent; but they
point out important exceptions to this rule.

The authors of *The American Voter* are interested not only in the
cognitive and affective components of attitudes, however; they are also
interested in individual action tendencies, particularly tendencies to
vote for certain parties or candidates and to engage in other political
activities.[5] Like attitude psychologists, they believe that an individual's
actions tend to be consistent with his beliefs and feelings. Much of
their work is devoted to showing this to be true in the case of political
behavior and to tracing the psychological and situational factors that
maintain consistency among all three components. In addition, Campbell et al. are interested in the factors that lead to inconsistencies
between occasional actions and enduring beliefs and feelings, and they
conclude that these are primarily powerful situational factors or
conflicting attitudes.[6]

The authors of *The American Voter*, therefore, say they are studying attitudes and regard attitudes as cognitive, affective, and behavioral constructs. They also clearly believe that attitudes are fairly persistent tendencies to evaluate objects. They are concerned primarily with evaluations of parties, candidates, and major government policies, and they take great pains to show that the evaluative tendencies which most people have toward these objects remain the same for many months, or even years. For example, they show that the party preferences of most individuals change little between elections and that their candidate preferences remain the same throughout a campaign period.[7]

In addition, Campbell et al. believe that an individual's attitudes are an integral part of his or her personality. We can see this clearly in their discussion of "attitude structures."[8] By "attitude structures" they mean groups of attitudes, all of which express a certain general political outlook, such as liberalism or conservatism. The authors write that such groups of attitudes are "functionally related" in the sense that all of the attitudes in the group are organized around an individual's basic needs and goals.[9] They also devote an entire chapter to analyzing differences in the degree of sophistication with which individuals conceptualize political objects.[10] Differences in political conceptualization were first identified as a basic personality dimension by Smith, Bruner, and White in their analysis of opinions and personality, and the authors of *The American Voter* acknowledge their debt to that analysis.[11]

Finally, Campbell et al. are clearly interested in consistencies among different attitudes. They argue that most of an individual's political attitudes are generally consistent, and they find that previously inconsistent attitudes tend to become consistent with the passage of time.[12] Campbell et al. devote a great deal of attention to explaining how these consistencies come about. They place particular emphasis on findings that individuals tend to form attitudes with consistent cognitive components and that most of an individual's political attitudes are generally consistent with his beliefs about political parties.[13] They seem to share Festinger's notion that individuals maintain consistencies among attitudes primarily by maintaining consistencies among beliefs and that they are more likely to maintain "important" attitudes than others. Chapter 4 (section entitled "Basic Assumptions of the Argument") explains more precisely how they believe different attitudes are related to each other.

In large parts of their work, therefore, the authors of *The American Voter* are clearly studying attitudes in a way consistent with the ideas of attitude psychologists. This is not surprising because the authors were trained as social psychologists, and they have made important contributions to the theory and methodology of attitude psychology. All of the authors of *Voting* are also leading social psychologists. The influence of attitude psychology on their work is equally strong, although they do not acknowledge that influence as explicitly as the authors of *The American Voter* do.

Berelson et al., the authors of *Voting,* say that their task is to analyze what they call the process of "implementation." They define this as the way in which an individual's "dispositions" may lead, finally, "to the performance of a specific act like buying a car, going on a trip, or voting for a candidate."[14] They identify dispositions with attitudes, and although they frequently use the words "attitude" and "opinion" interchangeably, like the authors of *The American Voter* they are clearly interested in an individual's enduring beliefs and feelings toward political objects. Berelson et al. study the way an individual's beliefs and feelings are related to political actions and the factors that create consistencies among all three attitude components.[15] They are also interested in the factors that lead individuals to hold consistent beliefs about political objects, and they devote a great deal of attention to selective perception.[16] Finally, like the authors of *The American Voter,* Berelson et al. believe that an individual's political attitudes tend to be consistent with each other, and they trace psychological and situational factors which they believe account for this.[17]

Attitude psychology also has a strong influence on the work of Key and of Lane and Sears. Key draws most of his data from the same surveys on which *The American Voter* is based, and therefore it is fair to say that if Campbell et al. are studying attitudes, so is he. Key is also concerned with many of the same psychological characteristics of attitudes that interest Campbell et al. and the authors of *Voting,* and he often refers to the work of attitude psychologists. For example, in discussing consistency among different attitudes, he relies on theories and findings developed by Sherif, Asch, and Festinger, and in discussing the stability of attitudes he refers to the work of Cantril, Sherif, and Klapper.[18]

Lane and Sears do not refer explicitly to attitudes, but *Public Opinion* is probably the most striking illustration of the relationship between contemporary public opinion analysis and attitude psychology. The book is intended to be an overview of public opinion research, and it is therefore significant that Lane and Sears divide their attention almost equally between the work of the authors of the other three books discussed in this chapter and the work of leading attitude psychologists. They review all the same characteristics of attitudes that the authors of other public opinion studies discuss. In addition, they are concerned particularly with the way attitudes are formed, how they are related to various aspects of an individual's personality, and how individuals can sometimes form feelings about objects on the basis of little information.[19]

What They Do.　As we have seen, the authors of the four studies under discussion claim that they are investigating political attitudes, and they make use of many of the ideas which psychologists have developed about the structure and functioning of attitudes. They also rely heavily on the techniques that psychologists have developed for assigning attitudes. This is particularly true of the authors of *The American Voter*. In their work they use all three of the scaling techniques discussed in Chapter 2.

Section 2 of *The American Voter*, "Political Attitudes and the Vote," is based almost entirely on data drawn from a series of unstructured interviews that were subjected to content analysis.[20] Campbell et al. asked their subjects to express any favorable or unfavorable feelings they had about political parties and candidates. They used the opinions gathered to assign attitudes toward the two political parties, the two presidential candidates, domestic issues, and foreign policy issues. These assignments of attitudes were analyzed together with demographic data, subjects' reports of their knowledge about politics, and their reports of their voting records. Most of the conclusions about attitudes found in *The American Voter* are based on these analyses. In their investigation of ideology, however, Campbell et al. adopted a different approach.[21] They recorded opinions on ten domestic issues and six foreign policy issues and subjected these to Guttman scale analysis to determine whether the opinions could be used to assign liberal and conservative attitudes to members of the public. The authors of *The American Voter* also make use of McClosky's analysis of political ideology, which is based on Thurstone scaling techniques.[22]

Although they rely heavily on scaling techniques, the authors of *The American Voter* at times assign attitudes in other ways. Sometimes they say an individual has an attitude solely because she or he expresses a single opinion about an object. For example, they assign attitudes toward government policies by simply asking an individual whether he or she agrees or disagrees with certain policies.[23] Also, Campbell et al. often use information about the relationship between expressions of opinion and other psychological factors to support their assignments.[24] Most of the data about attitudes found in *The American Voter*, however, were gathered by the use of scaling techniques.

The authors of *Voting* do not explain their techniques for assigning attitudes as clearly as the authors of *The American Voter* do. In separate articles, however, both Berelson and Lazarsfeld say that most modern public opinion studies, including the studies they conduct, rely heavily on attitude scaling techniques developed by psychologists.[25] Moreover, in *Voting* they frequently use Thurstone-type questionnaires to assign attitudes;[26] that is, to determine an individual's attitude toward a given object, they present him with several lists of statements about it and ask him to indicate which statements are closest to his own feelings. Each list consists of statements that are equivalent to statements on other lists, and an individual is assigned an attitude if he endorses equivalent statements. Berelson et al. do not say how they developed these lists of statements. But they do suggest that they have evidence that opinions of the individuals whom they interviewed tend to cluster around certain statements and that, as a result, those statements could be regarded as equivalent.[27] Although the authors of *Voting* may not go through all the steps that Thurstone suggests are needed to construct an attitude scale, their objective apparently is to construct scales similar to those Thurstone discusses.

When they do not use Thurstone-type scales to assign attitudes, the authors of *Voting,* like the authors of *The American Voter,* usually base their assignments on single opinions expressed by their subjects. They ask the individuals whom they interview to express agreement or disagreement with both government policies and statements of opinion about other political objects.[28] Unlike the authors of *The American Voter,* however, Berelson et al. repeat many of these single-opinion questions in several interviews. As a result, they have some indication of whether an individual's tendency to express certain opinions endures over a period of time.

As pointed out earlier, most of the data about attitudes on which Key's book is based are drawn from *The American Voter.* As a result, his work, like the work of Campbell et al., relies heavily on scaling techniques developed by attitude psychologists. In addition, Key devotes several pages to discussing these techniques and explaining how they are used in attitude studies of public opinion.[29] Lane and Sears draw heavily on assignments of attitudes made by the authors of both *The American Voter* and *Voting.* In addition they make use of data developed by McClosky, Newcomb, Maccoby, and other students of attitudes who rely heavily on scaling techniques.[30]

The authors of attitude studies of public opinion find scaling techniques useful for two reasons. First, like attitude psychologists, they believe those techniques provide accurate means of assigning attitudes and comparing the attitudes of different individuals. Second, scaling techniques allow them to assign attitudes to large numbers of people. As mentioned earlier, the authors of attitude studies often investigate the attitudes of representative samples of the American public. These samples may contain 1,000 people or more. It would be prohibitively expensive and time consuming to assign attitudes to that number of people by the use of in-depth interviews or personality tests. Most scaling techniques, however, enable psychologists to assign an attitude to an individual by asking him to express only a few opinions. As a result, these techniques make it possible to determine the attitudes of large numbers of people quickly and economically.

Because the authors of the four studies being discussed say they are investigating attitudes, because they describe attitudes in the same way psychologists do, and because they use the techniques psychologists have developed to assign attitudes, their work can be regarded as an application of attitude psychology to the study of politics. In fact, most standard textbooks on social psychology refer to these studies of public opinion as a branch of attitude psychology.[31] It would be wrong to regard such studies solely as applications of ideas developed by attitude psychologists, however. The authors of these studies also make use of ideas drawn from other schools of psychology, and they devote a great deal of attention to investigating political sociology. Nevertheless, much of their work consists of the investigation of political attitudes, and it is this part of their work that is of primary interest here.

Public Opinion and Attitude Studies

Just as they clearly state that they are studying political attitudes, the authors of the four studies under discussion clearly state that they are investigating public opinion. The studies by Key and by Lane and Sears contain the words "public opinion" in their titles, and the authors of both *The American Voter* and *Voting* frequently refer to their books as investigations of public opinion. However, are these four studies investigations of public opinion as understood by traditional political theorists? The authors repeatedly say that they are. For example, the authors of *The American Voter, Voting,* and *Public Opinion* all refer to Lippmann's definition of public opinion as "the pictures in our heads," and they say that they are studying these pictures.[32] In a frequently cited article, Berelson describes modern public opinion research as a continuation of a long tradition reaching back to Tocqueville and Bryce.[33] Key begins his book by tracing nineteenth- and early twentieth-century notions of public opinion and formulating a definition of the concept based on those notions.[34] It is public opinion in this sense that he claims to study.

While the authors of these studies believe they are investigating public opinion as it was traditionally understood, they also believe they have been able to add at least one important element to eighteenth- and nineteenth-century discussions of the subject. Berelson and Lazarsfeld point out that although traditional public opinion theory contained a strong empirical component, many of the conclusions traditional theorists drew about American public opinion were based on inadequate evidence.[35] For example, both Tocqueville and Bryce traveled extensively through the United States, talked with a number of people, and observed political events closely. They probably formed a good idea of what some Americans thought about some political issues, how their opinions were formed, and what effects those opinions had on politics. Bryce and Tocqueville assumed that the opinions of most Americans were similar to those of the people whom they encountered and that, as a result, they could draw conclusions about public opinion in the United States on the basis of their observations of the opinions of only a small part of the public. However, Berelson and Lazarsfeld point out that Tocqueville and Bryce had no way of knowing whether the individuals they encountered were a cross section of the American public and, as a result, whether many of their conclusions about American public opinion were accurate. Campbell et al. add that discussions of public opinion suffered from this difficulty until the late 1930s.[36]

The authors of the four studies believe they have been able to improve on traditional investigations of public opinion by strengthening their empirical components. They believe they have been able to accomplish this primarily through the use of scientific methods for determining the opinions of large national publics. These methods are the scaling techniques that have been discussed. The authors of attitude studies of public opinion claim that by using scaling techniques to measure the attitudes of representative samples of the American public, they can scientifically record public opinion as it traditionally was understood. In effect they identify attitudes, as understood by attitude psychologists, with opinions, as understood by traditional theorists, and claim that their findings about public attitudes are findings about public opinion.

This claim has a great deal of prima facie validity. As pointed out in Chapter 1, nineteenth-century political theorists often regarded opinions as likes and dislikes for such political objects as parties, candidates, and government policies. Attitudes are defined as tendencies to like or dislike, approve or disapprove of, particular objects; the authors of attitude studies of public opinion are generally concerned with attitudes toward the same sorts of objects that traditional theorists discussed, such as candidates or issues. Traditional theorists did not refer to opinions as "tendencies" or "dispositions," but they were certainly interested in enduring likes and dislikes rather than momentary expressions of opinion. For example, Bryce discusses how opinions formed at various points in time between elections eventually affect voting choices, and Tocqueville discusses how majority opinion acts on minorities over a period of time.[37] Thus it is reasonable to expect that traditional theorists would have agreed that the authors of attitude studies of public opinion are recording what they (traditional theorists) regarded as "opinions."

It is also reasonable to expect that nineteenth-century theorists would have agreed that the authors of the four studies under discussion are recording the attitudes of a "public." As pointed out in Chapter 1, traditional theorists believed a public consists of all the citizens of a nation-state. The authors of the four studies are interested only in political attitudes in the United States, and, although they do not interview all Americans, they use statistical techniques to select representative samples of the public. A manual prepared by the Survey Research Center of the University of Michigan, with which the authors of *The American Voter* were affiliated, states that their sampling method "enables us to select several hundred households which will mirror in every way all of the households in the United States."[38] They believe they can infer what opinions the mass of individuals outside government hold by recording the opinions of representative samples of Americans. Like traditional theorists, they sometimes focus on opinions held by members of a particular class or by people who live in a particular geographic region. For the most part, however, they study the characteristics of mass opinion.

The authors of attitude studies of public opinion, therefore, have good reasons to believe they are investigating public opinion as it was traditionally understood. Attitudes are in many ways similar to what traditional theorists called "opinions," and, like traditional theorists, the authors of attitude studies are concerned with the political views of the mass public. They believe that public attitudes have even more similarities to public opinion than those I have mentioned, however. To understand what these additional similarities are, it is necessary to consider why the authors of attitude studies are interested in investigating public attitudes.

The Significance of Public Attitudes

There are several reasons why the authors of the four studies being discussed believe it is important to investigate public attitudes. In part, they wish to study the psychological characteristics of those attitudes. They are interested in how attitudes about politics are formed, how they change, and whether they have the same characteristics that other sorts of attitudes have.[39] The authors of attitude studies of public opinion regard these findings as interesting in themselves because they increase our knowledge about the psychology of attitudes and extend the findings of attitude psychologists into a new domain. They are also interested in public attitudes because they wish to investigate certain aspects of political sociology. For example, they wish to determine what similarities there are among the political attitudes of members of the same class or the same religion.[40] In addition, they are interested in how an individual's political attitudes are influenced by his family and peer groups.[41]

Although they consider their findings about psychology and sociology important in themselves, the major reason the authors of attitude studies are interested in those findings and in public attitudes is that they believe those attitudes perform the same functions in political systems that traditional theorists attributed to public opinion. Traditional theorists considered public opinion important because they believed if a majority of the public hold a certain opinion, they often "tyrannize" the minority and because, in some countries, public opinion influences the decisions of government and the outcomes of elections. The authors of attitude studies are not interested in the tyranny of the majority but they frequently state that their major reason for studying public attitudes is that those attitudes influence the decisions of government and the outcomes of elections. These authors express their interest in the former effect of public attitudes quite explicitly. For example, Lane and Sears write, "Government policy, and, indeed, all important historical events are shaped by the opinions of the members of the political communities involved. That is why we are interested in public opinion."[42] Key writes that public opinion consists of "the opinions which government finds it prudent to heed," and he devotes one section of his book to discussing the "linkage" between public opinion and public policy.[43] In "Public Opinion and the Classical Tradition," Lazarsfeld reviews a number of studies of the influence of public opinion on government; he concludes that in the explanation of many government actions, "only attitude data can provide the components which produced the final result."[44] Finally, in a summary of the significance of their work, the authors of *The American Voter* describe the relationship of government to the public in the following way:

> The fact that public policy is tied to public opinion by the perceptions policy-forming elites and the electorate have of each other deserves the fullest appreciation. It means, at the very least, that the relation between governors and governed depends upon the intellective processes by which the electorate reviews and expresses its judgments of public affairs.[45]

In addition, the authors of many attitude studies believe that members of government are influenced by public opinion primarily because of the role it plays in the electoral process. For example, Campbell et al. write that "voting has provided the modern state with a way of connecting the actions of government with the preferences of the mass citizenry." They (as well as authors of other attitude studies) believe that this "connection" comes about because "the holders of elective or appointive office in democratic government are guided in many of their actions by a calculus of electoral effect."[46] In other words, the authors of many attitude studies believe that members of government are influenced by public opinion because they think that if they do not act in accordance with public wishes, they will not be reelected.

Like traditional theorists, therefore, the authors of attitude studies believe it is important to study public opinion primarily because it influences government decisions and the outcomes of elections. It will be remembered that traditional theorists often called the influence of public opinion on government decisions "rule by public opinion." Although the authors of the four studies under discussion do not often use this term, they clearly believe that public opinion "rules" in the United States.

Because they attach such great importance to the influence of public opinion on government decisions and the outcomes of elections, the authors of attitude studies devote most of their energies to investigating these two processes. It is in these investigations that they make the most extensive use of the techniques and theories of attitude psychology. In particular, they claim that those techniques and theories enable them to conduct two major kinds of analysis of the relationship between public opinion and government.

First, they say that by using the techniques of attitude psychology to record public attitudes and by comparing those attitudes with government actions, they can determine conclusively whether government members are influenced by public opinion.[47] They also believe they can use information about public attitudes together with other kinds of information to explain the political and social processes by which public views are transmitted to government members and affect their decisions.[48] In short, the authors of attitude studies claim that they can show whether and how the process of rule by public opinion operates in the United States.

Second, the authors of attitude studies often say that certain political attitudes held by members of the public "cause" or "motivate" their voting choices in the sense of determining which candidates they vote for.[49] In addition, the authors say that, collectively, the attitudes which motivate individual voting choices determine the outcomes of elections in the sense that they determine which candidates win elections. The authors claim that they are able to contribute to our understanding of the relationship between public opinion and government by using the techniques and theories of attitude psychology to determine which attitudes motivate voting choices and influence the outcomes of elections and by analyzing those attitudes in terms of theories of psychology, sociology, and political science.

The authors of the four studies believe that they make their major contribution to political science by using attitude psychology in these two ways, and most of their important conclusions about public opinion are based on the assumptions that they can investigate rule by public opinion and identify motives for votes. For example, they believe that by identifying motives for votes they can draw conclusions about what standards of judgment members of the public generally apply in selecting government officeholders. In particular, they believe that they are able to make an important contribution to the literature on public opinion by showing that party loyalties and attitudes toward the personal qualities of candidates are far more powerful determinants of voting choices than are attitudes toward political issues.[50] In addition, the authors believe that they can use findings about public attitudes to draw conclusions about electoral history, the functioning of many political institutions, and the "rationality" of the electorate, as well as many other subjects of interest to political scientists. Some of these conclusions are discussed in detail in following chapters.

There are also many conclusions found in attitude studies of public opinion that are not based on the two claims identified here. Some of them are reviewed in later chapters. However, the claims of authors of attitude studies that they can explain the influence of public opinion on government decisions and identify motives for votes, and the conclusions based on those claims, are the parts of attitude studies of primary interest in this book.

Summary and a Look Forward

It has been shown that the authors of attitude studies combine attitude psychology with traditional ideas about public opinion by attempting to use the techniques developed by attitude psychologists to record public opinion as traditionally understood and to study the two functions of public opinion in the political process that traditional theorists considered most important. Thus in many ways their work can be seen as a continuation of the work of Tocqueville, Bryce, and other traditional theorists. The authors of attitude studies claim to improve on traditional investigations of public opinion, however, because they believe that the techniques of attitude psychology enable them to record and analyze public opinion with a precision unknown until recent years. If the authors of attitude studies are correct in claiming they can combine attitude psychology with traditional ideas about public opinion in these ways, then those studies are, as Berelson says, truly remarkable examples of how modern social science can be used to further older traditions in political studies.[51]

In the chapters that follow, however, a major part of that claim is challenged. I think it is clear that public attitudes are very similar to public opinion as understood traditionally and that the authors of attitude studies are right in saying they can improve on the work of traditional theorists by recording public opinion with precision. However, they are wrong in making the two other major claims on which their work is based: that they can identify motives for votes and explain whether and how rule by public opinion operates in the United States. By demonstrating this, I shall show that the authors of attitude studies are not successful in combining attitude psychology with traditional ideas about public opinion in the ways they consider most important and that many of their major conclusions about public opinion are unacceptable. In addition, it will be shown that their lack of success is partly due to shortcomings in the ways they conduct their research and partly due to shortcomings in traditional theories of public opinion.

The next two parts of this book are devoted to criticizing the claims of authors of attitude studies that they can identify motives for votes and determine whether and how rule by public opinion operates in the United States. This will be a lengthy process because the arguments on which these claims are based must be examined in considerable detail. To reduce the task to manageable proportions, the way each claim is presented will be analyzed for only one of the four studies under discussion. In each case, the study in which the claim is most clearly articulated and most strongly defended has been selected. In Part II the way in which the authors of *The American Voter* claim to identify motives for voting choices is criticized. In Part III the way in which Key claims to explain the process of rule by public opinion is criticized. Strictly speaking, the conclusions drawn in each part apply only to the study discussed in that part. Nevertheless, the authors of all attitude studies of public opinion in which these claims are found make essentially the same mistakes in attempting to identify motives for votes and explain rule by public opinion. Therefore my conclusions apply to all four studies discussed in this chapter as well as to many other studies.

II. Motives for Votes

It was said in Chapter 3 that the authors of attitude studies believe they can determine which attitudes "cause" or "motivate" the voting choices of members of the general public. It was also pointed out that many of their conclusions about public opinion are based on this claim. In Part II it is argued that the authors of *The American Voter* are unsuccessful in their attempts to identify motives for votes.

My argument has five parts, and a chapter is devoted to each part. Chapter 4 explains the methods used by the authors of *The American Voter* to identify motives for votes and the reasons they believe these methods are successful. They attempt to establish that a few widely held attitudes (particularly preferences for parties and for the personal qualities of candidates) determine the partisan choices of most members of the public and, as a result, the outcomes of elections. Their procedure is to eliminate the possibility that issue attitudes have an influence on partisan choice and to demonstrate that among those attitudes which are influential, party preference exerts a more powerful influence than others.

Chapter 5 criticizes the procedures Campbell et al. use to determine whether issue attitudes motivate votes. It is shown that they do not consider all the attitudes which might influence partisan choices and that the ways in which they assign attitudes to members of the public and determine the influence of those attitudes on votes have certain limitations. In light of these criticisms, it is argued that the authors of *The American Voter* cannot claim to show that issue attitudes do not determine the outcomes of elections. When examined carefully, many of their findings are consistent with a contrary hypothesis: that the outcomes of elections are determined by many different issue attitudes, each of which influences a large number of people although not enough to affect the votes of a large percentage of the American public.

Chapter 6 is devoted to showing that the claims which the authors of *The American Voter* make about party preference are weak. In particular, it is argued that they cannot claim to have shown that party preference is the primary determinant of voting choices because they neglect certain evidence which suggests that party preference may simply result from other attitudes, socioeconomic factors, and information flow.

In Chapter 7 it is argued that because of the shortcomings in their work, the authors of *The American Voter* cannot claim to draw certain conclusions about public opinion which they regard as important parts of their study. However, it is shown that despite these shortcomings their work contains many valuable findings.

Finally, Chapter 8 considers the reasons the authors of *The American Voter* may have made the errors of which I have accused them. It is argued that many of the difficulties in their work are due to certain traditional ideas about public opinion they have adopted.

In the course of the discussion, demands are made of the authors of *The American Voter* that are, perhaps, more stringent than the demands which political scientists and social psychologists commonly make of social science researchers. I hope, however, that when my argument is concluded it will be clear that if Campbell et al. wish to draw the conclusions about politics which they claim to draw, they must meet these demands. The difficulty of doing so is probably less an indication of my perspective on their work than of how hard it is to use attitude psychology as Campbell et al. claim to use it.

4. The Argument of *The American Voter*

Before considering how the authors of *The American Voter* attempt to identify the attitudes that motivate votes, it is necessary to clarify exactly what task they set for themselves. Campbell et al. believe that many psychological and environmental factors have an influence on the voting choices of members of the American public.[1] Yet they claim that certain attitudes are "motives" for votes.[2] Presumably this means that certain attitudes are related to voting choices in some way that other factors are not. Unless we can define what this special relationship is, it will be difficult to understand what kinds of attitudes the authors of *The American Voter* are concerned with or to decide whether they have been successful in identifying them.

Fundamental Assumptions of the Argument

We can understand what Campbell et al. mean when they say that certain attitudes are motives for votes by considering how they believe these attitudes are related both to other factors that may influence voting choices and to those choices themselves. Fortunately, the authors discuss both these points fairly early in their work. They ask us to imagine a "funnel of causality," such as that represented in Figure 4.1.[3] The axis of the funnel is a time dimension running from the distant past, at the base of the funnel, to the present, at its apex. The present is the time at which an individual casts his vote in an election. Campbell et al. say that the funnel is filled with all the environmental influences plus all the psychological factors which, through a causal chain over many years, have combined to influence an individual's vote; that is, they are necessary conditions for his choosing one candidate rather than another. The model is funnel shaped because it is assumed that as time goes on there are fewer necessary conditions which must be fulfilled if the individual is to vote in a certain way. The attitudes that motivate votes, we are told, can be regarded as a cross section of the funnel fairly near its apex. It is not clear whether Campbell et al. regard the cross section as one attitude or several and whether, when they discuss the influence of attitudes on votes, they are discussing one funnel or several. Because they generally say that several attitudes rather than only one influence partisan choice, and because they generally refer to *the* funnel of causality, however, I assume that they place several attitudes at the bottom of the funnel.

To understand the funnel of causality model, it is necessary to understand that Campbell et al. devote most of their attention to two different kinds of attitude. First, they are interested in certain attitudes they often call "voting decisions."[4] These decisions are attitudes toward candidates, and they are formed only a few weeks or months before election day. Campbell et al. would place voting decisions very near the apex of the funnel of causality, below the cross section of attitudes they usually discuss; that is, voting decisions are the last attitudes bearing on the voting choice an individual forms before election day. The authors say that an individual has formed a voting decision if for a period of time before election day he believes a particular candidate should be elected and if he votes for that candidate. Voting decisions are, therefore, narrowly focused attitudes in that they are exclusively tendencies to favor

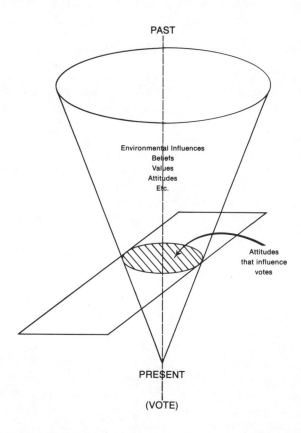

Figure 4.1. The funnel of causality. (Based on Angus Campbell, Philip E. Converse, Warren E. Miller, and Donald E. Stokes, *The American Voter* [New York: Wiley, 1960], pp. 24–33.)

the election of a particular candidate. Campbell et al. regard any other evaluative tendencies toward candidates or other political objects as attitudes that are different from voting decisions. They regard votes as expressions of the behavioral components of voting decisions. Strictly speaking, therefore, they do not believe that voting decisions cause votes; rather, they believe that votes are parts, or indications, of voting decisions. This way of discussing the relationship between attitudes and votes, is, of course, consistent with theories of attitude psychology because psychologists often say that attitudes have behavioral as well as cognitive and affective components.

The second kind of attitude with which Campbell et al. are concerned is any political attitude other than voting decisions. Among these are attitudes toward parties, the personal qualities of candidates, and issues.[5] The authors believe that these attitudes are generally formed before voting decisions are formed. Moreover, they believe that these attitudes cause voting decisions in the sense that each individual's attitudes toward parties, candidates, and issues are the major factors that determine which candidate his voting decisions will favor. This is consistent with theories of attitude psychology in that psychologists believe attitudes can influence the formation of other attitudes (see "Consistency of Attitudes" in Chapter 2). By this they may mean that either (1) if we know an individual holds certain attitudes we can predict with a high degree of accuracy that he holds or will form certain other attitudes or (2) attitudes are psychological forces that determine the content of other attitudes. As we shall see shortly, Campbell et al. regard attitudes as psychological forces. But they rely heavily on their ability to predict that members of the public hold or will form certain attitudes to determine which attitudes influence voting decisions.

Although they generally regard voting decisions as attitudes that are formed shortly before an election, the authors of *The American Voter* sometimes say that members of the public hold both voting decisions and other political attitudes during the period of time between campaigns, as well as during campaigns. An individual can be said to hold voting decisions between campaigns in the sense that if he were asked which of several politicians he would vote for if an election were held soon, he would express a preference for the same candidate over a period of time. Campbell et al. believe, however, that in some cases both voting decisions and attitudes toward parties, candidates, and issues change during and between campaigns. They say that changes in voting decisions are due to changes in the attitudes which determine them and due to the fact that as time goes on the field of potential candidates for a particular election is narrowed. As a result, each member of the public is restricted in the voting decisions he can hold if his vote is to be effective. According to Campbell et al., this shifting of attitudes and decisions settles down sometime during the campaign period, and members of the public form attitudes and decisions that persist at least until election day.[6] They refer to the attitudes that determine these decisions as motives for votes, and they attempt to identify them.

When they say that the attitudes with which they are concerned are "motives for votes," therefore, Campbell et al. mean that these attitudes determine the voting decisions which have as their behavioral components the votes cast by members of the public in a particular election. Because they believe that these attitudes determine voting decisions, and because they believe that votes are almost always consistent with those decisions, Campbell et al. often neglect to mention voting decisions when they are discussing the relationship between attitudes and votes. They simply say that attitudes toward parties, candidates, and issues cause votes. In the following sections, this way of discussing the relationship between attitudes and votes will be adopted because it avoids needless awkwardness of expression. It is important to realize, however, that Campbell et al. believe that the attitudes with which they are concerned affect votes by affecting voting decisions.

This discussion of the funnel of causality explains how the attitudes with which Campbell et al. are concerned are related to other factors in the funnel. To understand this relationship, it is necessary to consider why they say that the attitudes which motivate votes are cross sections of the funnel fairly near its apex. The fundamental reason for this is that, as already pointed out, they believe that many kinds of factors may influence what political attitudes members of the public form. Like most psychologists, they believe that any given set of attitudes is determined partly by environmental factors and partly by such psychological factors as values, goals, and other attitudes (see pp. 33–44).[7] They say that the attitudes with which they are concerned are cross sections of the funnel of causality fairly near its apex because they wish to indicate that all the elements in the funnel above those attitudes are the environmental and psychological factors which determine them.

There are three additional reasons why Campbell et al. portray motives for votes as cross sections of the funnel of causality fairly near its apex:

1. They wish to indicate that members of the public hold these attitudes on election day and for a few weeks or months beforehand. In contrast, they believe that members of the public may not have some of the other psychological characteristics in the funnel and that they may not be directly affected by some of the environmental factors it contains during that period of time. They believe that many of the psychological

and environmental factors which they place above motives for votes in the funnel influence voting choices only in the sense that they are links in causal chains which may stretch back many years. For example, an individual may hold a certain belief fairly early in life that leads him to adopt a certain attitude. The belief and the attitude may change before a particular election; but while the individual holds them, they may lead him to form another attitude which endures until that election and affects his vote. In this case, Campbell et al. would say that the first attitude and belief should be placed farther from the apex of the funnel than the second attitude and its associated beliefs and that they are primarily concerned with the second attitude. To take another example, an individual's childhood environment may lead him to form certain enduring political values. Later in life, after he has left that environment, those values may lead him to form certain attitudes that affect his vote in a particular election. In this case, Campbell et al. would say that the influences in the individual's childhood environment should be placed farther from the apex of the funnel than the attitudes with which they are concerned.

2. The authors wish to indicate that they believe most of the attitudes which motivate votes are formed at a later point in time than are other psychological elements in the funnel. Campbell et al. devote most of their attention to attitudes toward candidates, issues, and parties, which they believe are the major motives for votes. They think that the attitudes toward candidates and issues which influence votes are often formed within a few months of election day, whereas the values, beliefs, and other psychological traits that affect those attitudes and thus affect votes are generally formed earlier. They do not believe that this is true of all attitudes toward candidates and issues, or of all other psychological traits, however. And they certainly believe that attitudes toward parties which affect votes may be formed many years before a particular election.

3. The authors wish to indicate that the effect of all the previous environmental influences and previously acquired psychological traits which have a bearing on voting choices is "finally expressed" by the attitudes that motivate votes.[8] Campbell et al. sometimes say that other factors influence votes by acting "through" the attitudes which motivate voting choices.[9] They are not clear about exactly what they mean by this, but in light of what was said about different notions of attitudes in Chapter 2, two possibilities come to mind. First, they might mean that from a knowledge of certain of an individual's attitudes we can predict his political behavior with accuracy, whereas we cannot predict his behavior accurately from a knowledge of any other subset of elements in the funnel of causality. Second, they might mean that the attitudes with

which they are concerned can be regarded as the results of a variety of forces that have an influence on political behavior. The implications of these or other notions about the relationship between motives for votes and other factors that influence political behavior will not be explored here because those implications are not important for the discussion that follows. It is important to realize, however, that Campbell et al. believe that all the other factors which influence votes are in some sense reflected by or channeled through the attitudes with which they are concerned. Thus they believe that by examining those attitudes they can examine a microcosm of all influences on the outcomes of elections.

In short, Campbell et al. are concerned with a certain set of political attitudes which differ from other elements in the funnel of causality in that they are generally formed within a few months of election day and endure at least until members of the public cast their ballots. Moreover, these attitudes can be considered, in a sense, as summaries of all other factors that affect voting choices. They are more than summaries, however. As already pointed out, Campbell et al. believe that the attitudes with which they are concerned are major determinants of voting decisions and therefore votes.

Having discussed how the funnel of causality model should be interpreted, we are now in a position to understand, at least in part, what the authors of *The American Voter* mean when they claim they can identify motives for votes. I think they mean two things, the first of which is that they can identify what kinds of attitude held by representative samples of the American public occupy the position in the funnel of causality I have described. By different "kinds" of attitude I mean attitudes toward different objects. For example, when they claim they can identify motives for votes, Campbell et al. mean they can show whether attitudes toward parties, issues, or both determine the voting choices of the public. Second, they mean they can determine which of the kinds of attitude that determine voting choices have the strongest influence on the outcomes of elections.

Campbell et al. seem to regard the second claim as more important than the first. Most of their conclusions about public opinion are based on the assumption that they can determine which public attitudes have the strongest influence on the outcomes of elections, rather than on the assumption that they can determine which public attitudes determine at least some voting choices. The analyses they conduct to substantiate these two claims are closely related, however. As a result, we can conclude that when they say they can identify motives for votes, Campbell et al. are making both claims.

Although they attach great importance to their ability to determine what kinds of attitude have the strongest influence on the outcomes of elections, Campbell et al. unfortunately do not tell us exactly what they mean by this. I think we can understand what they mean, however, if we review the procedures they use to determine what attitudes affect voting choices and which of those attitudes have the strongest influence on the outcomes of elections.

The Specifics of the Argument

The authors of *The American Voter* do not attempt to identify motives for votes by using any one test or experiment. Rather, they present a series of arguments which they believe lead to the conclusion that certain attitudes affect votes and influence the outcomes of elections. For the purposes of discussion, this series of arguments is divided into seven parts.

Six Partisan Attitudes.   Campbell et al. identify six partisan attitudes. Almost every member of representative samples of the American public prior to the 1952 and 1956 presidential elections held at least one of these attitudes, and some of the attitudes were held by a majority of those sampled.[10] The authors claim to show that the combination of these attitudes which each member of the samples (and, by inference, of the American public) held determined his vote in the 1952 and 1956 elections. These attitudes are the following: attitude toward Eisenhower, attitude toward Stevenson, attitude toward parties as managers of government, group-related attitude, attitude on domestic policies, and attitude on foreign policies. Campbell et al. define the first two attitudes as tendencies to like or dislike the personal qualities of the candidates. They are concerned with whether members of the public tend to believe that the candidates are honest, intelligent, religious, and so on; not with whether members of the public agree with the policies advocated by the candidates. Attitudes toward the parties as managers of government are defined as tendencies to associate a certain party with hard times, for example, or to believe that it is more frugal in its administration of government than the other party is; they are not defined as tendencies to approve of the parties' leaders or the policies they advocated in particular elections. Group-related attitudes are defined as tendencies to approve or disapprove of the associations of parties or candidates with particular social or economic groups. For example, someone who expressed approval of the Democratic party's alliance with labor or the Republican party's alliance with business would be expressing a group-related attitude. Finally, attitudes toward foreign and domestic policies are defined as tendencies to approve or disapprove of the policies advocated by the candidates and parties.

The six partisan attitudes were assigned by the methods of content analysis discussed in Chapter 2.[11] Each individual interviewed was asked eight open-ended questions. The form of the questions was: "Is there anything in particular that you (like, don't like) about the (Republican, Democratic) party? What is that?" "Is there anything in particular about (Stevenson, Eisenhower) that might make you want to vote (for him, against him)? What is that?" Each statement made by an individual in response to these questions was recorded. Coders determined which of the six attitude objects each statement referred to, and an individual was assigned an attitude toward an object if he made at least one statement about it.

Campbell et al. also used coders to determine the favorableness or unfavorableness of each attitude; but they did not follow the same coding procedures for all six partisan attitudes. In dealing with attitudes toward the two candidates and the parties, their procedure was fairly simple. If an individual made more favorable than unfavorable statements about one of these objects, he was said to have a favorable attitude toward it. If he made more unfavorable than favorable statements about the object, he was said to have an unfavorable attitude. The authors also used the ratio of favorable to unfavorable statements as an index of the intensity of an individual's feelings toward an object if he had a favorable attitude; they used the ratio of unfavorable to favorable statements as an index of intensity if he had an unfavorable attitude. For example, if someone made four times more favorable than unfavorable statements, he was said to have a more favorable attitude than someone who made three times more favorable than unfavorable statements.

The techniques used by Campbell et al. to assign group-related attitudes and attitudes toward foreign and domestic policies were somewhat different from those they used to assign attitudes toward parties and candidates. Coders determined whether each statement made by a person interviewed was pro-Republican or pro-Democratic, rather than whether it was favorable or unfavorable to some object. If a majority of an individual's statements about foreign affairs, for example, were pro-Republican, he was assigned a "pro-Republican attitude." The intensity of attitudes toward policies and group-related attitudes was computed by determining the ratio of pro-Republican to pro-Democratic statements if an individual had a pro-Republican attitude or by determining the ratio of pro-Democratic to pro-Republican statements if he had a pro-Democratic attitude.

Campbell et al. regarded several sorts of statements as pro-Republican or pro-Democratic. For example, any statements about domestic affairs made in response to questions asking interviewees what they liked about Eisenhower or the Republicans were regarded as pro-Republican. Statements about domestic affairs made in response to questions asking what they disliked about Stevenson or the Democrats were also regarded as pro-Republican. Pro-Democratic statements on domestic policies were, correspondingly, statements about domestic affairs made in response to questions asking interviewees what they liked about Stevenson and the Democrats or what they disliked about Eisenhower and the Republicans. Similar procedures were used to determine pro-Republican and pro-Democratic statements about foreign policies and the group associations of parties.

Campbell et al. adopted these procedures for assigning group-related attitudes and attitudes toward foreign and domestic policies because they wished to determine whether members of the public held attitudes that were favorable or unfavorable toward the general postures on foreign and domestic policy and toward the whole range of group affiliations of each party and candidate. They wished to determine, for example, whether members of the public believed that Eisenhower advocated foreign policies which were, on the whole, better or worse than Stevenson's policies. According to the authors, broad attitudes of this sort should be distinguished from attitudes toward specific issues or groups.[12] They do not tell us exactly how they believe these two sorts of attitude differ, but we can infer from their discussion that they distinguish between them in three ways.

First, Campbell et al. believe that attitudes toward specific issues and groups often have different kinds of objects than do broad attitudes toward foreign and domestic policy postures and group affiliations of candidates and parties. According to the authors, if an individual has an issue attitude he tends to like certain policy alternatives and dislike other alternatives on a *particular issue*. If he has a broad attitude toward foreign and domestic policy, however, he tends to like or dislike policy alternatives on *several issues*. Likewise, when Campbell et al. say an individual has an attitude toward a group, they mean that he tends to like or dislike a *particular group;* when they say he has an attitude toward the group affiliations of candidates or parties, they mean that he tends to like or dislike *several different groups* with which he believes the candidates or parties are affiliated. Of course, as pointed out, Campbell et al. sometimes assign attitudes toward foreign and domestic policies and toward group affiliations to members of the public because they express approval or disapproval of policies on only one issue or of only one group. In this case, their assignments of these broad attitudes are indistinguishable from their assignments of attitudes toward issues and groups. In other cases, however, their assignments of these two sorts of attitude differ in the way I have just indicated.

Second, according to Campbell et al., attitudes toward the policy postures or group affiliations of candidates and parties are tendencies to like or dislike certain objects that the individuals who hold the attitudes associate with candidates and parties. When they say that a member of the public favors Eisenhower's foreign policy posture, for example, the authors mean that he favors policies which he believes Eisenhower advocates. When they assign attitudes toward particular issues or groups, however, they are not implying that the individuals to whom they assign those attitudes believe that certain candidates or parties advocate policies or are affiliated with groups which they like or dislike. Thus they might say that an individual favors better relations with Russia whether or not he believes that Eisenhower or Stevenson advocates that policy. As a result, when Campbell et al. assign broad pro-Republican and pro-Democratic attitudes toward policies and group affiliations, they are not necessarily measuring all of the individual's specific attitudes toward foreign and domestic issues or toward groups. They are measuring only his tendencies to evaluate policies or groups that he associates with candidates or parties in a particular election. The authors focus on these tendencies because they assume that an individual's attitudes toward policies and groups can affect his vote only if he associates those policies and groups with particular candidates and parties.

Third, it is possible for a number of people who are assigned the same broad attitudes toward policies or group affiliations to tend to like or dislike different policies or groups. For example, one individual may be assigned a pro-Republican attitude toward foreign affairs because he likes Eisenhower's policies toward Russia and Korea, whereas another individual may be assigned a pro-Republican attitude because he likes Eisenhower's policies toward Mexico and China. The first individual may have no tendency to evaluate policies toward Mexico or China consistently; indeed, he may not even know what policies Eisenhower favors toward those countries. Yet, assuming that he and the second individual express only these opinions on foreign affairs, they would both be said to hold pro-Republican attitudes which were favorable to the same degree because they both expressed the same ratio of pro-Republican to pro-Democratic statements about foreign affairs. In contrast, when Campbell et al. say that two individuals have the same attitude toward a specific issue or group, they mean that those individuals like or dislike the same policy or group.

More will be said later about the way the authors of *The American Voter* assign the six partisan attitudes. For the moment, however, what has been said gives a general idea of how those assignments are made.

Predictions of Votes.   Having assigned the six partisan attitudes to members of their sample, the authors of *The American Voter* set about the task of determining whether those attitudes affect votes.[13] The first step they take is to determine whether their assignments of attitudes enable them to predict which candidate members of the public voted for. They assume that the six partisan attitudes cannot possibly be motives for votes unless they can be used to predict the ways in which the public voted. Of course, this makes good sense. If, for example, someone had a favorable attitude toward Stevenson's foreign policy but voted for Eisenhower, we would not believe that his foreign policy attitude determined his vote. Some other attitude or factor must have been responsible for his preference for Eisenhower.

Campbell et al. begin by calculating how well each attitude, considered separately, enables them to predict votes. They find that the attitudes are all excellent predictors. For example, 75% of the people to whom they assigned attitudes toward Eisenhower did or did not vote for him depending on whether their attitude was favorable or unfavorable.[14] The authors then examine the groups of attitudes each individual held. They write that if the six partisan attitudes determine voting choices, we can think of the attitudes an individual holds as a "force field";[15] that is, each attitude can be considered a force that compels the individual to vote in a certain direction. For example, if an individual holds a pro-Republican attitude toward foreign policy, we can think of this attitude as a force compelling him to vote for Eisenhower. If the analogy to a force field is correct, we would expect that if all of an individual's attitudes have the same direction (i.e., if they are all favorable to the Republicans or to the Democrats), he will vote for the candidate of the party which they all favor. If an individual has attitudes that have different directions, however, his vote will depend on the number of attitude forces in each direction and their relative strengths. For example, if an individual feels very strongly that Eisenhower has good personal qualities and feels less strongly that Stevenson advocates good foreign policies, he will probably vote for Eisenhower.

Campbell et al. believe they can show that the analogy to a force field is correct by using their measures of the intensity of attitudes as measures of the strength of attitude forces. In considering each individual's attitudes, they add the intensities of his pro-Republican and of his pro-Democratic attitudes. They assume that if his attitudes are a force field determining his vote, he will vote for Eisenhower if the summed intensity of his pro-Republican attitudes is greater than the summed intensity of his pro-Democratic attitudes and that he will vote for Stevenson if the summed intensity of his pro-Democratic attitudes is greater than the summed intensity of his pro-Republican attitudes.

In fact, Campbell et al. find that 85% of the people in their sample vote in the way that they predict by using the model of a force field.[16] As a result, they conclude that although the six partisan attitudes may not cause the voting decisions of all members of the public, there is evidence that they cause the decisions of most people. The authors also take considerable encouragement from the finding that if they apply the force field model to less than all six attitudes, their ability to predict votes is decreased.[17] They believe this shows that each of the attitudes is to some extent an independent force which makes a difference in how some, but not all, members of the public vote. In other words, the voting behavior of all members of the public is not caused by some one attitude, such as attitude toward Eisenhower, because if it were we would be able to predict their votes by considering only their attitudes toward Eisenhower as well as we could by considering all six partisan attitudes.

Intensity. The authors of *The American Voter* believe that certain findings about the intensity of the six partisan attitudes support their contention that they are measuring attitudes which determine votes.[18] In the first place, they find that members of the public do not always hold a given attitude with the same degree of intensity and that, if we graph the distribution of intensity of any given attitude found in the public, it forms a normal distribution curve; that is, we find that only a few people hold very intense attitudes and that most people hold moderately intense attitudes. Campbell et al. believe this shows that they have developed a good measure of intensity. Moreover, they find that all of the attitudes which a particular individual holds do not have the same intensity. The authors believe this is an indication that they are measuring discrete attitudes. If their measure of pro-Republican attitudes on foreign affairs, for example, were simply another way of measuring attitudes toward Eisenhower, we would expect that people who were assigned both attitudes would be assigned the same intensity for each attitude. Campbell et al. do not assume that evidence about differences in intensity is conclusive proof that they are assigning discrete attitudes; but they do believe that it contributes to a body of evidence which supports that contention.

Given these indications that their assignments of intensity are meaningful, Campbell et al. take encouragement from the finding that attitude intensity is a good predictor of votes.[19] They believe that if attitudes are forces that determine partisan choice, then the stronger those forces are, the more likely they are to determine voting behavior. In fact, the authors find that people who hold a given attitude very intensely are more likely to vote in accordance with it than are people who hold it less intensely. For example, they find that 98% of the people with very strong favorable attitudes toward Eisenhower voted for him, as opposed to 65% of the people with very weak favorable attitudes.[20]

Political Involvement.   Campbell et al. believe that their findings about the relationship of the six partisan attitudes to voting choice are reinforced by findings about the relationship of those attitudes to certain measures of political "involvement."[21] Although they do not define political involvement, they do say that the more involved in politics an individual is, the more likely he is to make up his mind early in a campaign about which candidate to vote for, to express an interest in the outcome of an election, and to vote a straight ticket. They also say that these are characteristics of an individual who is "highly motivated" politically.[22]

Campbell et al. reason that if an individual's attitudes are forces determining his political behavior, individuals whose attitudes push them in different directions should be less involved in politics than individuals whose attitudes all push them in the same direction. The authors expect that an individual with conflicting attitudes will make up his mind about which candidate to vote for later in the campaign than an individual with consistent attitudes will because there will be no powerful forces compelling him to vote for one candidate rather than another. They think that he will express indifference to the outcome of the election for the same reason. Finally, they think that he will be more likely to split his ticket than will an individual with consistent attitudes, because his attitude toward either party will be balanced by certain other attitudes. Campbell et al. find that all these expectations are borne out by their data. Members of the sample who held consistent attitudes were much more likely than members who held inconsistent attitudes to make up their minds early in the campaign about which candidate they preferred, to express interest in the outcome of the elections, and to vote a straight ticket. The authors believe that these data add further support to their hypothesis that the six partisan attitudes can be considered a force field which affects political behavior.

Attitude Strength.   Having shown that the six partisan attitudes exert an influence on voting choice, Campbell et al. claim that they can show how strong the influence of each attitude is. One way to do this would be simply to determine what percentage of individuals holding each attitude vote in accordance with it. We could say that if attitude x predicts a greater percentage of votes than attitude y does, it must be a stronger psychological force because people who hold it are seemingly more likely to be influenced by it. There are two difficulties with this way of determining the strength of attitudes.

The first difficulty is that this method does not take account of differences in the distribution of intensity of attitudes. For example, if most people who hold attitude x hold it at a high level of intensity and most people who hold attitude y hold it at a low level of intensity, we would expect that attitude x would be a better predictor of votes simply because more intense attitudes are generally more closely associated with behavior than are less intense attitudes. In comparing the two attitudes, therefore, we might be comparing the effect on votes of differences in levels of intensity rather than attitudes toward different objects.

The second difficulty with determining the influence of an attitude by considering only what percentage of votes it predicts is that this procedure ignores the possibility that the accuracy with which an attitude predicts votes may be partly due to the way it is combined with other attitudes and to the psychological force it exerts on voting choices. If, for example, attitude x predicts votes only when it is held together with attitudes y and z, we would suspect that the relationship between attitude x and votes may be due, in part, to the influence which attitudes y and z exert; we would also suspect that y and z may have a stronger influence on votes than attitude x has even though x may predict more votes than either of them considered separately.

Because of these two difficulties, Campbell et al. generally do not say that the influence of the six partisan attitudes on votes is indicated by what percentage of the individuals who hold a certain attitude vote in accordance with it. Instead, they use the techniques of multiple regression analysis to determine the influence of attitudes on votes.[23] Multiple regression analysis is a highly sophisticated statistical technique, and it is beyond the scope of this work to explain it.[24] It is sufficient to say that, as applied by Campbell et al., multiple regression analysis enables the authors to determine how well each of the six partisan attitudes predicts votes while the influence of other attitudes on votes is held constant statistically. It also enables them to compensate for differences in the distribution of intensity of attitudes. As a result, multiple regression analysis enables Campbell et al. to determine how strong a relationship there would be between each attitude and voting choices if other attitudes did not exert an influence on those choices and if the distribution of the intensity of all attitudes were the same.

The precise results of the multiple regression analysis of the six partisan attitudes that Campbell et al. conduct are, for some reason, not reported in *The American Voter*. We are told, however, that attitudes toward Eisenhower and group-related attitudes are two of the attitudes which have the most powerful effect on votes.[25] The actual comparisons, reported in another publication, are presented in Figure 4.2. These comparisons support this conclusion, and they also show that attitudes toward parties as managers of government have an even stronger effect on voting choices than group-related attitudes have. Thus the authors of *The American Voter* claim that by the use of multiple regression analysis, they have shown that attitudes toward parties and candidates have a stronger effect on voting choice than attitudes toward issues have.

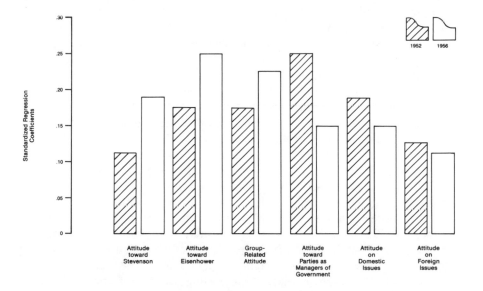

Figure 4.2. Results of the multiple regression analysis of the six partisan attitudes on votes. (Source: Donald E. Stokes, Angus Campbell, and Warren E. Miller, "Components of Electoral Decision," *American Political Science Review*, 52, no. 2 [1958]: 381.)

Party Preference.   Despite the importance they attach to the six partisan attitudes, the authors of *The American Voter* claim they have discovered another attitude that has an even more powerful effect on voting choices. This attitude is what they call "party preference" or "party identification."[26] Party preference differs from attitudes toward parties as managers of government in several ways. Probably the best way to understand these differences is to consider how the two attitudes are assigned. Attitudes toward parties as managers of government are assigned by content analyses of answers to free-response questions. The statements used to assign these attitudes are largely statements attributing such qualities as efficiency or fiscal responsibility to the parties or statements linking their periods in office to "good times" or "bad times." Measures of party preference are based on answers to two questions: "Generally speaking, do you think of yourself as a Republican or a Democrat, or what?" "Would you call yourself a strong (Republican or Democrat) or a not very strong (Republican or Democrat)?"[27] Independents are asked to classify themselves as closer to one party or the other.

These questions, of course, directly ask individuals only to express their self-images, not their evaluations of the parties. If we assume that people generally identify with things they like, however, we can expect that their answers to questions about party preference will be consistent with their tendencies to evaluate the parties. If, for example, an individual says he considers himself a Democrat, we can expect that he will tend to evaluate the Democrats favorably. Campbell et al. believe that their techniques for measuring party preference do, in fact, enable them to record attitudes toward parties because they find that party preference, as indicated by those techniques, correlates highly with the voting histories reported by members of the public.[28] Each member of their sample was asked whether he had always voted for the same party or for different parties in the past. Since an individual's pattern of votes can be regarded as a pattern of evaluative actions, his voting record can be considered a measure of his attitude toward parties. In 80% of the cases, people said that they had always voted for the same party, and in almost every case this was the party they identified with. Moreover, consistent voters were much more likely to say that they were strong party identifiers than were inconsistent voters. Hence the authors of *The American Voter* assume that, by recording party preference, they are also recording long-standing attitudes toward parties.

Campbell et al. believe that party preference has a powerful influence on voting choices because they find that it is a slightly better predictor of the way in which members of their sample voted than are all six of the partisan attitudes combined.[29] The authors see party preference as more than just a powerful attitude, however. They argue that it is the major influence on voting choices of members of their sample and that it causes individuals to adopt partisan attitudes consistent with it.[30] According to them, therefore, party preference determines both votes and the direction of the six partisan attitudes.

Campbell et al. present several sorts of evidence to support this claim.[31] First, they say that because party preference predicts more voting choices than all six partisan attitudes combined, there is reason to believe that it determines more voting choices as well.

Second, they report that most of the individuals they interviewed held attitudes consistent with their votes in the sense that they voted for the party which a majority of their attitudes favored. This is significant for discussions of party preference because the authors also found that interviewees almost always expressed a preference for the same party which a majority of their attitudes favored and that strong party identifiers were more likely than weak identifiers or independents to hold a majority of attitudes favoring the party they preferred. The authors believe these findings show that an individual's party preference determines the direction of the other political attitudes he forms and his voting choices and that the stronger his party preference is, the stronger its influence on other attitudes and voting choices will be. In addition, they believe these findings show that the relationships between the six partisan attitudes and voting choices which they have discovered are due to the influence of party preference on those attitudes and voting choices.

Third, Campbell et al. report that the party preferences expressed by the individuals they interviewed correlated highly with all the measures of political involvement—such as time of voting decision, interest in the election, and straight-ticket voting—with which the six partisan attitudes correlated. Weak party identifiers were much more likely than strong identifiers to make up their minds late in campaigns about which candidate to vote for, to be indifferent to the outcomes of elections, and to split their tickets. The authors believe these findings show that an individual's party preference determines the level of his political involvement and that the relationships between the six partisan attitudes and measures of political involvement they discover are due to the influence of party preference on both those factors.

In short, the authors of *The American Voter* believe there is a body of evidence which shows that the party preferences held by members of the public determined the direction of the six partisan attitudes which they held, their levels of political involvement, and their voting choices in the 1952 and 1956 elections. This same evidence, however, could be used to argue that the six partisan attitudes determine party preferences, voting choices, and political involvement. We could interpret the findings that members of the public generally hold political attitudes which are consistent with their party preferences and votes and that strong party identifiers are more likely to have consistent attitudes and to vote for the party they favor than are weak identifiers differently than Campbell et al. do. We could say these findings show that if most of the attitudes an individual forms favor a certain party, those attitudes will cause him to express a strong preference for the party and vote for it in most elections; alternatively, if his attitudes favor different parties, they will not cause him to form a strong preference for either party and he will vote for different parties in different elections. We could conclude, therefore, that the relationships between party preferences, the six partisan attitudes, and voting choices which Campbell et al. have discovered are due to the influence of the six partisan attitudes on party preferences and voting choices, rather than the influence of party preferences on the other two factors.

In addition, we could interpret findings that individuals with strong party preferences are generally more involved in politics than individuals with weak preferences differently than Campbell et al. do. We could explain these findings by saying that the six partisan attitudes determine both strength of party preference and the level of political involvement instead of saying that party preference determines the level of political involvement and the direction of the six partisan attitudes. Thus we could say that if an individual's partisan attitudes are very consistent, they cause him to adopt a strong preference for one party and to be highly involved in politics; but if they are not very consistent, they do not cause him to have a strong preference for either party or to take an interest in politics. If this is a correct description of the relationship between party preference, political involvement, and partisan attitudes, we would expect the level of political involvement to vary with the strength of party preference because both would be determined by the same factor, partisan attitudes. This explanation would only be plausible, however, if we found that individuals with more consistent partisan attitudes tend to be more involved in politics and to have stronger party preferences than individuals with less consistent partisan attitudes. In fact, I pointed out earlier (see "Political involvement") that Campbell et al. have shown that the level of political involvement among members of the public varies with the consistency of their partisan attitudes; I also demonstrated how these findings could be interpreted to show that the six partisan attitudes determine political involvement. Moreover, I have just pointed out that Campbell et al. show that individuals with highly consistent attitudes tend to express stronger party preferences than do individuals with less consistent attitudes.

Finally, we might say that findings that party preference predicts more voting choices than do the six partisan attitudes indicate only that party preference may have determined the voting choices of those few individuals who did not vote for the party which most of their attitudes favored. We can argue that the votes of the vast majority of the individuals who did vote for the party which most of their attitudes favored were determined by those attitudes rather than by party preference.

Campbell et al. are aware that their findings can be interpreted to show that the six partisan attitudes determined party preference rather than vice versa, and they discuss this problem at length. They write:

Our conviction on this point [that their data show the influence of party preference on the six partisan attitudes rather than the influence of those attitudes on party preference] is rooted in what we know of the relative stability and priority in time of party identification and the attitudes it may affect. We know that people who identify with one of the parties typically have held the same partisan tie for all or most of their adult lives. But within their experience since coming of voting age many of the elements of politics have changed. For example, the 1952 campaign brought two new candidates to presidential politics and a set of new issues arising very recently from the Korean War and the charges of corruption during the later Truman years. Yet the reactions to the personalities of Eisenhower and Stevenson, to the issues of the Far Eastern war, and to the probity of the Democratic Administration differed markedly according to the individual's party allegiance. If we trust the evidence on the stability of party identification, these differences must be attributed to the capacity of general partisan orientation to color responses to particular political objects.[32]

In other words, Campbell et al. believe that party preference must have influenced the six partisan attitudes in 1952 and 1956 because individuals formed their party preferences before they formed their partisan attitudes and because party preferences are more stable than partisan attitudes.

Issue Attitudes. So far I have shown how the authors of *The American Voter* argue that certain attitudes determine which candidates members of the public vote for. An equally important part of their argument is that certain other attitudes cannot cause votes. By eliminating other attitudes, they hope to show that the six partisan attitudes and party preference are the only attitudes which influence votes and the outcomes of elections.

Campbell et al. devote an entire chapter to showing that attitudes toward specific political issues cannot have a strong effect on voting choices.[33] In each of the campaigns they studied, they selected 16 issues they believed were among those receiving most attention by the press and politicians; for example, whether suspected Communists should be fired from government service and whether the United States should give foreign aid to neutral countries. Each member of their sample was asked whether he agreed or disagreed with a certain statement of opinion about each issue. He was also asked if he knew what the government was doing about each issue and what positions the two parties had taken on it. The authors found that only about 60% of the people in their sample both expressed an opinion about any given issue and offered any explanation, whether correct or incorrect, of what the government was doing about it. In addition, only a small percentage of the interviewees expressed opinions and offered explanations of government actions on a majority of the 16 issues. Finally, only about 30% of those people who offered an opinion and claimed to know what the government was doing on any given issue said they could perceive any difference between the stands of the two parties on that issue. Moreover, people who could perceive differences between the parties often disagreed about which party held which position.[34]

Campbell et al. believe these findings show that attitudes toward specific issues cannot have a strong effect on voting choices. Most people do not have attitudes toward many issues and, if they do, they seldom know what positions the government or the parties have taken. The authors reason that unless members of the public hold beliefs which link their attitudes toward issues with government and parties, those attitudes cannot possibly affect votes.

In addition to their other findings about issue attitudes, Campbell et al. report that members of the public generally express opinions about issues which are consistent with their party preferences and that when they perceive policy differences between parties, they generally assume that the party which they favor holds a position similar to their own.[35] From these two findings the authors conclude that party preferences probably determine attitudes toward specific issues as well as the six partisan attitudes. They draw this conclusion for the same reason they conclude that party preference determines, rather than is determined by, the six partisan attitudes. In other words, they assume that any consistencies between party preference and issue attitudes must be due to the influence of party preference on the formation of issue attitudes, rather than the influence of issue attitudes on the formation of party preference. This is because they believe that party preference is formed prior to most issue attitudes and is more stable than those attitudes are.

Summary of the Argument

When they claim they can identify motives for votes, Campbell et al. are claiming that they are able to show (1) what kinds of public attitudes determine the voting choices of members of the American public and (2) which of these attitudes have the strongest influence on the outcomes of elections. Regarding the first claim, the authors believe they have shown that a fairly small number of attitudes determine voting choices. These are the six partisan attitudes and party preference. A substantial percentage of members of the American public held each of these kinds of attitudes during the election campaigns which Campbell et al. studied, and all of them tended to make a variety of evaluations.[36] The authors claim to have shown that these broad, widely held attitudes determined voting choices by showing that they (1) enable us to predict votes, (2) interact with each other like elements in a force field and (3) are related to measures of political involvement in certain interesting ways. They also claim to have shown that attitudes toward specific issues did not influence the voting choices of many members of the American public.

Regarding their second claim, Campbell et al. believe they have shown that party preference had a stronger influence on the outcomes of the elections they studied than the six partisan attitudes had and that both party preference and the six partisan attitudes had a stronger influence than issue attitudes had. I said earlier that we would be in a better position to understand what the authors mean when they say that certain kinds of attitudes have a stronger influence on the outcomes of elections than other kinds after we had reviewed the techniques they use to identify motives for votes. We can now see that they mean at least three things:

1. Campbell et al. mean that certain kinds of attitude affect the voting choices of more members of the public than other kinds do. (When I say an attitude "affects" someone's vote, I mean that it is one of the attitudes which occupies the position in the funnel of causality relative to his vote which the authors assign to motives for votes.) For example, they say that party preference had a stronger influence than issue attitudes on the outcomes of the elections they studied because they believe that party preference affected the voting choices of almost all members of the public in those elections, whereas issue attitudes affected the voting choices of very few members of the public.

2. Campbell et al. say that if a member of the public holds several attitudes which are consistent with his voting choice, and if there is evidence that one of these attitudes has determined the direction of the other attitudes (i.e., has determined whether they are favorable or unfavorable to a certain party, candidate, or issue), that attitude has a stronger influence on his voting choice than the other attitudes have. If, therefore, they find that certain kinds of attitude which are generally consistent with the voting choices of members of the public often determine the direction of other kinds of attitudes which are also generally consistent with those choices, they say that attitudes of the first kind have a stronger influence on the outcomes of elections than attitudes of the second kind. For example, the authors say that party preference had a stronger influence on the outcomes of the elections they studied than the six partisan attitudes had because they believe that the direction of the six partisan attitudes was often determined by party preference.

3. Campbell et al. say that attitudes of type x have a stronger influence

on the outcomes of elections than attitudes of types y and z if, when the relationship between attitudes of types y and z is held constant, attitudes of type x predict voting choices more accurately than do attitudes of types y and z when they are analyzed in a similar way. The authors use multiple regression analysis to determine which kinds of attitude have the strongest influence on the outcomes of elections in this sense. For example, they say that, of the six partisan attitudes, attitudes toward the personal qualities of candidates had the strongest influence on the outcomes of the elections they studied because a multiple regression analysis indicated that attitudes toward the personal qualities of candidates were better predictors of voting choices than were the other partisan attitudes.

The authors of *The American Voter* believe that their argument is significant primarily because they believe they have shown that members of the American public do not vote for candidates on the basis of what those candidates say or do about issues. Their votes are determined primarily by long-standing habits of loyalty to parties and by feelings about the personal qualities of candidates. Campbell et al. believe this shows that members of the public are not as "rational" as they are often supposed to be and that many optimistic theories about American democracy are wrong. They also believe their findings enable us to understand certain political strategies that candidates and parties do or might adopt. The conclusions that Campbell et al. draw from their findings are reviewed in more detail in Chapter 7. First, it is important to determine whether their interpretation of those findings is, in fact, correct.

5. Issue Attitudes

In this and the following chapter, two parts of the argument of *The American Voter* are criticized. In this chapter it is argued that Campbell et al. do not show that attitudes toward particular issues have only a minor influence on voting choices. This is a criticism of the part of their argument outlined in the section of Chapter 4 entitled "Issue attitudes." In Chapter 6 it is argued that Campbell et al. do not show that party preference has a much stronger influence on voting choices and the outcomes of elections than any other attitudes have, or that it in fact determines the attitudes toward issues and candidates which members of the public hold. This is a criticism of the part of their argument outlined in the section of Chapter 4 entitled "Party preference." I have no quarrel with the other parts of the argument of *The American Voter*. I concede that Campbell et al. have shown that the six partisan attitudes influence voting choices and the outcomes of elections. By criticizing their arguments about issue attitudes and party preference, however, I shall show that many of their general conclusions about political attitudes, including many based partly on findings about the six partisan attitudes, must be reconsidered.

Summary of the Argument

The authors of *The American Voter* say that attitudes toward specific issues are not very widely held, are often not linked to perceptions about candidates and parties, and seem to be influenced strongly by party preference. Beyond this, Campbell et al. tell us little about issue attitudes. They claim, nevertheless, that the information about issue attitudes which they present is sufficient to show that those attitudes cannot possibly have a great effect on voting choices and, therefore, on the outcomes of elections. I have two criticisms of this claim.

First, the information about issue attitudes that Campbell et al. present does not enable them to draw any firm conclusions about the relationship between those attitudes and votes. Second, the authors are, therefore, remiss in not using the same techniques to determine whether issue attitudes influence voting choices and the outcomes of elections that they use to analyze other kinds of attitude. As a result, they cannot claim to show whether issue attitudes are motives for votes. These two criticisms are elaborated separately, and several objections to them are considered. In the course of considering these objections, it is shown that there is reason to believe that if Campbell et al. had analyzed issue attitudes differently, they would have found that those attitudes have a substantial influence on voting choices and the outcomes of elections.

Where the Argument of *The American Voter* Fails

Issue Publics.   The authors of *The American Voter* claim that issue attitudes cannot influence voting choices and the outcomes of elections because they are not widely held, are not often linked to perceptions of candidates and parties, and are strongly influenced by party preference. The first of these three claims is the most perplexing. It is certainly true that no one of the issue attitudes which Campbell et al. record could have as strong an influence on the outcomes of elections as party preference and the six partisan attitudes have because party preference and each of the six partisan attitudes are held by a majority of members of the public, whereas each issue attitude is held by only a small percentage of members of the public. This does not mean, however, that *collectively* issue attitudes could not affect the voting choices of a majority of members of the public and, as a result, have a strong influence on the outcomes of elections. If every member of the public holds at least one issue attitude, and if it affects his vote, then issue attitudes would be powerful political forces.

Campbell et al. do not tell us how many members of their sample held at least one issue attitude, but Key has thrown some light on this question by analyzing the data they used to assign issue attitudes. It will be remembered that Campbell et al. assigned these attitudes by asking members of their sample whether they agreed or disagreed with statements about 16 issues. If an individual expressed an opinion about one of the statements, he was said to have an attitude about the issue to which it corresponds. Because Key was interested in the influence of issue attitudes on votes, he analyzed only data about the individuals interviewed by Campbell et al. who voted in the year they were interviewed. He reports that 84% of these individuals expressed an opinion about at least one of the 16 issues and said that they could perceive a difference between the stands of the parties on some of the issues about which they expressed opinions.[1]

Key also reports that 34% of the voters expressed opinions about 6 to 16 issues. It is, therefore, quite possible that issue attitudes could have affected the votes of a substantial percentage of members of the American public. In fact, it is conceivable that they could have had a stronger influence on the outcomes of elections than any one of the six partisan attitudes had. Campbell et al. report that the most influential attitude they recorded, attitude toward Eisenhower, predicted the votes of only 75% of their sample.[2] If everyone who held an issue attitude voted in accordance with it, however, issue attitudes would have predicted 84% of the votes in the elections Campbell et al. studied. As already pointed out, the authors assume that if an attitude predicts voting choices this can be considered at least partial evidence that it determines them. If we accept this assumption, we can say that if everyone who held an issue attitude voted in accordance with it, there would be some reason to believe that issue attitudes have a stronger influence on the outcomes of elections than any one of the six partisan attitudes have.

We can describe the way Campbell et al. analyze issue attitudes by saying that they neglect the importance of "issue publics." By an issue public, I mean a fairly small percentage of members of the general public who are more concerned about a particular issue than are other members of the public. If most people belonged to at least one issue public, and if the votes of the members of such a public were determined by their attitudes toward the issue of common concern to them, then issue attitudes would have a strong influence on voting choices and the outcomes of elections even though they were not widely held.

It is surprising that in *The American Voter* Campbell, Converse, Miller, and Stokes do not consider the possibility that issue attitudes might influence the outcomes of elections by affecting the votes of limited sectors of the public because, in another study, Converse seems to consider issue publics quite important.[3] Moreover, the importance of these publics has been stressed by many other political scientists in recent years. It has been shown that members of certain economic and social groups are more likely to hold attitudes about some issues than are other members of the public.[4] For example, farmers are more likely to hold attitudes about farm issues than are other members of the public, and blue-collar workers are more likely to hold attitudes about labor issues.[5] In addition, some studies suggest that issue attitudes may influence voting choices and the outcomes of elections by showing that the distribution of opinions in certain economic and social groups is often not the same as the distribution in the general public and that members of these groups often vote in accordance with their issue attitudes.[6] For example, studies have shown that a larger percentage of Jews than other members of the public hold liberal issue attitudes and also vote for the more liberal candidates in elections.[7] Indeed, Campbell et al. themselves present evidence that the distribution of issue attitudes and the voting tendencies in certain groups often distinguish them from the general public; but they do not conclude on the basis of this evidence that issue attitudes affect voting choices.[8] Unfortunately studies of issue publics generally cover only a ˜ew groups and issues, and the existing literature does not provide the basis for firm conclusions about the overall influence of issue attitudes on American electoral history. Nevertheless, it at least suggests that there may be some validity to the notion that those attitudes affect electoral results by affecting the votes of issue publics.

Relationship to Party.   I think, therefore, that Campbell et al. are wrong in claiming that issue attitudes cannot be motives for votes simply because those attitudes are not widely held. In addition, I think they are wrong in claiming that issue attitudes cannot influence voting choices and the outcomes of elections because members of the public who express an opinion about an issue are often unable to state which party has taken a stand they favor on the issue. The authors argue that issue attitudes cannot motivate individuals to vote for parties or candidates unless the individuals have some idea of what positions the parties or candidates have taken on the issues in question. This is, of course, a reasonable argument; but it does not provide sufficient grounds for rejecting all issue attitudes. It may well be that many of the issue attitudes held by members of the public have no effect on their votes. This does not mean, however, that some issue attitudes—those which are linked to parties and candidates—have no effect. As I have pointed out, Key reports that 84% of the voters whom Campbell et al. interviewed held at least one issue attitude which was linked to their perceptions of parties and candidates. It is, therefore, conceivable that if Campbell et al. were to study only these attitudes, they would find that issue attitudes have as strong an influence on voting choices and the outcomes of elections as the six partisan attitudes have.

The only way we can reject all issue attitudes because some of them cannot affect votes is to assume that unless an attitude determines the votes of everyone who holds it, it cannot determine the votes of anyone. I think this is an assumption no psychologist would accept. As I pointed out in Chapter 2, psychologists believe that attitudes do not always have behavioral components and that the behavioral components of attitudes are not always consistent with their cognitive and affective components. They devote a great deal of attention to why particular attitudes have behavioral components and why these components are consistent with beliefs and feelings when the attitudes are held by some people but not others. As a result, I think it is fair to say that psychologists do not believe that unless an attitude is always related to the behavior of all members of the public who hold it, it cannot be related to the behavior of any members of the public.

Moreover, Campbell et al. themselves do not assume that unless attitudes affect the votes of everyone who holds them, they cannot affect the votes of anyone. As already pointed out, the authors assign the six partisan attitudes by analyzing opinions expressed in answer to free-response questions about parties and candidates. Because all the opinions they record are about parties and candidates, there is no reason for Campbell et al. to assume that the six partisan attitudes cannot affect votes because they are not linked to perceptions of parties and candidates. They do, however, sometimes say that these attitudes cannot possibly affect the votes of certain individuals for another reason. If, for example, an individual's broad attitudes on domestic policies are pro-Republican and if he voted for the Democrats, Campbell et al. would conclude that his attitude could not possibly have determined his vote. In fact, they find that each of the six partisan attitudes fails to predict the votes of many individuals whom they interviewed.[9] There are, therefore, many cases in which each of these attitudes, like each of the 16 issue attitudes, could not affect votes. The authors do not conclude, however, that the six partisan attitudes cannot affect voting choices because each of them cannot affect the votes of all members of the public who hold it. Rather, they go on to determine how strong an effect each attitude has on the voting choices of some members of the public. As a result, there seems to be no reason why they should assume that issue attitudes cannot influence the outcomes of elections because no one issue attitude can determine the votes of everyone who holds it.

Party Preference.   The final reason why Campbell et al. claim that issue attitudes cannot have a strong influence on voting choices and the outcomes of elections is that those attitudes appear to be determined by party preference. I do not think the arguments that the authors use to show that party preference has a powerful effect on other attitudes are conclusive, however, and those arguments are discussed at length in Chapter 6. Even if we accept them, we should bear in mind that the authors of *The American Voter* believe that the six partisan attitudes as well as the 16 issue attitudes are determined by party preference. In fact, they say that party preference influences votes primarily by acting "through" the six partisan attitudes.[10] If it is reasonable for Campbell et al. to conclude that issue attitudes cannot have a strong influence on voting choices and the outcomes of elections because they are determined by party preference, it would also be reasonable for them to draw the same conclusion about the six partisan attitudes. Instead they conclude that the six partisan attitudes strongly influence votes and election outcomes, but not as strongly as party preference does, and that issue attitudes have little influence on votes and election outcomes. Clearly, therefore, it is inconsistent with what they say elsewhere for Campbell et al. to claim that evidence that issue attitudes are determined by party preference by itself provides sufficient grounds for concluding that those attitudes cannot be motives for votes.

The three arguments I have reviewed are the only arguments Campbell et al. use to show that issue attitudes cannot influence voting choices and the outcomes of elections. I have shown that these arguments are inconclusive. Judging from the evidence the authors present, it is of course possible that issue attitudes do not have a strong effect on votes; but we cannot conclude that this is the case simply because they are not widely held, are often not linked to perceptions of parties and candidates, or appear to be influenced by party preference. None of this evidence precludes the possibility that issue attitudes might have a powerful influence on the outcomes of elections by affecting the votes of issue publics. I do not deny that Campbell et al. have performed a valuable service by showing that issue attitudes are not as widely held as attitudes toward parties and candidates. It is shown later that this is the basis for several important conclusions which they draw. I think, however, that Campbell et al. are wrong in claiming they have shown that, collectively, issue attitudes are not motives for votes.

The Argument Not Presented by *The American Voter*

Because they believe the evidence shows that issue attitudes do not influence the voting choices of many members of the public, Campbell et al. make two important and problematic assumptions.

First, they assume that it is superfluous to apply to issue attitudes the same techniques they use to determine whether other kinds of attitude affect voting choices. In particular, they do not determine how well those attitudes predict voting choices and whether they are related to each other like elements in a force field.[11] If we grant that their analysis of issue attitudes is correct, it makes good sense for the authors to neglect these techniques. They believe they have shown that issue attitudes cannot possibly determine the voting choices of many members of the public by a series of analyses which have been outlined earlier. As a result, it would surely be a waste of time and energy for them to conduct another series of analyses that would only show the same thing. In addition, the analyses of issue attitudes that Campbell et al. conduct are much simpler than their analyses of other kinds of attitude in the sense that they require collecting less data and performing fewer and less sophisticated computations. Given these circumstances, it surely makes sense for the authors to analyze the relationship between issue attitudes and voting choices in the way that they do, rather than attempt to determine whether those attitudes predict voting choices or form a force field.

Second, Campbell et al. assume that it is superfluous to apply the same techniques to issue attitudes which they use to determine whether other kinds of attitude have a strong or weak influence on the out-comes of elections. In particular, they do not include issue attitudes in their multiple regression analyses, and they do not attempt to find out whether those attitudes determine other attitudes that predict vot-ing choices. The authors do not tell us why they fail to analyze issue attitudes in these ways. Because the only findings about issue atti-tudes that they report are those which I discussed earlier, however, they must base their conclusion that issue attitudes do not have a strong influence on the outcomes of elections on those findings. Thus the most likely reason Campbell et al. do not apply the same tech-niques to issue attitudes which they use to analyze the relationship of other kinds of attitude to electoral outcomes is that they believe their findings about issue attitudes show they cannot possibly have a strong influence on the outcomes of elections in any of the three senses men-tioned earlier.

It might well be reasonable for Campbell et al. to believe this if their interpretations of their findings about issue attitudes are correct. To begin with, they claim to show that those attitudes cannot possibly influence the voting choices of many members of the public. This finding indicates that issue attitudes do not have a strong influence on the out-comes of elections in the first sense mentioned in Chapter 4. In addition, Campbell et al. claim to have shown that issue attitudes are determined by party preference. They might believe that this shows that those atti-tudes cannot have a strong influence on the outcomes of elections in the second sense mentioned in Chapter 4 (i.e., in the sense that they are determined by rather than determine other attitudes). Finally, Campbell et al. might believe that because they have shown that voting choices and issue attitudes are determined by party preference, they can also assume that issue attitudes do not influence the outcomes of elections in the third sense mentioned in Chapter 4. I have pointed out that they use the techniques of multiple regression analysis to determine whether atti-tudes have a strong influence on the outcomes of elections in this third sense. I have also pointed out that if attitude x and attitude y often predict voting choices, and if attitude y generally predicts voting choices only because both it and those choices are determined by attitude x, a multiple regression analysis will probably show that attitude x has a stronger influence on voting choices than attitude y has. Campbell et al. may believe, therefore, that if they have shown that party preference determines both voting choices and issue attitudes, and that issue atti-tudes cannot determine votes, they are probably safe in assuming that a multiple regression analysis would show that issue attitudes do not have a strong influence on the outcomes of elections.

The assumptions that it is superfluous to test whether issue attitudes

affect voting choices or how strong an influence they have on the outcomes of elections make sense only if Campbell et al. are correct in
claiming they have shown that issue attitudes do not affect the voting
choices of many members of the public and that they are determined by
party preference. If, as I have argued, they are wrong in making these
claims, we can criticize their work in two important ways.

First, we can say that they are wrong in not using the same techniques
to determine whether issue attitudes affect voting choices which they
use to determine whether other attitudes affect voting choices. Those
techniques seem to be sound and if, as Campbell et al. claim, they are
valid ways of analyzing the six partisan attitudes and party preference,
they should also be valid ways of analyzing issue attitudes. Assuming I
am correct to argue that the techniques the authors use to analyze issue
attitudes do not produce valuable findings, it is surely reasonable to say
that they should have used other valid techniques which they had at
their disposal to determine whether those attitudes affect voting choices.

Second, if Campbell et al. are wrong in claiming they have shown that
issue attitudes do not affect the voting choices of many members of the
public and that those attitudes are determined by party preference, then
they are also wrong in not applying the same techniques to those attitudes which they use to determine whether other kinds of attitude
influence the outcomes of elections. The most likely explanation of why
they neglect those techniques is that they believe they have shown that
issue attitudes cannot have a strong influence on the outcomes of elections by showing that they do not determine many voting choices and
are determined by party preference. If, however, their findings about the
relationship of issue attitudes to voting choices and party preference are
inconclusive, they have not shown whether those attitudes influence the
outcomes of elections, and there is no apparent reason why they should
not apply the same techniques to those attitudes that they apply to
determine whether other kinds of attitudes influence electoral outcomes.

In short, it seems that Campbell et al. should have used the same
techniques to determine whether issue attitudes influence voting choices
and the outcomes of elections that they use to analyze other kinds of
attitude. Of course, there may be other techniques that would be equally
effective for these purposes. Nevertheless, if they had applied the same
techniques to the six partisan attitudes, party preference, and issue attitudes, the authors could easily have compared their findings about different kinds of attitude. In any event, if my criticisms of their analysis of
issue attitudes are correct, we can say that because they do not analyze
those attitudes in the same ways that they analyze other kinds of attitude
or in any other acceptable way, Campbell et al. do not demonstrate
whether issue attitudes affect voting choices or how strong an influence

they have on the outcomes of elections. It is possible, therefore, that if they had included issue attitudes in their multiple regression analyses, and if they had attempted to determine whether those attitudes (1) can be used to predict voting choices, (2) seem to form a force field, and (3) determine the directions of other attitudes, Campbell et al. would have found that issue attitudes affect the voting choices of many members of the public and have a powerful influence on the outcomes of elections.

What *The American Voter* Might Have Done

If the authors of *The American Voter* had wished to analyze issue attitudes in the same way they analyze the six partisan attitudes and party preference, there are at least two points in their work where they might have done so. The first point is obviously in their discussion of the 16 issue attitudes. Since Campbell et al. asked all their subjects how they voted, it would have been fairly easy for them to have determined how well each of the 16 issue attitudes predicts votes. They would simply have had to calculate what percentage of the people who held each attitude and who linked it to a candidate or party voted consistently with it. The authors could also have determined whether issue attitudes could be considered a force field. To accomplish this, they would have had to begin by determining which party a majority of the attitudes held by each individual favors. They could then have determined whether individuals tend to vote in accordance with the majority of their attitudes and whether, for example, individuals with a higher ratio of pro-Republican to pro-Democratic attitudes are more likely to vote for the Republicans than are individuals with a lower ratio. Finally, Campbell et al. could have included issue attitudes in their multiple regression analyses of the six partisan attitudes. How such an analysis could have been conducted will be demonstrated later.

In addition, Campbell et al. might have attempted to determine whether issue attitudes determine the direction of other attitudes. This point is discussed at length in Chapter 6.

The second point in their work where Campbell et al. might have analyzed issue attitudes in the same way they analyze the six partisan attitudes is in their discussion of broad attitudes toward foreign and domestic policy. If they had interpreted the data they use to assign broad policy attitudes differently, they might well have been able to determine how strong an effect attitudes toward specific issues have on votes without greatly modifying the course of their analysis.

As explained previously the authors of *The American Voter* assigned broad attitudes toward foreign and domestic policy to members of their sample on the basis of statements about issues made in answer to free-

response questions about parties and candidates. They recorded statements about a variety of issues being discussed in 1952 and 1956. For
example, some people liked the Republicans because they advocated a
tough line toward Russia and promised to maintain the Taft-Hartley Act,
and other people liked the Democrats because they favored more foreign
aid and more federal aid to education.[12] Campbell et al. assume that
these statements are not merely casual expressions of opinion. Rather,
they believe that answers to free-response questions are indicative of
enduring evaluative tendencies. Thus they could assume that these
answers are expressions of attitudes toward specific issues. In other
words, there is seemingly no reason why they should assume that if an
individual says he favors Eisenhower's policy toward Russia, he is expressing a broad attitude toward Eisenhower's general posture on foreign affairs rather than an attitude toward a specific policy.

Moreover, the assumption that individuals are expressing several issue attitudes when they answer free-response questions would be perfectly consistent with the way in which Campbell et al. assigned the 16
issue attitudes. Each of these attitudes was assigned to an individual if
he expressed only a single opinion about an issue. If they had applied
the same rule in analyzing answers to free-response questions, the authors could have used these answers to determine how strong an
influence issue attitudes have on votes; that is, they could have assigned
each individual several attitudes toward specific issues on the basis of
his or her answers to free-response questions and then analyzed those
attitudes in the same way they analyzed attitudes toward candidates and
parties. This would require some modification in the way in which they
record and analyze opinions about issues, but the modification need not
be major (see pp. 98–115).

Campbell et al. do not proceed in this way, however. Rather, they
combine all the opinions an individual expresses in answer to free-
response questions into indices of broad attitudes toward foreign and
domestic policies. They present no explanation of why they believe it is
more correct to interpret those opinions as expressions of broad policy
attitudes rather than as expressions of attitudes toward specific issues.
One possibility is that the authors are simply more interested in broad
policy attitudes than in attitudes toward specific issues because broad
attitudes are more widely held. They are able to assign attitudes toward
foreign and domestic issues to a majority of the members of their
sample, whereas only a small percentage of their sample expresses opinions about any one specific issue. If they assume that only widely held
attitudes can possibly influence votes, and if they are interested in studying the factors which influence the outcomes of elections, Campbell et
al. might simply believe that it is useful to employ answers to free-

response questions to assign broad policy attitudes. I have already pointed out, however, that there is no reason to believe that widely held attitudes exert a stronger influence on the outcomes of elections than specific issue attitudes do. Therefore there is no reason to think that it is either more correct or more useful to use answers to free-response questions to assign broad policy attitudes, rather than specific issue attitudes, simply because broad attitudes are more widely held.

Another reason Campbell et al. might use expressions of opinion about issues to assign broad policy attitudes is that they might believe that those attitudes differ in some important respect from specific issue attitudes and that there is some evidence which suggests that the opinions they record are expressions of broad policy attitudes rather than specific issue attitudes. In fact, as pointed out in Chapter 4, they say that broad policy attitudes differ from issue attitudes in three major ways: broad policy attitudes are tendencies to evaluate several issues rather than only one; they are linked to perceptions of parties and candidates; and individuals who are assigned the same broad policy attitudes may not have evaluative tendencies toward the same issues.

Although these are indeed significant differences, I do not think they are reasons why Campbell et al. should not use the opinions expressed in answer to their free-response questions to assign specific attitudes. To begin with, we could interpret findings that an individual expresses opinions about several specific issues by saying that he is expressing several specific issue attitudes. This would certainly be consistent with the way Campbell et al. assign attitudes because, as pointed out in Chapter 4, they often assign both broad policy attitudes and specific issue attitudes to individuals solely on the basis of evidence that those individuals express single opinions. In addition, we could interpret findings that individuals express opinions which are linked to perceptions of candidates and parties by saying that they are expressing several specific issue attitudes. This would also be consistent with the way Campbell et al. assign attitudes because, as pointed out earlier in this chapter, Key shows that the specific issue attitudes they assign are often linked to perceptions of parties and candidates. Finally, we could interpret findings that individuals express opinions about different issues by saying that they are expressing specific issue attitudes; we need only say that they are expressing different issue attitudes.

In short, given the ways in which Campbell et al. distinguish between broad policy attitudes and specific issue attitudes, there is every reason to believe that, when they say an individual has a broad policy attitude, they would be equally correct in saying that he has one or more specific issue attitudes. One qualification to this general conclusion is that answers to the free-response questions in *The American Voter* could not be used to identify all the specific issue attitudes which members of the public hold. They could only be used to identify those attitudes that are linked to perceptions of candidates and parties. Nevertheless, if our objective is to determine which attitudes motivate votes, and if Campbell et al. are right in claiming that only attitudes linked to perceptions of candidates and parties can be motives for votes, then the evidence they use to assign broad policy attitudes would be sufficient to assign all the specific issue attitudes that need concern us.

There are two other ways in which one might attempt to distinguish between broad policy attitudes and specific issue attitudes. First, it might be said that an individual with a broad policy attitude tends to evaluate several issues consistently. For example, he might tend to favor the positions advocated by the Republicans on all the issues, whereas an individual with several specific issue attitudes does not. Second, it might be said that in addition to expressing opinions about several specific issues, an individual with a broad policy attitude tends to express other kinds of opinions as well. He might express approval for certain general characteristics of the foreign and domestic issue postures of candidates or parties. For example, he might say that he approves of Eisenhower's "moderation" in foreign affairs. Moreover, he might express opinions linking the policy positions of candidates and parties to certain belief systems. For example, he might say that Eisenhower has a "conservative" domestic policy posture.

These may be reasonable ways of distinguishing between broad policy attitudes and specific issue attitudes, but Campbell et al. do not adopt either distinction, and it would be inconsistent with the ways they assign attitudes to do so. To begin with, if we find that an individual expresses several consistent opinions about issues and if, like the authors, we believe an attitude can be assigned on the basis of evidence that an individual expresses a single opinion, then we should be able to say that the individual is expressing several consistent issue attitudes. To deny that this would be a valid way of interpreting the evidence would be to deny that attitudes can be assigned on the basis of a single opinion or that individuals can express consistent issue attitudes. In addition, Campbell et al. indicate that all the opinions expressed by individuals to whom they assign broad policy attitudes are not always consistent and that many of the individuals to whom they assign specific issue attitudes have consistent attitudes.[13] As a result, it would be inconsistent with the ways they assign attitudes for them to distinguish between broad policy attitudes and specific issue attitudes in the first way I suggested. Moreover, it would be inconsistent for them to make this distinction in the second way I mentioned. The authors tell us that they assign broad policy attitudes to individuals solely on the basis of evidence that those individuals express opinions about specific issues.[14] As a result, there is no reason to believe that all or most of those individuals would express other kinds of opinion as well. In addition, Campbell et al. present evidence which they claim shows that members of the public rarely have commitments to broad belief systems or think of candidates and parties in ideological terms.[15]

I do not think, therefore, that there is any reason why the answers to free-response questions which Campbell et al. record should not be used to assign attitudes toward specific issues rather than broad policy attitudes. I do not mean to imply that the interpretation the authors place on their data is necessarily wrong. My argument is, rather, that it is no more correct than another interpretation. Furthermore, I do not mean to imply that Campbell et al. use answers to free-response questions to assign broad policy attitudes because they purposely wish to avoid discussing specific issue attitudes. They may have good reasons for taking an interest in broad policy attitudes, and they may have some unexplained reason for believing that members of the public hold broad policy attitudes rather than specific issue attitudes. In light of what they say, however, I think it is fair to conclude that in their discussion of attitudes toward foreign and domestic policies, as in their discussion of the 16 issue attitudes, Campbell et al. fail to use available data in a way which would enable them to determine how strong an influence issue attitudes have on voting choices and the outcomes of elections.

Objections to My Argument

If we accept the criticisms I have made of the way Campbell et al. analyze issue attitudes, there is no reason to believe they have shown that those attitudes do not have a powerful influence on voting choices and the outcomes of elections. They leave this point moot because the information they present about issue attitudes does not enable them to draw conclusions about whether those attitudes affect the voting choices of many members of the public and whether, as a result, they have a strong influence on the outcomes of elections. The authors leave this point moot also because they fail to make use of techniques and data that would enable them to determine fairly easily how strong an influence issue attitudes have on voting choices and the outcomes of elections. Having shown this, I can rest my case against the first part of the argument of *The American Voter*.

It is important to consider one possible objection to what I have said so far, however. Someone might argue that meaningful analyses of the influence of issue attitudes on votes have, in fact, been conducted and that those analyses show that issue attitudes are less influential than attitudes toward parties and candidates. Thus it might be argued that there are findings which confirm the conclusions Campbell et al. draw about issue attitudes. There are several studies of issue attitudes that seem to support this contention. I think, however, that these studies suffer from at least one serious difficulty. Moreover, I think they suggest that if political scientists conducted careful analyses of the relationship between issue attitudes and votes, they would find that those attitudes have a powerful effect on voting choices and the outcomes of elections.

Someone who wished to challenge my argument might begin by admitting that, as I have suggested, the way to determine the influence of issue attitudes on votes and elections is to analyze those attitudes in the same way Campbell et al. analyzed the six partisan attitudes; that is, we should determine whether issue attitudes can be used to predict votes and whether they seem to form a force field related to voting choice. We should then conduct a multiple regression analysis of the relationship between voting choices and both issue attitudes and the six partisan attitudes to determine which sort of attitude has the stronger influence on the outcomes of elections.

Attitudes as Predictors and the Force Field Analogy.   If the objector wished to show that political scientists have determined whether issue attitudes predict voting choices and whether they seem to form a force field, he might point to an analysis found in V.O. Key's *Public Opinion and American Democracy*. The results of that analysis are reported in Figure 5.1, taken from Key's book. The figure is based on data about the 16 issue attitudes that Campbell et al. recorded prior to the 1956 election. The cell entries are the percentages of people holding a certain number of pro-Republican and pro-Democratic attitudes who voted for the Democrats.

If at least some issue attitudes predict voting choices and if those attitudes form a force field, we would expect to find that individuals who have more pro-Democratic attitudes would tend to vote for the Democrats and that the higher the ratio of their pro-Democratic to pro-Republican attitudes, the more likely they would be to cast a Democratic vote. Correspondingly, we would expect that people with more pro-Republican than pro-Democratic attitudes would tend to vote for the Republicans and that the higher the ratio of their pro-Republican to pro-Democratic attitudes, the more likely they would be to cast a Republican vote. These expectations are, in fact, fulfilled by the findings presented in Figure 5.1. In every case well over a majority of the individuals with more pro-Democratic than pro-Republican attitudes voted for the Democrats. Notice, for example, that 81% of the individuals with 3 to 5 pro-Democratic attitudes and no pro-Republican

Number of pro-Democratic Issue Attitudes	Number of pro-Republican Issue Attitudes			
	0	1–2	3–5	6–16
0	36%	14%	3%	2%
1–2	72	41	16	3
3–5	81	60	33	14
6–16	89	78	—[2]	—[3]

[1]Entries are percentages of those in each cell reporting a Democratic presidential vote in 1956.
[2]Only 12 cases fell in this cell; 8 reported a Democratic vote.
[3]No cases in this cell.

Figure 5.1 Key's analysis of data from *The American Voter*. (Presidential vote in relation to voter's perception of closeness of the parties to his position on 16 policy issues.)[1] (Source: V.O. Key, Jr., *Public Opinion and American Democracy* [New York: Knopf, 1961], p. 461.)

attitudes voted for the Democrats and that 60% of the individuals with 3 to 5 pro-Democratic attitudes and one or two pro-Republican attitudes voted for the Democrats. Notice too that the higher the ratio of pro-Democratic to pro-Republican attitudes which individuals hold, the more likely they are to vote for the Democrats. For example, 89% of the people with 6 to 16 pro-Democratic attitudes and no pro-Republican attitudes voted for the Democrats, whereas only 78% of the people with 6 to 16 pro-Democratic attitudes and one or two pro-Republican attitudes voted for the Democrats.

Figure 5.1 also shows that people who have more pro-Republican than pro-Democratic attitudes tend to vote for the Republicans and that the higher the ratio of pro-Republican to pro-Democratic attitudes, the greater is the likelihood of a Republican vote. In reading the figure to determine whether this is true, however, it is necessary to remember that the percentages reported are percentages of individuals voting for the Democrats. Thus, for example, the figure indicates that 2% of the people with 6 to 16 pro-Republican attitudes and no pro-Democratic attitudes voted for the Democrats. We can read this entry, however, as an indication that 98% of these individuals voted for the Republicans.

I think the findings reported in Figure 5.1 are important because they indicate that issue attitudes can be used to predict votes, often with startling accuracy. They also indicate that the force-field analogy does have some applicability to issue attitudes. It should be noted, however, that if we consider issue attitudes to be a force field, we are not able to make perfect predictions of votes. Not everyone who has more pro-Democratic than pro-Republican attitudes, for example, tends to vote for the Democrats. Moreover, a majority of the people who hold an equal number of pro-Republican and pro-Democratic attitudes tend to vote for the Republicans. Key points out that if issue attitudes were the only forces influencing votes, we would expect everyone with a majority of pro-Democratic attitudes to vote for the Democrats and everyone with a majority of pro-Republican attitudes to vote for the Republicans. Moreover, we would expect that people with an equal number of pro-Democratic and pro-Republican attitudes would choose a candidate at random, because no psychological forces would determine their votes. If this were true, 50% of these people should vote for each party.

Key says that because the findings reported in Figure 5.1 do not meet these expectations, we can infer that some psychological factors other than the 16 issue attitudes must influence votes. Moreover, he suggests that because people with equal numbers of pro-Republican and pro-Democratic attitudes tend to vote for the Republicans, there is reason to believe that the most important influences on votes in addition to issue attitudes are attitudes toward Eisenhower and the Republican party.[16]

Someone who wished to criticize my argument against *The American Voter* might point out, therefore, that just as Campbell et al. have shown that the six partisan attitudes can be used to predict voting choices and can be considered a force field, Key has shown that issue attitudes can be used to predict voting choices and they can be considered a force field. He claims, however, to show that this does not prove that issue attitudes determine voting choices. If we believe that the way to analyze the relationship between issue attitudes and votes is to follow the steps Campbell et al. take in their analysis of the six partisan attitudes, therefore, we must credit Key with taking at least two of these steps and with showing that some of the conclusions of *The American Voter* are correct.

Multiple Regression Analysis.   After discussing the force-field model, the next step Campbell et al. take in analyzing the six partisan attitudes is to subject them to a multiple regression analysis. They claim that this enables them to determine which of these attitudes have the strongest influence on votes. If we wish to follow the procedures the authors use in analyzing the six partisan attitudes, therefore, our next step after absorbing Key's analysis should be to conduct a multiple regression analysis of the relationship between voting choices and attitudes toward parties, candidates, and specific issues. This would presumably enable us to compare the effect of issue attitudes on the outcomes of elections with the effect of attitudes toward parties and candidates.

Someone who wished to criticize my argument against *The American Voter* might point to two studies in which multiple regression analyses of attitudes toward parties, candidates, and issues have been conducted. The first study is *The American Voter* itself. I pointed out earlier that the opinions Campbell et al. use to assign broad attitudes toward foreign and domestic policies might be used to assign attitudes toward specific issues. If I am right about this, we can say that when they assign broad attitudes toward foreign and domestic policies, the authors are, in effect, applying the force-field model to issue attitudes. They say that an individual has a broad pro-Republican attitude if he expresses more pro-Republican than pro-Democratic opinions; they also say he has a pro-Democratic attitude if he expresses more pro-Democratic than pro-Republican opinions. If each of these opinions indicates attitude forces, then when Campbell et al. say that an individual has a broad pro-Republican attitude toward domestic policies, for example, they are saying in effect that the result of all of his specific attitudes toward domestic issues is a force pressuring him to vote for the Republicans. If assignments of broad policy attitudes indicate the results of attitudes toward specific issues, therefore, it might be argued that to determine how much influence issue attitudes have on the outcomes of elections, we only need to conduct a multiple regression analysis of the relationship between votes, broad policy attitudes, and attitudes toward candidates and parties. This is, of course, precisely what Campbell et al. do in their investigation of the six partisan attitudes. Thus, if we interpret their work differently than they do, we might say that it does in fact show how strong an effect issue attitudes have on the outcomes of elections.

The second multiple regression analysis to which a critic of my argument might point is reported in an article by RePass that has received a great deal of attention.[17] RePass uses data from a survey of public attitudes conducted by the authors of *The American Voter* prior to the 1964 presidential election. In this survey, 25 attitudes toward specific issues were assigned to members of the public. Like Campbell et al., RePass assumes that if an individual holds a majority of pro-Republican attitudes, his attitudes must be pressuring him to vote for the Republicans; if he holds a majority of pro-Democratic attitudes, his issue attitudes must be pressuring him to vote for the Democrats. RePass assigns each individual an overall issue attitude on the basis of whether he has a majority of pro-Republican or pro-Democratic attitudes, and he conducts a multiple regression analysis that compares the influence of these attitudes on votes with the influence of attitudes toward parties and candidates.

These two multiple regression analyses together with Key's force field analysis support my contention that issue attitudes may determine votes and the outcomes of elections to some extent. Key shows that they predict the votes of a large percentage of the public, and the multiple regression analysis conducted by Campbell et al. shows that they have a considerable influence on the outcomes of elections when compared to attitudes toward parties and candidates (see Figures 4.2 and 5.2). Moreover, RePass reports that attitudes toward issues have almost exactly as strong an influence on the outcomes of elections as attitudes toward candidates have.[18]

A critic of my argument might point out, however, that Key shows that issue attitudes do *not* predict the votes of a substantial percentage of the public and that Campbell et al. show that the influence of those attitudes on votes is considerably weaker than the influence of attitudes toward parties and candidates. Moreover, RePass reports that party preference has a stronger effect on the outcomes of elections than attitudes toward candidates or issues. Thus it might be argued that although analyses of the relationship between issue attitudes and votes do not show that those attitudes have a negligible effect on voting choices and the outcomes of elections, they do show that the influence of issue attitudes on votes is weaker than the influence of certain other attitudes. As a result, it might be argued that Campbell et al. are right to attach more importance to attitudes toward candidates and parties than to issue attitudes.

Rebuttal

My reply to this objection is that there is reason to believe that Campbell et al., Key, and RePass underestimate the influence of issue attitudes on votes or, at least, that their estimates of the strength of that influence are not to be relied on. This is because they accept the force-field analogy; that is, they believe that if, for example, an individual has more pro-Republican than pro-Democratic issue attitudes, his issue attitudes are pressuring him to vote for the Republicans. If he does not report a Republican vote, they conclude that his issue attitudes have had no effect on his electoral decision. This is a democratic view of attitudes: Each attitude has some influence on votes, and the majority rules. To understand the difficulties that the analyses conducted by Campbell et al., Key, and RePass face, it is necessary to understand that there is another view of attitudes they might adopt. They might say that some issue attitudes which an individual holds have no effect on his voting choices at all, that some have only a slight effect, and that others have a powerful effect—so powerful in fact that regardless of what other attitudes the individual holds, he will vote in accordance with these attitudes.

Attitude Strength.   The notion that attitudes do not have an equal influence on behavior has a great deal of commonsense appeal. We often say that an individual who is faced with a choice between several things he values chooses the thing he values most. For example, given the choice between writing this page and going to dinner and the theater tonight, I have decided to write this page because I consider it more important, even though there are many more things I like about dinners and theaters than about writing.

The notion that attitudes do not have an equal influence on behavior is reflected in attitude psychology in a number of ways. To begin with, as I pointed out in Chapter 2, psychologists have found that individuals do not always behave in accordance with their beliefs and feelings. They have also found that if several individuals hold the same beliefs and feelings, some people will behave in accordance with them and others will not. Psychologists believe that the latter finding is due partly to the fact that individuals are exposed to different situational influences. In addition, however, they have found that consistency of behavior with beliefs and feelings is often related to certain psychological factors. For example, many psychologists, including the authors of *The American Voter*, have found that individuals are often more likely to behave in accordance with very intense than with less intense attitudes.[19] In other words, an individual's behavior is more likely to be consistent with his feelings toward an object if those feelings are very favorable or unfavorable than if they are only moderately favorable or unfavorable. (I pointed out in Chapter 2 that this is only one way of discussing the intensity of attitudes; but it will suffice for my purposes here.)

Moreover, some psychologists say that individuals are more likely to act in accordance with attitudes that are highly "salient" than with attitudes which are less salient.[20] "Salience" is often defined as a measure of how important an attitude object is to an individual under study or how closely it is related to his major concerns. As a result, the degree of salience of an attitude may differ from the degree of its intensity. We would expect highly intense attitudes to be highly salient because we do not think that people generally have strong feelings about things which do not concern them greatly. We would also expect, however, that less intense attitudes would sometimes differ in salience.

The notion that attitudes differ in motivational strength, therefore, is held by many psychologists. The notion is also implicit in the way the authors of *The American Voter* analyze how strong an influence the six partisan attitudes as a group have on voting choices.[21] If they had assumed that all these attitudes have the same strength, they would have calculated whether each individual has a majority of pro-Democratic or pro-Republican attitudes; they would also have said that his vote was influenced by the six partisan attitudes if it was consistent with the majority of his attitudes. Instead, as I have explained, they sum the intensity of an individual's pro-Republican and pro-Democratic attitudes and say that his or her vote was influenced by the six partisan attitudes if it is consistent with those attitudes which have the greater summed intensity.

Campbell et al. seem to regard attitude intensity as important in their investigation of the six partisan attitudes, but they do not discuss attitude salience. Other political scientists have analyzed salience, however, and they have reported findings which suggest that salient attitudes may have a stronger effect on political behavior than other attitudes have. For example, the authors of *Voting* conducted an analysis of individuals who held some attitudes favoring one party and some attitudes favoring the other party.[22] Berelson et al. asked these "cross-pressured" individuals which attitude objects they considered "most important." They found that the individuals generally voted in accordance with their attitudes toward the more salient objects.

Key reports similar findings.[23] He also reports an interesting body of data about salience collected by the Gallup organization in 1960.[24] Members of a national sample were asked what they considered the "most important" problem facing the country and which candidate they believed would be best able to handle that problem. From the data we can deduce that almost 90% of the people who expressed an opinion in answer to this question voted for the candidate who they believed would do the best job handling the issue they considered most salient.[25] If we compare this finding with other findings about issue attitudes, we can easily see that these salient issue attitudes are far better predictors of voting choices than most other sets of issue attitudes.

There are, therefore, reasons to believe that all attitudes do not have an equal influence on political behavior. It might be argued, however, that in his analysis of how well issue attitudes fit the force-field model, Key has shown that these attitudes are equal in strength and that, as a result, Campbell et al. are right to treat them as equal influences on votes. One might argue this because Key has shown that if we determine whether individuals have a majority of pro-Democratic or pro-Republican attitudes and assume that their votes will be consistent with a majority of their attitudes, we can predict votes with a high degree of accuracy. This suggests that attitudes are equal in strength because it shows that we can predict votes by considering only how many attitudes favoring each party people hold.

Key's Analysis Reconsidered.   My answer is that although Key has shown that we can predict the votes of some individuals by considering only how many pro-Republican and pro-Democratic attitudes they hold, he has also shown that we cannot predict the votes of all individuals in this way. For example, only 60% of the people with three to five pro-Democratic attitudes and one or two pro-Republican attitudes voted for the Democrats. (see Figure 5.1). Key says that the remaining 40% probably voted for the Republicans because they held favorable attitudes toward Eisenhower and the Republican party that outweighed their issue attitudes. This might have been the reason those people voted for the Republicans; but the reason might instead have been that the one or two pro-Republican attitudes they held were simply stronger than the three to five pro-Democratic attitudes they held. In other words, Key might have been able to show that attitudes toward issues predict votes even better than they do in Figure 5.1 if he had introduced a measure of the strength of attitudes into his work.

I do not deny that Key has shown that the number of issue attitudes favoring each party which individuals hold has an influence on their votes. The importance of the number of attitudes is shown by his finding that the likelihood that individuals will vote for a certain party increases as the ratio of their attitudes favoring that party to their attitudes favoring the other party increases. Thus, for example, individuals who have 15 pro-Republican attitudes and one pro-Democratic attitude are more likely to vote for the Republicans than are individuals who have two pro-Republican attitudes and one pro-Democratic attitude (see Figure 5.1). This finding certainly shows that 15 attitudes are more likely to outweigh one attitude than two attitudes are. As a result, it suggests that the number of attitudes toward each party which individuals hold has a bearing on how they vote. The finding does not enable us to conclude that the strength of attitudes is unimportant, however. We can say that the reason individuals with 15 pro-Republican attitudes and one pro-Democratic attitude almost always vote for the Republicans is that any 15 attitudes, regardless of how weak, are bound to have a greater influence on behavior than any one attitude has, regardless of how strong it is. In contrast, we can say that the reason many people who hold two pro-Republican attitudes and one pro-Democratic attitude vote for the Democrats is that two pro-Republican attitudes, regardless of their strength, may *not* be stronger than one pro-Democratic attitude. Key's findings may indicate, therefore, that while one strong attitude may not be 15 times as strong as other attitudes, it may be twice as strong. The sheer weight of numbers of attitudes may, therefore, account for the votes of many people, such as those who have 15 weak attitudes and one strong attitude; but the strength as well as the number of attitudes may account for the votes of other people, such as those who have two weak attitudes and one strong attitude.

It is reasonable to assume, therefore, that individuals hold attitudes of different strengths. Key's evidence does not show conclusively that all attitudes have the same strength. This is important because it obviously implies that Key's analysis of how issue attitudes form a force field is not as precise as it might be. If he considered the strength of attitudes, he might find an even closer relationship between issue attitudes and votes than he, in fact, finds. More important, the fact that attitudes can differ in strength suggests that the multiple regression analyses conducted by Campbell et al. and RePass may not accurately determine how strong an influence issue attitudes have on the outcomes of elections.

Another View of the Multiple Regression Analyses.   It will be remembered that Campbell et al. and RePass begin their analyses by determining which party a majority of each individual's issue attitudes favor. They then assign each individual an overall issue attitude favoring that party. This enables them to determine what percentage of members of the public vote consistently with their attitudes. Campbell et al. and RePass then use the techniques of multiple regression analysis to compare the influence that issue attitudes exert on election outcomes with the influence exerted by attitudes toward candidates and parties.

If they were to consider the strength of particular issue attitudes, Campbell et al. and RePass might have to revise their conclusions about the relationship between issue attitudes and the outcomes of elections. One reason is that if they were to assign overall issue attitudes on the basis of the strength of particular issue attitudes as well as their number, they would probably assign different overall attitudes to some individuals. For example, if they considered only how many attitudes favoring a certain party each individual holds, they would say that an individual with two weak pro-Democratic attitudes and one strong pro-Republican attitude had an overall attitude favoring the Democrats. If, however, they considered the strength of the attitudes individuals hold as well as their number, Campbell et al. and RePass might say that the individual had an overall attitude favoring the Republicans (i.e., if his one pro-Republican attitude was stronger than his two pro-Democratic attitudes combined).

Changes in the way Campbell et al. and RePass assign overall attitudes might also lead to changes in their conclusions about how many people vote consistently with their issue attitudes. If they considered only the number of attitudes favoring each party which each individual holds, and if an individual with two weak pro-Democratic attitudes and one strong pro-Republican attitude voted for the Republicans, they would say that he *did not* vote in accordance with his attitudes. If, however, they considered the strength of his attitudes, they might say that this individual *did* vote in accordance with his attitudes. If there were many individuals of this sort in their samples, therefore, Campbell et al. and RePass might revise their conclusions about how many people held attitudes consistent with their votes.

If Campbell et al. and RePass had assigned more people overall attitudes consistent with their votes, it is possible that when they conducted multiple regression analyses of those attitudes together with attitudes toward parties and candidates, they would find that issue attitudes have a stronger influence on election outcomes than indicated by the multiple regression analyses. This would not necessarily occur, however, because the strength of the relationship between an attitude and votes indicated by a multiple regression analysis depends partly on how the attitude is combined with other attitudes in addition to how well it predicts votes considered by itself.[26] Nevertheless, there is a reasonable chance that other things being equal, a multiple regression analysis of the relationship between issue attitudes and votes would show that issue attitudes would have a stronger influence on the outcomes of elections if we had considered the strength of those attitudes and if we had found that their predictive power increased.

Thus, by considering the strength of issue attitudes, Campbell et al. and RePass might find that those attitudes have a stronger influence on votes than they had previously thought; but, depending on the nature of their data, they might find that their previous conclusions were correct or that they had, in fact, overestimated the influence of issue attitudes. To illustrate how the authors might draw any of these three conclusions, I will discuss how a consideration of the strength of attitudes might lead them to draw different conclusions about whether individuals with three pro-Republican and two pro-Democratic attitudes vote consistently with their attitudes. For clarity of exposition, I will say that people who vote consistently with their attitudes are "consistent" or simply that they "vote consistently."

As the top part of Figure 5.2 shows, individuals with three pro-Republican and two pro-Democratic attitudes can be divided into four different types. The types are based on which party they vote for and how a consideration of the strength of their attitudes would affect conclusions about whether they vote consistently. Type I people are individuals whom we would regard as consistent regardless of whether we considered the strength of their attitudes. A Type I person is exemplified in Figure 5.2 by an individual who holds three strong pro-Republican and two weak pro-Democratic attitudes and who votes Republican. Whether or not we considered the strength of this individual's attitudes, we would say he voted consistently because the attitudes that are consistent with his vote are both more numerous and stronger than the attitudes which are inconsistent with his vote. Individuals with three strong pro-Republican attitudes and two weak pro-Democratic attitudes are not the only kinds of individual we would regard as consistent whether or not we considered the strength of their attitudes, however. For example, this would also be true of individuals with two strong and one weak pro-Republican attitude and two weak pro-Democratic attitudes who voted Republican. These and several other kinds of individual would all fall under the rubric of Type I.

X=WEAK ATTITUDE		X̲=STRONG ATTITUDE	
TYPE I		**TYPE II**	
Pro-Republican	Pro-Democratic	Pro-Republican	Pro-Democratic
X̲X̲X̲	XX	X̲X̲X̲	XX
Votes Republican		Votes Democratic	
TYPE III		**TYPE IV**	
Pro-Republican	Pro-Democratic	Pro-Republican	Pro-Democratic
XXX	X̲X̲	XXX	X̲X̲
Votes Democratic		Votes Republican	

No Measure of Strength		Measure of Strength	
Consistent	Inconsistent	Consistent	Inconsistent
I	II	I	II
IV	III	III	IV

TYPE V		**TYPE VI**	
Pro-Republican	Pro-Democratic	Pro-Republican	Pro-Democratic
XXX	X̲	XXX	X̲
Votes Republican		Votes Democratic	

Figure 5.2. Effects of introducing a measure of strength into analyses of the relationship between attitudes and votes.

Type II people are individuals we would regard as *inconsistent* regardless of whether we considered the strength of their attitudes. A Type II person is exemplified in Figure 5.2 by someone with three strong pro-Republican and two weak pro-Democratic attitudes who votes for the Democrats. We would say that this individual's vote was inconsistent even if we did not consider the strength of his attitudes, because a majority of his attitudes are pro-Republican and he voted for the Democrats. We would draw the same conclusion if we considered the strength of his attitudes, because the attitudes inconsistent with his vote are stronger than the attitudes consistent with his vote. Another example of a Type II individual would be someone with one weak and two strong pro-Republican attitudes and two weak pro-Democratic attitudes who voted for the Democrats.

If their entire samples consisted of Type I and Type II people, it would not make any difference in the analyses Campbell et al. and RePass conduct whether or not they considered the strength of issue attitudes because they would say that these people voted consistently or inconsistently in either case. Type III individuals raise problems for the authors, however. These are individuals we would regard as inconsistent if we did not take the strength of their attitudes into account. If we did consider the strength of their attitudes, however, we would say that the votes of Type III people are consistent. A Type III person is exemplified in Figure 5.2 by an individual who holds two strong pro-Democratic and three weak pro-Republican attitudes and who votes for the Democrats. If we considered only how many pro-Republican and pro-Democratic attitudes this individual holds, we would say his vote was inconsistent because he does not vote in accordance with the majority of his attitudes. If, however, we considered the strength of his attitudes, we would say his vote was consistent, assuming that the two pro-Democratic attitudes are considerably stronger than the three pro-Republican attitudes. Another example of a Type III person would be someone who holds one strong and three weak pro-Republican attitudes and three strong pro-Democratic attitudes and who votes for the Democrats.

Type IV people are the opposite of Type III people; they are individuals we would regard as consistent if we did not consider the strength of their attitudes. If we did consider the strength of their attitudes, however, we would say that Type IV people had voted inconsistently. A Type IV person is exemplified in Figure 5.2 by someone who holds three weak pro-Republican and two strong pro-Democratic attitudes and who votes for the Republicans. If we did not consider the strength of this individual's attitudes, we would say his vote was consistent because he holds a majority of pro-Republican attitudes and votes for the Republicans. If we did consider the strength of his attitudes, however, we would say this individual's vote was inconsistent, assuming that the two pro-Democratic attitudes are stronger than the three pro-Republican attitudes. Another example of a Type IV person would be someone who holds one strong pro-Democratic attitude and two weak pro-Republican attitudes and who votes for the Republicans.

The overall effect of considering differences in the strength of attitudes is shown in the middle section of Figure 5.2. If we did not consider differences in strength, we would say that Type I and Type IV people voted consistently and that Type II and Type III people voted inconsistently. This is the way Campbell et al. and RePass would rate individuals who have three pro-Republican and two pro-Democratic attitudes. If we did consider the strength of their attitudes, we would say that Type I and Type III people were consistent and that Type II and Type IV people were inconsistent. The difference between the two cases is that Type III and Type IV people are shifted to different columns. If there is an equal number of people of each type, considering the strength of attitudes would make no difference to our conclusions about how well those attitudes predict votes. If, however, there were more Type III than Type IV people in our sample, we would say that more people voted consistently if we considered the strength of attitudes than if we considered only how many pro-Republican and pro-Democratic attitudes each individual held; that is, we would find that issue attitudes are better predictors of votes than Campbell et al. and RePass claim they are.

Moreover, as I pointed out earlier, there is a good possibility that if attitudes are better predictors of votes than Campbell et al. and RePass claim, a multiple regression analysis will show that they have a stronger influence on votes. As a result, there is a good possibility that if there were more Type III than Type IV people in our sample, we would find that issue attitudes have a stronger influence on the outcomes of elections than the authors' studies indicate. If, on the other hand, there are more Type IV than Type III individuals in our sample, we would find that introducing a measure of the strength of attitudes into our analysis would have the opposite effect. We would find that attitudes are worse predictors of votes than Campbell et al. and RePass claim, and a multiple regression analysis might show that they are less powerful influences on the outcomes of elections than the authors' analyses suggest. If we believe that the political behavior of an individual is probably influenced by his strongest attitudes if he votes in accordance with those attitudes, therefore, we would have to say that Campbell et al. and RePass have probably underestimated the influence of issue attitudes on votes if there are more Type III than Type IV people in their samples and that they have probably overestimated the influence of issue attitudes on votes if there are more Type IV than Type III people in their samples.

It is possible, therefore, that the conclusions Campbell et al. and RePass draw about the relationship between issue attitudes and votes are not correct because they do not consider the strength of those attitudes. Without actually analyzing the same expressions of attitudes that they study in a way which takes the strength of attitudes into account, it is impossible to say for sure whether their conclusions are correct or whether they have overestimated or underestimated the influence of issue attitudes on votes. Unfortunately, such an analysis cannot be conducted because the necessary data about the strength of the attitudes that Campbell et al. and RePass study do not exist. As pointed out in Chapter 4, the authors of *The American Voter* do not believe that the answers to free-response questions on which their regression analysis is based are expressions of attitudes toward specific issues. As a result they do not ask members of their sample how strongly they feel about objects toward which they express opinions in answer to free-response questions. Moreover, the assignments of attitudes on which RePass bases his analysis do not enable us to compare the strength of different attitudes.[27]

RePass Reconsidered.   Fortunately, however, it is possible to get some idea of how introducing a measure of the strength of attitudes would affect conclusions about the influence of issue attitudes on elections by affecting the outcome of a multiple regression analysis of the relationship between those attitudes and votes. We can get an idea of how introducing a measure of strength of attitudes would affect findings about issue attitudes by considering certain differences between the procedures and findings of the analyses conducted by Campbell et al. and the procedures and findings of RePass's analysis. RePass finds that issue attitudes influence votes almost as strongly as attitudes toward candidates do, whereas the authors of *The American Voter* find that issue attitudes are considerably less influential than attitudes toward candidates. RePass's study has received so much attention because of this difference. He has apparently shown that the authors of *The American Voter* have underestimated the importance of issue attitudes.

The reason for the difference between RePass's findings and the findings reported in *The American Voter* may simply be that different elections were being studied. The analysis conducted by Campbell et al. is based on data about the 1952 and 1956 elections, whereas RePass's analysis is based on data about the 1964 election. It may be that issue attitudes had a stronger influence on votes in 1964 than in 1952 and 1956. RePass believes, however, that there is another reason for the difference. As pointed out earlier, in their surveys of attitudes during the 1952 and 1956 campaigns, Campbell et al. recorded issue attitudes in two ways: they asked members of the public whether they agreed or disagreed with statements about 16 issues; and they recorded opinions about issues that were expressed in answer to their free-response questions. In a survey of attitudes conducted before the 1964 election (but not included in *The American Voter*), however, Campbell et al. recorded issue attitudes in a third way.[28] They asked each individual which issues he considered most important in the campaign and which party he considered closest to his own position on each of the issues he mentioned. Campbell et al. claim that this procedure enabled them to measure only the most salient issue attitudes held by members of the public. As already pointed out, there is reason to believe that the more salient an individual's attitudes are, the more likely he is to act in accordance with them. Thus measures of the salience of issue attitudes can be considered measures of the strength of the influence they exert on votes. Campbell et al. claim, therefore, that in their 1964 survey they measured the strongest issue attitudes which members of the public held: the issue attitudes most likely to determine votes.

RePass's analysis is based on the assignments of issue attitudes that Campbell et al. made in 1964. RePass claims that the reason for the difference between his findings and those of Campbell et al. in *The American Voter* (which did not include the 1964 data) is that he is considering only highly salient attitudes, whereas they are considering both salient and nonsalient attitudes.[29]

By referring to Figure 5.2, it is easy to see how RePass might reach different conclusions about the influence of issue attitudes on votes than Campbell et al. reach simply because he considers only salient attitudes. Let us assume that the samples of individuals Campbell et al. studied in 1952, 1956, and 1964 all contained individuals of all four types represented in Figure 5.2. Let us also assume that all three samples contained the same percentage of individuals of each type. In *The American Voter*, Campbell et al. make no effort to record only salient attitudes. As a result, we can assume that if they were studying the imaginary individuals represented in Figure 5.2, they would record both the strong (salient) attitudes and the weak (nonsalient) attitudes. Because they assume that an individual votes consistently if he votes in accordance with the majority of his attitudes, they would group the individuals as indicated in the "No Measure of Strength" section of the figure.

RePass records only salient attitudes, which means that if he were studying the imaginary individuals in Figure 5.2, he would record only the strong attitudes. He too says that individuals vote consistently if they vote in accordance with the majority of their attitudes; but if he considered only salient attitudes, he would group individuals as indicated in the "Measure of Strength" part of Figure 5.2. In other words, RePass would say that Type III individuals voted consistently, whereas Campbell et al. would say that they voted inconsistently. Moreover, RePass would say that Type IV people voted inconsistently, whereas Campbell et al. would say they voted consistently. If there were no Type III and Type IV people in their samples, Campbell et al. and RePass should reach the same conclusions about the influence of issue attitudes on the outcomes of elections. If there were an equal number of Type III and Type IV people, they should also reach the same conclusions. If, however, there were more Type III than Type IV people in the samples, and if differences in the ways researchers determine whether individuals vote in accordance with their attitudes are reflected in the results of multiple regression analyses of the sort I have been discussing, RePass would conclude that the influence of issue attitudes on the outcomes of elections is stronger than Campbell et al. say it is. Moreover, if we believe that it is correct to say that the votes of individuals of Type III are influenced by their issue attitudes, we will have to conclude that Campbell et al. underestimate the influence of issue attitudes on electoral outcomes and that RePass's findings are more correct.

As I have indicated, RePass does in fact conclude that issue attitudes are stronger influences on the outcomes of elections than Campbell et al. say they are. His findings, therefore, are consistent with the hypothesis that Campbell et al. have underestimated the influence of issue attitudes because they have failed to take into account the strength of those attitudes. RePass's findings also suggest that multiple regression analyses of the sort which he and the authors of *The American Voter* conduct reflect differences in the ways researchers determine whether individuals vote in accordance with their attitudes. The results of a multiple regression analysis of the relationship between issue attitudes and votes will show that those attitudes have a stronger influence on the outcomes of elections if researchers consider the salience of issue attitudes than if they do not. These findings are consistent with my hypothesis that if researchers consider the salience of attitudes, they will say that more individuals vote in accordance with their attitudes than if they do not consider salience; also, if they base their multiple regression analyses of the relationship between issue attitudes and votes on a larger estimate of the number of people who vote in accordance with their attitudes, those analyses will show that issue attitudes have a stronger influence on the outcomes of elections than if researchers base their multiple regression analyses on a smaller estimate of the number of people who vote in accordance with their attitudes.

RePass's work does not provide conclusive support for the points I have just made, however, for at least two reasons. First, we might theorize that in 1964 people expressed pretty much the same kinds of opinion when asked what issues they considered most important as they would have expressed if they were asked whether there was "anything" they liked or disliked about the parties or candidates. We could conclude, therefore, that the difference between RePass's findings and those reported by Campbell et al. is that in 1964 issues were more important to members of the public than they were in 1952 and 1956. As a result, a greater number of people voted for the party that a majority of their attitudes favored in 1964 than they did in 1952 and 1956. We could determine whether this was the reason for the differences between the findings Campbell et al. report and those reported by RePass if Campbell et al. had asked members of their 1964 sample (which RePass used) whether there was "anything" they liked or disliked about the parties and candidates and if these opinions could be compared with the opinions that RePass analyzed. Unfortunately, the 1964 questionnaire (which elicited the data RePass used) did not contain this question; as a result, it is difficult to say how much of a difference asking people what issues they considered most important made.

The second reason RePass's analysis does not show conclusively that Campbell et al. underestimated the influence of issue attitudes on votes is that RePass does not consider that, when combined with each other, even attitudes which are not highly salient may have some influence on voting choices. By failing to consider issue attitudes that are not highly salient, he may either underestimate or overestimate the influence of issue attitudes on votes. An example of a case in which he might overestimate the influence is listed as Type V at the bottom of Figure 5.2. RePass would say that Type V people who have one strong pro-Democratic attitude and three weak pro-Republican attitudes and who voted for the Democrats had voted consistently. This is because if he studied only highly salient attitudes, he would have considered only the pro-Democratic attitude. If the three pro-Republican attitudes were, in total, stronger than the pro-Democratic attitude, however, it would be more correct to say that Type V individuals had voted inconsistently. This is, of course, what Campbell et al. would say, because Type V individuals have a greater number of pro-Republican than pro-Democratic attitudes and vote for the Republicans. If his sample consisted of a great number of Type V individuals, therefore, RePass would overestimate the influence of issue attitudes on the outcomes of elections.

Type VI individuals present a case in which RePass would underestimate the influence of issue attitudes on votes. A Type VI person is exemplified in Figure 5.2 by an individual who holds one strong pro-Democratic attitude and three weak pro-Republican attitudes and who votes Republican. RePass would say that such individuals voted inconsistently because he would only consider their pro-Democratic attitude. Campbell et al. would say that such individuals voted consistently because they voted in accordance with the majority of their attitudes. If the three pro-Republican attitudes are collectively stronger than the pro-Democratic attitude, we would have to conclude that Campbell et al. were correct. If RePass's sample consisted of a great number of Type VI individuals, therefore, he would underestimate the influence of issue attitudes on the outcomes of elections.

These are simply illustrative examples of the ways RePass might overestimate or underestimate the influence of issue attitudes on the outcomes of elections. They show, however, that because he does not take into account the relative strengths of all attitudes, RePass does not show conclusively how strong an influence those attitudes have. As a result, his analysis, like the analysis conducted by Campbell et al., is not entirely satisfactory, and I think it is correct to assert that political scientists have not adequately analyzed the relationship between issue attitudes and votes. Nevertheless, there is a limit to the precision of all analyses, and RePass certainly analyzes issue attitudes in a more acceptable way than do Campbell et al. because he makes some attempt to consider the strength of those attitudes. Moreover, his analysis at least suggests, even if it does not conclusively prove, that if we introduce a measure of the strength of attitudes into a multiple regression analysis of the relationship between issue attitudes and votes, we will reach different conclusions about how strong an influence those attitudes have on elections than if we consider only how many attitudes favoring each party members of the public hold. As a result, RePass's analysis suggests that because they do not consider the strength of issue attitudes, Campbell et al. may underestimate the significance of those attitudes in the electoral process.

Conclusion and One Final Objection

I have presented arguments to show that the authors of *The American Voter* have not demonstrated that attitudes toward specific issues do not have a strong influence on voting choices or the outcomes of elections. First, I have argued that the evidence they present about the 16 issue attitudes does not enable them to draw firm conclusions about the relationship of issue attitudes to votes. Second, I have shown that they have not made use of techniques and data which would have enabled them to determine how strong an influence issue attitudes have on voting choices and the outcomes of elections. Third, I have admitted that if we interpret their findings somewhat differently than they do, we can say that Campbell et al. apply at least one technique—multiple regression analysis— to the study of issue attitudes which might enable them to determine how strong an influence those attitudes have on the outcomes of elections. I have argued, however, that because of the way they organize the data to which they apply multiple regression analysis, they may underestimate the influence of issue attitudes on elections. I have also shown that the results of their regression analysis and of the regression analysis conducted by RePass suggest that issue attitudes may, in fact, be important factors in the electoral process.

I have argued, therefore, that the first part of the argument of *The American Voter* with which I am concerned is unacceptable. Campbell et al. do not show that issue attitudes do not influence voting choices and the outcomes of elections or how strong the influence of those attitudes is. In fact, the conclusion which is supported best by their study, as well as by the studies of Key and RePass I have reviewed, is that issue attitudes have a strong influence on elections rather than a negligible influence, as Campbell et al. claim.

One final objection might be raised against my argument, however. I have criticized the authors of attitude studies for not paying adequate attention to the salience of issue attitudes. It might be argued, however, that since 1968 the Survey Research Center at the University of Michigan (with which two authors of *The American Voter* are still affiliated) and other research groups have in fact been measuring attitude salience in most of their studies and have been including considerations about it in their analyses.

My response to this objection is partially included in the body of my argument. I have shown that although the authors of attitude studies of public opinion may measure salience, they do not necessarily make good use of the data in their analyses. In addition, even assuming that they did handle data about salience properly, an important question of historical interpretation arises. It has become common among public opinion researchers to say that there has been a great change in the psychological determinants of voting since the 1950s.[30] This argument holds that whereas party preference seemed to be the major motivation for voting when the earliest studies were carried out in the 1940s and 1950s, this changed in the 1960s and 1970s. Now, it is said, issue attitudes play a much larger role in determining partisan choice than they did before, although party preference is still the major determinant of voting. As a result, it is contended that voting studies have surveyed a great historical watershed in American political history in which issues have become more important determinants of election outcomes than they were previously.

If my criticisms of classical public opinion studies are correct, however, this conclusion should be questioned strongly. I have argued that classical, and even recent, studies of public opinion have not taken proper account of the salience of issue attitudes and that if they had done so they might have found that those attitudes were major determinants of votes even in the 1950s. It may be, therefore, that the proper interpretation of political history recorded by attitude studies of public opinion is not to say that Americans vote more in accordance with issue attitudes today than they did 20 years ago. The proper interpretation may be that students of public opinion have simply begun to study issue attitudes more carefully than they did 20 years ago. Their findings may be due to the fact that they have been paying more attention to attitude salience than they did in previous studies. Thus the findings of attitude studies may not reflect any major historical change. Rather, they may be an artifact of a change in social science methodology. Issue attitudes may always have been major determinants of votes, but students of public opinion may have begun to study them seriously only in the mid-sixties. Even assuming that the authors of attitude studies have begun to take attitude salience into account, my arguments still have important consequences for understanding recent American political history.

6. Party Preference

The Argument of *The American Voter* in Brief

The second part of the argument of *The American Voter* which I shall consider is the contention that the influence of party preference on voting choices and the outcomes of elections is stronger than the influence of any other attitudes. Campbell et al. argue that party preference affects the outcomes of elections by determining the six partisan attitudes and issue attitudes, which in turn determine voting choices (see "Party Preference" and "Issue Attitudes" in Chapter 4). In other words, they claim that because people favor a particular party, they adopt favorable attitudes toward its candidates and the policies those candidates advocate. Campbell et al. believe that these attitudes determine voting choices. We can also say, however, that they believe party preference determines those choices because they regard the six partisan attitudes and issue attitudes as mirrors of party preference and because they find that most people vote in accordance with their party preferences even if they hold practically no other political attitudes.

Campbell et al. provide support for their argument about party preference by showing that a majority of the six partisan attitudes and of the issue attitudes which people hold are generally consistent with their party preferences, by showing that people generally vote in accordance with their party preferences, and by showing that people who are more involved in politics are more likely to have strong party preferences than people who are less involved. I pointed out earlier (pp. 77–79), however, that all this evidence could be used to argue that party preference is determined by other attitudes rather than that it determines them. The crucial point in the argument about party preference which Campbell et al. present is their contention that party preference determines issue attitudes and the six partisan attitudes because it is formed before these other attitudes and because most people hold the same party preference for many years. It is this argument, based on the primacy and stability of party preference, that will be addressed.

Conflicting Evidence

The major reason the argument based on the primacy and stability of party preference seems so compelling is that we find it hard to imagine any mechanism other than the influence of long-standing party preferences on other attitudes and voting choices which could lead members of the public to favor the same party year after year and, usually, to hold other attitudes consistent with their party preferences. Certainly we believe that these phenomena could not be caused by the influence of attitudes toward candidates and issues on party preferences and voting choices because national affairs and the leadership of the parties change greatly over periods of only a few years. As a result, we believe that if votes and party preferences were determined by attitudes toward candidates and issues, there would surely come a time when people would conclude that the party they have supported traditionally no longer advocates the superior positions on issues which concern them or no longer endorses the better candidates. We would expect, therefore, that party loyalties would change from time to time and that people would not always vote for the same party. Because Campbell et al. present evidence which indicates that members of the public favor and vote for the same party during most of their lifetimes, however, we conclude that consistencies among party preferences, other political attitudes, and voting choices must be due to the influence of long-standing party preferences on other attitudes and voting choices, rather than being due to the influence of attitudes toward candidates and issues on party preference or to any other mechanism.

Strong though this argument is, it should be assessed against the background of certain other findings. To begin with, members of the public do not always vote in accordance with their long-standing party loyalties. Campbell et al. report that party preference fails to predict the votes of 20% of the public in any given election, and 30% of the public report that they have not always voted for the same party.[1] Moreover, both Key and the authors of *The American Voter* point out that in the past there have been considerable changes of party loyalties.[2] For example, in what Key calls the "realigning election" of 1932, a large percentage of the public changed their party loyalties and maintained their new loyalties for many years.[3] In short, in the elections studied by Campbell et al. a substantial number of people deviated from their long-standing party preferences, and even more people have deviated in other elections.

We may wonder, however, what role attitudes toward issues or candidates have in bringing about these deviations. The authors of *The American Voter* present data that bear upon this question. Approximately 70% of those people whose votes failed to correspond with their party identifications in 1952 and 1956 were people whose attitudes toward candidates and issues conflicted with their party identifications.[4] To put this differently, of those people whose attitudes toward candidates and issues conflicted with their party identification, approximately 60% voted in accordance with their attitudes toward candidates and issues. This evidence suggests that people may not vote for the party they have supported in the past regardless of what attitudes toward candidates and issues they hold; rather, they may vote for that party only when they hold attitudes toward candidates and issues which favor it. As a result, the same evidence suggests that the reason people deviate from their long-standing party loyalties may be that they form attitudes toward candidates and issues inconsistent with those loyalties. Key provides further support for this conclusion by showing that in elections from 1932 through 1960, a large percentage of the people who crossed party lines held attitudes toward candidates and issues favoring the party for which they voted.[5]

The final finding against which we must assess *The American Voter*'s argument about party preference is that there are a number of nonpsychological factors which are good predictors of voting choices. These include occupation, religion, level of education, and opinions of family and peer-group members. No one of these factors by itself is as good a predictor of voting choice as party preference is; but, taken together, they enable us to predict votes with a high degree of accuracy. This has been shown by the authors of *Voting* and by a number of other political scientists who are interested in the sociological as well as the psychological correlates of voting choices.[6]

The Information Flow View of Party Preference

The findings discussed suggest that we can legitimately interpret the three-cornered relationship among parties, candidates, and issues in a different way than the authors of *The American Voter* interpret it. This alternative interpretation is by no means my invention. Rather, it is a collection of ideas that political scientists often oppose to the interpretation offered by Campbell et al., although they rarely articulate those ideas clearly.[7]

The alternative interpretation is as follows. People form political attitudes because they believe that certain sorts of policy and certain candidates will best serve their needs, wants, interests, and so on, and because they are persuaded to adopt attitudes by their friends and by communications they receive through the mass media. They vote for the party that advocates the policies and endorses the candidates which they believe are most consistent with their political attitudes. The reason people repeatedly vote for the same party is that, year after year, most of the information they receive suggests that one of the parties advocates policies and endorses candidates which are more consistent with their attitudes than are the policies and candidates of the other party. As long as they continue to receive information of this sort, they will continue to vote for the same party and, if asked, they will say they consider themselves members of that party. If, however, they receive information which suggests that the party they have favored in the past no longer advocates policies or endorses candidates consistent with their attitudes, they will change their party loyalties or at least vote for the other party in the next election. Therefore people will vote for the party they have traditionally supported only as long as its policies and candidates are consistent with their attitudes.

In short, the alternative interpretation I am suggesting is that people vote repeatedly for the same party and hold attitudes favoring the candidates and policies of that party not because party preference determines other attitudes and votes, but because they generally receive information which leads them to believe that the candidates and policies of one party are superior to those of the other party. Party preference is, therefore, a resultant of many specific attitudes that people have formed over the years and many specific pieces of information which they have received; party preference is not a powerful attitude that by itself determines votes and attitudes toward candidates and issues.

Why do people generally receive information which suggests that one rather than the other party has superior candidates and policies? The alternative interpretation I am discussing suggests that this is because each party serves some constituencies which are not as well served by the other party. Each of these constituencies is comprised of people who hold many of the same political attitudes and share many other characteristics. For example, organized labor and blacks are constituencies that have been served by the Democratic party in recent years. Year after year the Democrats attempt to take those positions and endorse those candidates that will appeal most strongly to the leaders of these groups and are consistent with the most salient political attitudes held by the groups' rank and file. Moreover, party and group leaders make use of propaganda techniques and chains of personal influence specially suited to reaching members of their constituencies. By these means they attempt to inform the rank and file of each constituency of the ways in which the party is serving their interests; leaders also attempt to persuade group members to adopt attitudes that favor the party's policies and candidates. Year after year, therefore, an individual usually receives information which leads him to regard the same party favorably because that party tries harder than the other party to act in accordance with the most salient attitudes held by people like him, and because it has better control of the mechanisms for informing and persuading him than the other party has. The correspondence between party preferences held by members of the public and their attitudes toward candidates and issues can be explained, therefore, by saying that parties do a good job of serving certain constituencies.

This interpretation can be summarized by saying that party loyalties persist because there is a communications system linking party and group leaders with members of their constituencies. At one end of this system are the leaders who attempt to inform and persuade their constituents. At the other end are the ordinary members of the public who hold certain attitudes and who live in information environments, partly created by the leaders, which are consistently favorable to one party. We can regard this interpretation as plausible only if we can be convinced of at least five things:

1. We must be convinced that the leaders of each political party devote special attention to maintaining the loyalties of certain constituencies and that they command the means of communicating information and opinions favorable to their parties to the members of their constituencies. This would suggest that the first part of the communication process operates as I have said it may operate.

2. We must be convinced that a substantial majority of the members of each group to which the parties pay particular attention hold the same beliefs, party preferences, and attitudes on many important issues. This would suggest that it is possible for party leaders to maintain the loyalties of these groups by adopting policies and endorsing candidates consistent with the attitudes of a majority of their members. In addition, it would suggest that it is possible for party leaders to maintain the loyalties of these groups by inducing group members to adopt attitudes and beliefs favorable to their parties.

3. We would have to be convinced that most members of the public live in environments where they usually receive information favoring one party but not the other. This would suggest that the efforts of party leaders to provide members of their constituencies with information favoring their party may be successful.

4. We would have to be convinced that the information which members of the public receive influences their attitudes and political behavior. This, together with the other evidence mentioned, would suggest that the reason most members of certain groups often hold the same attitudes and support the same party over a period of time may be that they are exposed to and influenced by information from the same party leaders.

5. It would be useful, although not necessary, for us to be convinced that the political attitudes held by members of the public are determined by some psychological factors other than attitudes toward parties, candidates, and issues. This would suggest that a variety of psychological factors, rather than simply party preference, may predispose each member of the public to be receptive to the appeals of one party rather than the other.

If we had evidence of these five sorts, it would be reasonable to believe that a combination of information flow, group loyalties, issue attitudes, and other psychological factors, rather than the influence of party preference, may lead members of the public to favor the same party over many years, to vote for it, and to hold attitudes toward issues and candidates which are consistent with their party preferences. In fact, social scientists have provided us with evidence of all five types, and that evidence will be reviewed briefly.

How Parties Play to Constituencies.   Studies of the two American political parties have shown that each is, in fact, more sensitive to the interests of some groups over a long period of time than to the interests of other groups.[8] For example, in recent years the Democratic party has attempted to adopt policies and endorse candidates that would please union members, blacks, and intellectuals. Truman's opposition to the Taft-Hartley Act, Kennedy's and Johnson's advocacy of federal aid to education, and the support that all three presidents provided for civil rights legislation are examples of the ways the Democrats have served these constituencies. This is not to deny that the Democrats have sometimes adopted policies which were not approved by union members, blacks, and intellectuals. Their record of service to these constituencies has, however, been good enough for them to retain control of certain means of communication particularly suited for reaching members of each group. The labor press is consistently pro-Democratic, and union funds and personnel are used for election-year canvasing on behalf of Democratic candidates. Likewise, local and national black leaders in recent years have endorsed Democratic candidates and have attempted to mobilize their communities to support those candidates. Finally, leaders of the intellectual community, as well as such intellectual journals and newspapers as *The New York Times* and *The Washington Post,* express consistently pro-Democratic views. In short, there is a great body of evidence that the parties attempt to serve certain constituencies and command powerful methods of informing and persuading members of those constituencies.

How Constituencies Share Views.   There is also a great deal of evidence which suggests that most of the members of the constituencies which political parties serve hold the same attitudes about at least some issues that the parties emphasize. For example, it has been shown that in 1968 blacks overwhelmingly believed that the United States was moving too slowly on civil rights issues, and Key has shown that in 1952 a majority of union members who held attitudes about the Taft-Hartley Act opposed it.[9] In both cases findings are reported which show that a majority of the members of each group voted for the party which advocated policies consistent with their attitudes.[10] As already pointed out, studies of the attitudes held by large social groups have been far too few to allow for any firm conclusions about how often most group members hold the same attitudes on a number of issues or how closely their votes are related to commonly held attitudes (see pp. 84–86). But the evidence just cited, together with the findings of other studies, suggests that this is not an infrequent occurrence. Researchers have suggested that group members may share many of the same attitudes because they share certain common characteristics (e.g., values or interests) which lead them to form the same attitudes, because party leaders persuade them to adopt the same attitudes, or for a combination of these and other reasons. In any event, it is possible that by attempting to take positions which would be consistent with the attitudes held by most members of particular constituencies, party leaders might insure the loyalty of those constituencies for many years.

Many students of social behavior have pointed out, however, that each member of the public should not be regarded as a member of only one social group.[11] This is true whether we say an individual is a member of a group because he identifies with it or because other people regard him as a member of it. In either case, an individual may be considered a member of several large social groups, and it is possible that most members of one group to which he belongs may not hold the same attitudes as most members of another group to which he belongs.

An individual may adopt the attitudes shared by most members of one group rather than the attitudes shared by most members of another group for a variety of reasons. For example, he may identify more strongly with one group rather than with another; the persuasive communications he receives from the leaders of one group may be stronger than the communications he receives from the leaders of other groups; or the basic beliefs and values that he shares with members of one group may have a stronger influence on the formation of his attitudes than the beliefs and values he shares with members of other groups. We can say that for any one or a combination of these reasons membership in a certain group may be more salient for an individual than membership in other groups. We should expect, therefore, that if we determine which of several group memberships is most salient for an individual at a particular point in time, we should be able to predict whether he will share the attitudes of most members of one group to which he belongs rather than the attitudes of most members of another group. In fact, Lane reports findings which show that members of the public who have conflicting group memberships often adopt the attitudes of the groups with which they identify most closely.[12]

Multiple group memberships create a problem for my explanation of party loyalties. If an individual is a member of several groups, if most members of each group to which he belongs do not hold the same attitudes as most members of other groups to which he belongs, and if the individual shares the attitudes of most members of one group at one time and the attitudes of most members of another group at another time, the parties cannot attempt to win his long-standing loyalty simply by serving a few constituencies. For example, if an individual is a black businessman, he may sometimes share the largely pro-Democratic attitudes of blacks; at other times he may share the largely pro-Republican attitudes of businessmen. In addition, it is possible that he may hold some pro-Democratic and some pro-Republican attitudes at the same time. If his membership in a pro-Democratic group and the attitudes he shares with that group are more salient for him in one election, he may vote for the Democrats in that election; if his membership in a pro-Republican group and the attitudes he shares with that group are more salient for him in the next election, he may vote for the Republicans. Therefore neither Democratic nor Republican leaders will be able to insure his loyalty simply by serving their normal constituencies. Moreover, if most members of the public have conflicting group memberships, the parties will not be able to maintain the loyalties of large sectors of the public by serving only a few groups.

Conflicting group memberships would not be problematic for my argument, however, if most members of almost all the groups to which individuals belong generally hold the same attitudes and are generally served by the same parties. In fact, the authors of *Voting* have shown that this is the case. In addition, they have shown that individuals who do not have conflicting group memberships are much more likely to have consistent party loyalties over a long period of time and to vote in accordance with those loyalties than are individuals who have conflicting group memberships.[13] Thus it is possible that although members of the public may be members of several large social groups, party leaders may create long-standing party loyalties by attempting to serve a few constituencies over a long period of time.

Information Environments.　　The evidence mentioned so far suggests only that political leaders attempt to provide members of groups with political information favoring their party and that many group members do, in fact, share attitudes favoring the same party. This evidence does not show, however, whether members of the public hear more information and opinions favoring the party they have supported in the past than the other party. But, in fact, there are findings that suggest they do. For example, the authors of *Voting* (Berelson et al.) found that most people reported hearing more information and opinions favoring one party than the other party during a campaign. Moreover, the people interviewed by those authors also reported that most of the information they heard favored the party they had supported in the past.[14] In addition, Berelson et al. found that most of the people with whom an individual has face-to-face contacts—family, friends, and colleagues at work—held attitudes which favored one party and were similar to his or her own attitudes.[15] It is likely, therefore, that in face-to-face contacts individuals hear more opinions favoring the party they have traditionally supported than the other party. Finally, Berelson et al. and other students of mass media usage suggest that members of the public generally subscribe to newspapers and listen to television and radio commentaries which convey information and opinions favoring the party they have traditionally supported, rather than the other party.[16]

Unfortunately, no one has been able to show how strong an effect the efforts of political leaders to portray their parties in a favorable light have on the immediate information environment of the average citizen. It may be that an individual and his friends generally hear information and opinions which support a particular party as a direct result of those efforts. An individual and his friends may all be members of many of the same groups and may all be responsive to the same party's efforts to serve those groups. It may be, however, that the relationship between party leaders and followers is either weaker or more complex than this. In any event, there are findings which suggest that the parties try to create favorable information environments for members of certain groups over a period of time and that many people live in such environments, even if there is not strong evidence about how these two sets of findings are related to each other.

The Influence of Information.   Even if we accept that people live in somewhat uniform information environments, however, we may wonder whether the information they receive has any influence on their attitudes and voting decisions. There are numerous findings that suggest it does. First, if people live in environments where most of the information available over a period of time favors a certain party, and if they are affected by the information they receive, we would expect that the more information they receive, the more likely they will be to vote for that party in succeeding elections. Receiving more information will maximize the chance that they will learn about the party's efforts to serve their interests. Also, as the sheer weight of information they receive increases, it is more likely to become a motivational force. If individuals are not influenced by the information they receive, however, we would not expect that differences in the amount of that information would be related to differences in the consistency of their voting records. In fact, Converse has shown that the higher the level of information people receive, the greater the probability they will vote for the same party in two succeeding elections. He has also shown that the greater the number of mass media of communication from which people draw their information, the more likely they are to vote consistently over time.[17] These findings do not prove conclusively that the information which people receive influences their voting behavior. For example, we might argue that the findings indicate that people with strong party loyalties seek out information which supports their loyalties. Nevertheless, the findings reported by Converse are at least consistent with the hypothesis that information flow influences votes, even if they are also consistent with other hypotheses.

A second example which suggests that people are influenced by the information they receive is reported by the authors of *Voting*.[18] Berelson et al. found that during the 1948 campaign a great number of people who had voted for the Democrats in the past and whose social and demographic characteristics indicated they would vote for the Democrats in that year reported early in the campaign that they intended to vote Republican. A significant number of these people reported that they considered social and economic issues highly salient and that they intended to vote for the Republicans primarily because they disliked some of the personal characteristics of Truman, the Democratic candidate. Berelson et al. found, however, that many of these people decided to vote for Truman just before election day. After examining these "shifters" more closely, the authors found that many of them had been dissatisfied with Truman because he had taken a weak stand in opposition to the Taft-Hartley Act. After they learned that his stand on that issue toughened at the very end of the campaign, they changed their attitude and voted for him. In this case, therefore, as long as the information people received was not consistent with their traditional party loyalties, they were prepared to cross party lines. Truman shifted his position to catch just such voters, and as soon as he did they resumed their traditional support for the Democrats. This evidence strongly suggests that the last-minute shifters were influenced by the information they received and that their party loyalty was maintained only because the information they received continued to favor the Democrats.

How Attitudes Are Formed.   There is evidence which suggests, therefore, that members of the public may be exposed to information which favors the same party year after year and that they may support the same party for a long period of time because the information they receive indicates that it takes positions and endorses candidates consistent with their political attitudes. But how do members of the public form these attitudes in the first place?

The evidence discussed suggests that the information flow to which individuals are exposed may contain expressions of opinion and other communications that persuade them to adopt attitudes toward candidates and policies. In addition, there is evidence which suggests that an individual's political attitudes may be determined by certain psychological factors other than party preference. To begin with, the evidence that individuals share some political attitudes with other members of groups to which they belong suggests that they may form attitudes favoring certain policies because they perceive that those policies will be in their interest. In fact, many of the attitudes shared by group members are about political objects that vitally affect their interests. The attitudes of union members about labor policy and the attitudes of blacks about civil rights issues are two examples mentioned earlier. Unfortunately, evidence that people in fact perceive the objects of shared attitudes to be in their interest is hard to find. Nevertheless, because there is a scarcity of firm evidence on the subject, it is possible that perceptions of self-interest may determine many attitudes.[19]

Many researchers have attempted to discover whether political attitudes and votes are determined by psychological characteristics shared by large numbers of people, such as ideologies and common personality traits.[20] This research has been far from conclusive, but it certainly has not shown that ideologies or common personality traits have an important influence on votes. Researchers who have attempted to discover whether an individual's political attitudes are consistent with the mix of psychological characteristics (whether commonly held or not) that make up his personality have been more successful, however. Intensive interviews of a few individuals conducted by Lane and by Smith, Bruner, and White, among others, have shown that people generally adopt political attitudes which are consistent with many facets of their personalities, such as their needs, habits, aspirations, and temperaments.[21] Of course, because these studies focus on small numbers of individuals, they do not show conclusively that the attitudes held by all or even a majority of the public are influenced by personality traits. Nevertheless, they at least suggest that there is a strong possibility that these traits (which, for convenience, will be called "needs" in the discussion that follows) may play an important role in determining political attitudes.

Possible Objections by the Authors of *The American Voter*

The five kinds of evidence I have reviewed suggest that the arguments about the primacy and stability of party preference which Campbell et al. present are not conclusive. Exactly how this evidence is related to their arguments will be discussed shortly. First, however, it is important to consider several objections Campbell et al. might raise to the interpretation I have placed on some of the findings just reviewed. I said that much of this evidence suggests that members of the public may be exposed to a strong information flow which is favorable to the same party over many years and that this may be the reason they express a preference for and vote for the same party during most of their lives. Campbell et al. might challenge this conclusion in a number of ways.

To begin with, they might argue that studies show that members of the public have very little political information and, as a result, it cannot have a strong effect on their votes. This would be similar to their argument that issue attitudes cannot influence votes because most people do not hold many issue attitudes. As pointed out in discussing that argument, most people have enough information to associate one of the parties with a stand they favor on at least one issue. If this stand is sufficiently important to them, that small amount of information may be sufficient to determine their votes.

Campbell et al. might also argue that certain of their findings about the 16 issue attitudes show that the voting choices and party preferences of many members of the public cannot be determined by a strong flow of information coming from the parties. They report that a large percentage of the people they interviewed incorrectly identified the stands of the parties on the 16 issues.[22]

They also report that, on some of these issues, there was practically no agreement among the people interviewed about which party held which position; that is, an approximately equal number of people identified each party with each of two opposing positions on the issues. The authors reason that if people attribute positions to parties because of information they have received more or less directly from political leaders, most people would correctly identify the positions of the parties and there would be general agreement about which party held which position. Because they find that this is often not the case, and because they also find that members of the public generally report that the party they favor holds positions on the 16 issues which they also favor, Campbell et al. conclude that members of the public are not exposed to or influenced by strong information flows from the parties. Rather, they conclude that in many cases people simply imagine, on the basis of no information at all, that the party they favor holds positions similar to their own.[23] Believing on the basis of no information that a favored individual or group shares one's own views is an example of a psychological phenomenon often called "projection." As a result, Campbell et al. might argue that findings that people report hearing more information favoring the parties they have traditionally supported than information favoring the opposition parties do not show that they are exposed to strong information flows favoring their parties or that they live in fairly uniform information environments. These findings only show that members of the public project their own attitudes onto the parties they have traditionally supported.

It is hard to know what to make of the evidence about misperceptions of party positions which Campbell et al. present, but I do not think that the interpretation they place on it is conclusive. Their interpretation does not take account of the possibilities that some people may be genuinely misinformed about the positions of parties on particular issues or that those positions may be genuinely, and perhaps intentionally, ambiguous. In addition, their interpretation overlooks the possibility that in many cases people may tell interviewers they have received more information than they have or may invent stories about candidates and parties on the spur of the moment simply to seem knowledgeable. They may not, therefore, believe some of the information they report, and it may have no bearing on their political behavior. If we could determine what information reported by members of the public they do believe, however, we might find that most people agree on which positions are held by which parties and candidates. Furthermore, Campbell et al. stress that on some issues there was virtually no agreement among the people they surveyed about which party holds which position; at the same time the authors put less emphasis on the fact that, on a majority of issues, between 65 and 75% of the people they interviewed agreed on which positions the parties held.[24] These considerations suggest that the authors of *The American Voter* may overemphasize the degree to which members of the public project policy positions on parties and candidates. Certainly they present no evidence which suggests that all or most of the beliefs members of the public report they hold about parties and candidates are projections.

Campbell et al. also suggest that other psychological mechanisms— most notably selective exposure, perception, and retention—may lead people to report they receive more information favoring the party they have traditionally supported than the other party;[25] that is, people may expose themselves more often to information favoring their own than the other party. They may also tend to notice and remember information favoring the party they have traditionally supported more readily than information favoring the opposition. In short, Campbell et al. believe that through selective mechanisms, members of the public may screen out information which is inconsistent with their long-standing party loyalties. Unfortunately, however, they present no evidence which shows that selective exposure, perception, and retention play important roles in determining what political information members of the American public hold. It may be that these psychological mechanisms, like projection, are partly responsible for the fact that members of the public hold information which is generally consistent with their party preferences. Nevertheless, because Campbell et al. present no findings which show that selective mechanisms screen out a large part of the average individual's information environment, there is no reason to assume that the beliefs of most individuals about politics are not, to a large extent, a result of that environment.[26]

The Direction of Causality

All in all, the possible objections which Campbell et al. might raise do not show that the interpretation I have placed on evidence about information flow is incorrect. Having reviewed these objections, we are now in a position to see precisely how that evidence and my interpretation are related to the argument about the primacy and stability of party preference which Campbell et al. present. To make this relationship clear, it will be discussed in terms of Heider's theories of psychological balance that were outlined in Chapter 2.

Heider and The American Voter. It will be remembered that Heider was interested in the relationships among an individual's attitude toward another person, his attitude toward an object, and his beliefs about the other person's attitude toward the object. Heider represented these relationships by triangular diagrams, such as Figure 6.1*a.* The person, *o*, the other person, *p*, and the object, *x*, are at the corners of the triangle. The lines, or "bonds," between these elements represent attitudes or beliefs. A + sign indicates a favorable attitude or belief, and a − sign indicates an unfavorable attitude or belief.

In their discussion of party preference, the authors of *The American Voter*, like Heider, are interested in the relationship between an individual's beliefs and attitudes. In particular, they are interested in the relationships among his attitudes toward parties, his attitudes toward policies, and his beliefs about the positions parties adopt on policies toward which he holds attitudes. (They are also, of course, interested in the relationships among an individual's attitudes toward candidates, his attitudes toward parties, and his beliefs about the party affiliations of the candidates. Only slight modifications of the argument to follow are

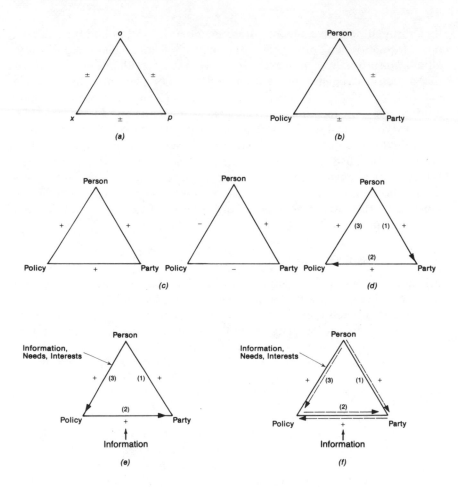

Figure 6.1. The direction of causality.

needed to substitute attitudes toward candidates for attitudes toward policies, however; but for the sake of brevity, only attitudes toward policies will be considered.)

Following Heider, we can represent the attitudes and beliefs by a triangular diagram such as Figure 6.1b. A person, the party for which he has traditionally voted, and a policy are at the three corners of the triangle. The lines between the person and the party and between the person and the policy represent his attitudes toward the party and policy. A + sign indicates a favorable attitude, and a − sign indicates an unfavorable attitude. The line between the policy and the party represents the individual's belief about the party's position on the policy. A +

sign indicates that he believes the party endorses the policy, and a −
sign indicates that he believes the party opposes the policy.

As already pointed out, Campbell et al. base their argument about
party preference on three kinds of findings: that individuals generally
report they have held the same party preference for many years, vote in
accordance with their party preference, and hold favorable attitudes
toward policies they believe their party endorses and unfavorable attitudes toward policies they believe their party opposes. The third finding
can be represented in terms of Heider's theory by Figure 6.1c. Campbell
et al. find that the bonds between a person, the party he has traditionally
supported, and a policy toward which he has an attitude and on which
the party has a position are all positive or that the bonds between a
person and a policy and between the party and a policy are negative,
while the bond between the person and the party is positive.

Campbell et al. claim that their findings show a causal relationship
between the three elements in the triangular relationships represented in
Figure 6.1. They believe this causal relationship takes the form indicated
by the direction of the arrows in Figure 6.1d. An individual holds a
favorable attitude toward a party (bond 1), and he learns that the party
favors a certain policy (bond 2). This creates two positive bonds; Heider
would say that in a situation of this sort, individuals tend to achieve
psychological balance by forming a third positive bond. The authors of
The American Voter also believe there is a tendency for individuals to
form a third positive bond in a situation of this sort, but they do not
discuss this tendency in terms of Heider's theories about psychological
balance. They simply say that once an individual who has a favorable
attitude toward a party learns that the party endorses a certain policy, he
tends to form a favorable attitude toward that policy. His attitude toward the policy is caused by his attitude toward the party in the sense
that he would not have formed his policy attitude if he had not held a
certain party preference and a certain belief about his party's position.

There is another way in which these attitudes and beliefs might be
causally related. My alternative interpretation is represented by Figure
6.1e. A person might form a favorable attitude toward a policy (bond 3),
learn that a party endorses the policy (bond 2), and, as a result, form a
favorable attitude toward the party (bond 1). Alternatively, he might
learn that a party favors a certain policy (bond 2), decide, upon consideration, that he likes the policy (bond 3), and, as a result, adopt a
favorable attitude toward the party (bond 1).

The authors of *The American Voter* argue that their interpretation of
the relationships depicted in Figure 6.1 must be correct because people
hold attitudes toward parties (bond 1) before they acquire attitudes toward policies or information about which policies the parties endorse in

a particular election year (bonds 3 and 2). They believe that the primacy of party preference is shown by the fact that people who are asked about their party preference in several interviews conducted over a number of years generally report the same party preference and by the fact that people generally say they have voted for the same party in many elections.[27] Campbell et al. argue that because party preference is developed prior to attitudes toward policies and beliefs about party positions, it cannot be caused by those attitudes and beliefs. Rather, any causal chain linking party preference, policy attitudes, and beliefs about party positions must begin with party preference. Given this initial assumption, the authors believe there are only two possible causal chains which might link the three elements in such a way that people would always hold policy attitudes consistent with the policy positions adopted by the party they have traditionally favored.

To begin with, the second link in the causal chain might be that an individual learns that the party he favors takes a certain position on a policy. Having formed bonds 1 and 2 in the triangular relationship indicated by Figure 6.1*d*, the individual would have to form a third bond having the same sign as bond 2 to maintain psychological balance. In this chain of causality, therefore, his policy attitude would be caused by his party preference and his perceptions about the policy positions of the party he favors. Alternatively, the second link in the causal chain might be that the individual would form an attitude toward a policy (bond 3). To maintain psychological balance, therefore, he would then have to form bond 2 with the same sign as bond 3; that is, having formed a positive attitude toward a party and an attitude toward a policy, he could only maintain psychological balance by assuming that the party endorsed the policy if he favored it or by assuming that the party opposed the policy if he opposed it. As already pointed out, the phenomenon of assuming that one's party shares one's views about politics is an example of the psychological phenomenon of projection. Given their findings about the primacy of party preference, therefore, Campbell et al. believe that consistencies between policy attitudes and beliefs about party positions must be caused by the influence of party preference on policy attitudes or the projection of policy attitudes onto parties.

Campbell et al. claim that both the causal chain in which party preference influences policy attitudes and the causal chain in which policy positions are projected onto parties operate fairly frequently. It is important to realize, however, that their conclusions about these two causal chains imply different assumptions about the relationship between party preference and policy attitudes. The causal chain that brings about projection is not a chain in which party preference determines policy attitudes. It is, rather, a chain in which party preference and policy attitudes that are not influenced by party preference together determine beliefs. Thus, by claiming that projection can account for their findings about party preference, Campbell et al. in effect are admitting that simply because party preference is formed prior to policy attitudes and beliefs about party positions, and because policy attitudes and beliefs about party positions are generally consistent, we cannot assume that party preference determines policy attitudes. Even if we admit the primacy of party preference, we can explain the consistencies between policy attitudes and beliefs about party positions by saying that all or most of those consistencies might be caused by projection rather than the influence of party preference on policy attitudes. This is possible because, as pointed out previously, Campbell et al. present no evidence that shows how frequently projection operates. Thus we could argue that they have not shown that party preference determines policy attitudes because all the evidence on which they base this conclusion can be explained by the phenomenon of projection.

Heider and the Author.   I do not, however, base my argument against Campbell et al.'s conclusions about party preference on the possibility that their findings might be explained by the phenomenon of projection because, as just mentioned, they present no evidence about how frequently projection operates. It is possible that projection has a strong influence on the beliefs which members of the public hold; but it is also possible that its effect is minor. My argument against the conclusions Campbell et al. draw is that when people report their party preferences, they may simply be indicating that they have generally found the policies and candidates of a certain party to be superior to the policies and candidates of the other party; they are not necessarily expressing an attitude that has motivational force over a period of time. We cannot, therefore, assume that the causal chain which brings about consistencies between party preference, policy attitudes, and beliefs about party positions must begin with party preference. Referring to Figure 6.1, we cannot assume that bond 1 must be formed before bonds 2 and 3.

Why, then, do people generally have policy attitudes that are consistent with their perceptions of the policy positions endorsed by the parties they favor? I have suggested, as indicated by Figure 6.1e, that this may be because the flow of information to which an individual is exposed and his needs and interests constantly lead him to adopt certain attitudes and to believe that the policies endorsed by the same party are consistent with those attitudes over a long period of time. It may be information flow and an individual's needs and interests, therefore, rather than his party preference, that create bond 3 and insure its consistency with bond 2. Moreover, bond 1 may be generally consistent with these two bonds because they are usually consistent with each other. In other words, an individual may express a preference for the same party over a long period of time because the information flow to which he is exposed and his needs and interests generally lead him to form attitudes which are consistent with the positions advocated by that party.

I have demonstrated that this is a possible hypothesis by showing that when people who have favored a particular party for many years form attitudes which are opposed to the party's policies, they change their attitude toward the party; that is, to return to Figure 6.1, when bonds 2 and 3 are negative bond 1 is also negative. This would not be the case if the causal chain linking these attitudes and beliefs always began with party preference. In that case an individual would always have a favorable attitude toward the party he has supported in the past (bond 1 would always be positive). I have also shown that my alternative hypothesis is supported by findings that there is, in fact, a flow of information and opinions favoring the same party directed at each member of the public year after year and that members of the public live in fairly uniform information environments. In addition, I have shown that members of the public hold political attitudes similar to those of other members of groups to which they belong. This suggests that they may adopt attitudes favoring certain policies and candidates partly because party propaganda which urges them to adopt those attitudes is directed toward their groups and partly because they share certain interests and values with other group members. Finally, I have shown that there is evidence from intensive psychological interviews that people adopt attitudes toward policies and candidates which are consistent with many of their fundamental personality traits. This at least suggests that there are psychological factors other than party preference which might determine political attitudes.

All the evidence reviewed shows that both party preference and attitudes toward candidates and issues may be determined by information flow and basic psychological traits. In addition, it suggests that party preference may be more stable and long lasting than attitudes toward candidates and issues because parties are enduring political institutions which create information flows to members of the public. Year after year each member of the public receives information that reinforces his attitude toward the same party; however, every few years he forms new attitudes toward candidates and issues and his old attitudes change because of altered political conditions and changes in the messages he receives from the parties. As a result, party preference is bound to be more stable and long lasting than other attitudes. We should not assume, however, that findings about the stability and primacy of party preference and evidence that members of the public generally hold other attitudes which are consistent with their party preferences show that party preference determines other attitudes. On the contrary, the evidence reviewed suggests that attitudes toward candidates and issues may possibly be determined by information flow and a variety of psychological traits and that these factors may determine party preference.

I have based my argument about party preference on the same evidence Campbell et al. use to support their argument, as well as on certain other evidence. At the least I have shown that on the basis of the evidence reviewed, it is as reasonable to accept my interpretation of the role of party preference as it is to accept the interpretation offered by Campbell et al. I believe, therefore, that to show that party preference determines attitudes toward candidates and policy attitudes, those authors would have to offer evidence which would enable us to choose between their interpretation and the one I have offered. Campbell et al. present no such evidence, however. Their argument about party preference is based entirely on the evidence I have discussed, and this evidence does not enable them to choose between their interpretation and the one I have offered.[28] As a result, I think we can conclude that they are wrong in claiming they have shown that party preference has a stronger influence on the outcomes of elections than any other attitudes or that party preference in fact determines issue attitudes because the evidence they present to support this conclusion is consistent with a contrary conclusion.

I am not arguing that the alternative explanation of findings about party preference which I have offered is necessarily superior to the explanation Campbell et al. offer. My argument is, rather, that their evidence does not enable us to choose between the two explanations. I concede that most of the evidence I have presented to support my alternative explanation could also be used to support the conclusion that party preference determines issue attitudes. In other words, we could argue that findings about the efforts of party leaders to influence certain groups and findings about the uniformity of information environments show only that the information people receive reinforces their party preferences or leads them to adopt attitudes they are already predisposed to adopt. In addition, we could argue that findings about group consistencies in attitudes and votes may simply show that people adopt party preferences consistent with group norms and that those preferences determine policy attitudes. Moreover, we could argue that Converse's findings that level of information correlates with consistency in voting show only that party preference is strengthened by information. Finally, we could say that the findings about the influence of information on votes which the authors of *Voting* present are inconclusive. Berelson et al. showed that a certain group of people were prepared to vote inconsistently with their party loyalties until they received certain information. It may be, however, that their party preferences rather than the information swayed their votes in the end. I admit, therefore, that most of these findings can be explained by the theory Campbell et al. elaborate as well as by my alternative theory. My argument is, however, that Campbell et al. do not present evidence which enables us to determine which theory is correct.

A Compromise Interpretation

It is not realistic to think that most members of the public form their party preferences anew during each election campaign with no thought of their party's past performance or of their own past votes, nor would I suggest that they receive each new piece of political information as if they had no previous political information or commitments. It is probable, as the authors of *The American Voter* suggest, that people have predispositions favoring the parties they voted for in the past and that they are more receptive to information which supports rather than contradicts those predispositions. I have shown, however, that people are prepared to depart from their party preferences if they receive information which indicates that the party they have supported in the past no longer presents policies and candidates they approve of. There may be some resistance to such information; but there is evidence that when it is available, it is often accepted and often influences votes. The evidence I have discussed suggests, however, that information which is inconsistent with their party preferences is not generally available to most people. For the most part, respondents to sample surveys report that their information environments are fairly uniform. It may be that various psychological processes lead them to report that the information available to them is more uniform than it actually is. Nevertheless, no one has shown how strong an influence those processes have.

There is reason to believe, therefore, that the information environments in which most people live at least support their party preferences even if those environments are not entirely uniform. If this is true, the proper way to describe the relationship between information flow and party preference is to say that they are two mutually reinforcing processes: An individual's political experiences and the information he receives generally support and strengthen his party preference over the years, and his party preference predisposes him to receive and pay attention to information that is consistent with his past votes. As long as these two processes continue to act in tandem, as they do for most people most of the time, individuals will vote for the same party in each election. If political information and issue attitudes become seriously inconsistent with party preference, however, an individual will deviate from his past voting pattern.

We can represent these two processes in terms of Heider's theory as two parallel causal chains that create pressures for consistency between attitudes and beliefs. These two chains are represented by the clockwise and counterclockwise sets of arrows in Figure 6.1f. In this diagram individual issue attitudes, needs, and interests, together with an overall tendency to maintain psychological balance, create a constant pressure for consistency between attitudes and beliefs in the counterclockwise direction; at the same time party preference and perceptions of party positions, together with an overall tendency for balance, create pressures for consistency in the clockwise direction. If this is an accurate representation of the way party preference, issue attitudes, and beliefs about party positions are related, then, to show that party preference is a more powerful influence on the outcomes of elections than are other attitudes, Campbell et al. would have to show that the clockwise pressures are stronger than the counterclockwise pressures; that is, they would have to show that party preference exerts a stronger influence on other attitudes than information flow, issue attitudes, needs, and interests exert on party preference.

I am not sure how they might go about doing this. Certainly evidence that information flow is weak or inconsistent with an individual's issue attitudes would argue for the strength of the clockwise forces, as would evidence that individuals do not form attitudes consistent with their needs and interests or that they do not form issue attitudes until after they have received information about the policies of the party they have traditionally supported. Evidence which would support my alternative hypothesis would be that information flow is strong and consistent with issue attitudes and that there are factors—either information flow or psychological factors—which would lead people to form the issue attitudes they hold even if they did not have loyalties to a particular party or beliefs about its positions on particular issues. Also, as I have pointed out, information that people sometimes form issue attitudes which are inconsistent with their past party preferences and that this leads them to change those party preferences would support my alternative hypothesis. I do not know, however, exactly how these different sorts of information could be combined in a way that would make it possible to compare precisely the strength of the clockwise and counterclockwise forces in Figure 6.1. Campbell et al. certainly provide no way of doing this. As a result, they do not show how strong an influence party preference has on votes compared to the influence of other attitudes, and they are certainly wrong in claiming to have shown that it determines most other attitudes.

7. The Conclusions of *The American Voter*

What Campbell et al. Do Not Show

In the two preceding chapters I have criticized two parts of the argument of *The American Voter*. I think my criticisms are significant because they cast doubt on the most important claim which Campbell et al. make about their work: that they can identify motives for votes. Certainly there is a sense in which this claim is justified. The relationships between attitudes and votes which they discover strongly suggest that attitudes toward parties, candidates, and issues all have *some* effect on voting choices and the outcomes of elections. Campbell et al. may overestimate the strength of that effect in the case of party preference, and they may underestimate it in the case of issue attitudes; but they at least show that these are among the major psychological factors which determine political behavior.

As pointed out earlier (pp. 73–82), however, the authors of *The American Voter* claim to do more than simply show that attitudes toward parties, candidates, and issues have some effect on voting choices and the outcomes of elections. After all, this general conclusion has been affirmed by students of politics ever since public opinion became the subject of serious study in the nineteenth century. Campbell et al. claim to go beyond the work of traditional public opinion theorists by using attitude psychology to show that certain kinds of attitude have a far stronger influence on voting choices and the outcomes of modern American elections than other kinds of attitude have. It is in this sense that they claim to identify motives for votes, and it is on this claim that my argument in the two preceding chapters casts doubt.

I have argued that Campbell et al. do not show that issue attitudes have only a minimal effect on voting choices and the outcomes of elections or that party preference has a stronger effect than any other attitudes have. Moreover, although I have not criticized their analysis of the six partisan attitudes, it is difficult to determine the significance of that analysis if their findings about issue attitudes and party preference are inconclusive. I do not doubt that Campbell et al. have been able to determine the relative strength among the six partisan attitudes. Because they are unable to determine the strength of the influence that attitudes toward issues and parties exert on votes and elections, however, they are unable to say whether the influence exerted by the six partisan attitudes is stronger or weaker than the influence exerted by party preference and issue attitudes. Like traditional public opinion theorists, therefore, Campbell et al. are able to show only that attitudes toward parties, candidates, and issues have *some* effect on votes and the outcomes of elections; they are not able to show that certain sorts of attitude have a stronger effect than others.

The Political Process and *The American Voter*

This conclusion is important in itself because it shows that Campbell et al. do not accomplish what they set out to accomplish. It is also important because a great number of the specific conclusions they draw about American politics are based on the assumption that they can compare the influence which different attitudes have on votes and elections. For example, the general picture of the American voter that emerges from their study is not very flattering.[1] They claim that the average voter cares little about the specific policies and actions of government or the promises made by aspirants to government office. Instead, his voting choices are usually motivated by a combination of blind party loyalty and preferences for the personal qualities of candidates. As a result, politicians need not stress issues to win the support of the great majority of voters. The politicians' task is to stress their images as candidates and to relate themselves to parties. Moreover, when they achieve office, politicians have a great deal of freedom in their actions. They need not fear being dismissed from office at the next election because they pursue certain policies. Their constituencies will support them as long as their actions are not greatly inconsistent with the prevailing image of their parties.

Given this state of affairs, American electoral history can be seen as a series of long periods of stability in the strength of either of the two parties. During a stable period, one party generally enjoys the loyalty of more members of the public than does the other party. For example, in recent years more members of the public have identified with the Democratic than with the Republican party, whereas during the early part of this century more people identified with the Republicans than with the Democrats. Members of the public exercise no effective control over public policy by their votes during such stable periods because they do not vote for candidates on the basis of the policies they advocate. Stable periods are interrupted only by such cataclysmic events as wars and depressions, which lead to realignments of party loyalties. In elections held at the time of these historic cataclysms, issues may play an important role; but such elections only set the stage for new periods of stability.

It is, of course, puzzling that during the periods of time in which, according to Campbell et al., party loyalties are stable, the party with which most people identify does not always win elections. For example, from 1932 through 1972 a majority of the people who identified with a party considered themselves Democrats; even so, the Republicans won the presidential elections of 1952, 1956, 1968, and 1972. Campbell et al. explain this by distinguishing between strong party identifiers, weak party identifiers, and uncommitted voters. Strong party identifiers are people who consider themselves members of a party and almost always vote for it; weak identifiers are people who consider themselves members of a party but often vote for the other party; and uncommitted voters are people who do not consider themselves members of a party and report no strong consistencies in their voting records.

Campbell et al. believe that the Republicans can win elections during periods of Democratic predominance because, separately, neither the strong identifiers of the Republicans nor the strong identifiers of the Democrats add up to a majority of the voters in many elections although, collectively, they add up to well over a majority. As a result, weak identifiers and uncommitted voters often hold the balance of power in particular elections, and the Republicans can achieve victory by attracting the support of enough of them so that their votes plus the votes of strong Republicans add up to an electoral majority. Campbell et al. believe that the votes of weak identifiers and uncommitted voters are motivated primarily by attitudes toward the personal qualities of candidates and, in a sense, we can say that those attitudes determine the outcomes of elections. The authors also say, however, that the outcomes of elections are determined by both party preference and attitudes toward the personal qualities of candidates in the sense that, taken together, these two factors generally determine the votes of almost all members of the public.

If my criticisms of the argument of *The American Voter* are correct, all of these conclusions about how the American political system operates are groundless. Campbell et al. do not show that the average voter is not motivated by issue attitudes or that he is motivated primarily by party preference. Thus they do not show that the unflattering picture they paint of him is correct. Moreover, if they cannot assume that party preference determines most votes and that issue attitudes are unimportant, Campbell et al. cannot claim that the parties have great freedom to pursue whatever policies they wish to pursue or that they can maintain the loyalties of large segments of the public simply by stressing party and candidate images. On the contrary, it may be that parties can maintain the loyalties of the people who have traditionally supported them only by continuing to advance policies which are consistent with the most salient political attitudes held by those people and by persuading their constituents to adopt attitudes consistent with party policies.

In addition, we are led to different conclusions about electoral history than Campbell et al. draw if we believe that attitudes toward issues as well as candidates and parties may play an important part in determining voting choices and the outcomes of elections. According to this view, the difference between cataclysmic realigning elections and elections during periods of stability is not that issue attitudes play an important role in one sort of election but not in the other. Periods of stability are simply periods during which the parties have found a way to act in accordance with the attitudes of the same people year after year and also to form those attitudes. They are, therefore, periods during which the relationship between the public and the parties is in equilibrium. The equilibrium is dynamic, however: It is maintained only by the efforts of the parties to respond to changing public views and to changing political, social, and economic events. Periods of stability indicate that both the parties and the public are organized in such a way that this equilibrium can be maintained. Realigning elections are, therefore, elections in which the relationships between the parties and some of their supporters break down. The parties do not adjust fast enough to external events that create major changes in the attitudes of their constituents and, possibly, in the organization of the parties themselves. Thus, if my criticisms of the argument of *The American Voter* are correct, the difference between elections during periods of stability and realigning elections is that the parties are more successful in presenting positions which will hold the loyalties of their constituents in the one case than the other; the difference is not that in the one case issue attitudes are unimportant in determining the outcomes of elections, but are important in the other case.

Finally, if my criticisms of the argument of *The American Voter* are correct, the outcomes of elections during periods of stability may not be due to deviations from weak party loyalties or voting choices by uncommitted voters that are determined by candidate images. The outcomes of these elections may instead be due to the success of the winning party in presenting policies that attract voters outside its usual constituencies, while at the same time presenting policies which continue to appeal to its past supporters.

What Campbell et al. Succeed in Demonstrating

Because Campbell et al. do not show how strong an effect attitudes toward parties, candidates, and issues have on the outcomes of elections, therefore, we cannot accept many of the conclusions they draw about the American political system. This is not to deny that their work makes a substantial contribution to political science. I have discussed only certain sections of *The American Voter* in Part II, and I do not doubt that other sections are of great value. For example, Campbell et al. conduct extremely interesting analyses of the voting patterns of different social classes and of the effects of differences in election laws on the outcomes of elections.[2] Because these analyses are not based on the findings I have discussed in this part, however, my criticisms do not apply to them. Moreover, even the findings I have discussed in this chapter provide the basis for many important conclusions, and it is worthwhile to consider briefly what some of these are.

To begin with, it is of no small importance that Campbell et al. have shown that attitudes toward parties, candidates, and issues have at least some effect on voting choices and the outcomes of elections, even if they have not been able to show that the influence of some of these attitudes is stronger than that of others. As pointed out earlier, traditional political theorists concluded that opinions about these three kinds of political objects determine votes on the basis of questionable evidence. Their conclusions were based, for the most part, on informal interviews with groups of individuals that may or may not have been cross sections of the American public. Techniques for drawing representative samples of the general public, together with reliable techniques for recording attitudes and processing data, have enabled Campbell et al. to marshal an impressive amount of evidence that shows the importance of attitudes toward parties, candidates, and issues.

Moreover, the techniques just mentioned have enabled Campbell et al. to provide a powerful refutation of at least one traditional notion about the relationship between public opinion and government: that, in one of its forms, the mandate theory of elections is incorrect. The mandate theory holds that in an election members of the public are asked to choose between two candidates who hold opposite positions on most major issues. People decide to vote for a particular candidate because they prefer his policies to those of the other candidate. The winning candidate can therefore claim an electoral mandate to carry out his policies because, having received a majority of the votes, he can assume that a majority of the voters prefer his policies to those of his opponent. This is what I call the "crude form" of the mandate theory.

Many of the statements about the relationship between public opinion and government made by such traditional public opinion theorists as Tocqueville and Bryce suggest that they would have approved of the crude form of the mandate theory. As pointed out in Chapter 1, traditional theorists believe that elections are one of the means by which the public exercises control over government policy. They say that this control is effective because if a member of government adopts policies which are contrary to majority opinion, there is a good chance that a majority of the voters will oppose him in the next election. As a result, it can be concluded that the policies of a successful candidate must be approved by a majority of the voters. Tocqueville and Bryce sometimes seem to draw this conclusion, but at other times they seem to believe that the way in which elections force government to act in accordance with public opinion is more complex. Regardless of their beliefs, however, the mandate theory in its crude form is often adopted by contemporary journalists and other influential political commentators.[3] Campbell et al. could claim that they have accomplished a great deal by refuting that theory.

Whatever else they do or do not show about issue attitudes, Campbell et al. at least show that attitudes toward any one issue are not widely held and that most people do not hold attitudes toward many issues (see "Issue Attitudes" in Chapter 4). As a result, they show that a successful candidate usually cannot claim that a majority of voters even consider any of his policies let alone that all, or even one, of those policies are approved by a majority of voters. The most he might claim is that a majority of the people who care about some of the issues on which he takes stands approve of his policies on those issues and that those people, together with a majority of the people who care about other issues and who approve of his positions on those issues, form a majority of voters. Thus he might be able to claim that, overall, his policies appeal to the varied interests of a majority of voters; but he cannot generally say that any one or all of those policies are endorsed by a majority of voters. In fact, he may not even know which policies are endorsed by a majority of the people who are concerned with them.

Of course, this does not necessarily mean that a candidate is free to adopt whatever policies he wishes. It may be that he must adopt policies which are approved by a majority of at least some issue publics. This might be called the "sophisticated" form of the mandate theory because it takes into account empirical findings about public opinion. If this form of the mandate theory is correct, we can still say that public opinion exerts a degree of control over government policies through elections. Campbell et al. do not show whether politicians must adopt policies favored by issue publics to be elected and, as a result, do not show conclusively whether public opinion influences government policies. They do at least show, however, that the crude form of the mandate theory does not accurately describe the relationship between government policies and public opinion.

Another valuable contribution Campbell et al. make is to show that many of the theories and techniques which attitude psychologists have developed can be applied to the study of political attitudes. For example, they have shown that the homeostatic principle applies to public opinion. As we would expect if we adopted that principle, an individual generally tends to hold political attitudes which are consistent with each other and with his beliefs about politics (see pp. 33–37). Moreover, like attitude psychologists, Campbell et al. have found that attitude intensity appears to influence the degree of consistency between different attitudes and between the cognitive and affective components and the behavioral component of a given attitude (see "Intensity" in Chapter 4). Finally, Campbell et al. have shown that scaling techniques developed by attitude psychologists can be applied to public opinion research (see pp. 37–44, 50–54). All these findings are important because they provide further validation for the general theories and techniques developed by attitude psychologists. They are also important because they show that attitude psychology can be a useful tool in the study of public opinion if applied carefully.

Finally, the authors of *The American Voter* develop findings that enable them to draw important conclusions about electoral history, although in a different way than they claim. Campbell et al. see their task in analyzing electoral history as that of comparing the psychological factors which determine the outcomes of different elections over a period of many years.[4] One way to do this would be to list the attitudes toward parties, candidates, and issues that influence the outcome of each election. Because candidates and issues are not the same in each election, however, this would be a lengthy task. Moreover, this procedure would emphasize differences between elections and neglect any similarities they might have. A more elegant way to analyze electoral history would be to compare different elections in terms of the same factor; that is, we could say that differences in the outcomes of elections occur wholly or partly because some factor operates with greater strength or in a different direction in some elections than in others. This procedure would allow us to deal with fewer variables and would take into account similarities as well as differences between elections. Obviously, if we are to develop an explanation of this sort using attitude psychology, the common factor in terms of which we must compare different elections must be an attitude or attitudes that exert an influence on the outcomes of all the elections to be explained. Moreover, because attitudes are individual traits, if one attitude is to exert a major influence on the outcome of a particular election, it must be held by a large percentage of the public.

Campbell et al. believe they have identified an attitude of the sort just described: party preference. By comparing different elections in terms of how strong an influence party preference exerts on their outcomes, the authors are able to produce extremely elegant explanations of electoral history, and this is undoubtedly one reason their work should be admired. For example, they can explain the elections from 1948 through 1960 by saying that party loyalties were largely responsible for Truman's 1948 victory, that their influence was diminished somewhat by the influence of candidates and issues in 1952 and 1956, and that they again determined most votes in 1960. In addition, explanations such as this can be elaborated by determining which groups of voters deviated from their party loyalties in different years and by determining what factors led to their deviations.[5] Thus we might say that most people who crossed party lines in 1952 and 1956 were Democrats who were impressed by Eisenhower's personality, whereas most people who crossed party lines in 1960 were Democrats who did not approve of Kennedy's liberal policies.

Explanations of electoral history that combine information about the influence of party preference on several elections with information about the influence of other factors on each election are highly valuable. Moreover, their value is not greatly diminished if we assume that party preference is a resultant of several other attitudes rather than an attitude which, in itself, has motivational force. We can simply consider party preference an index of several factors that tend to make people vote for the same party over many years. From this point of view, we can say that in their analysis of electoral history, Campbell et al. are, in effect, comparing how strong an influence these several factors which determine party preference (rather than a single attitude) have on the outcomes of different elections. In this case, party preference is still a useful standard for comparing different elections, although we would have to conclude that it is a different kind of standard than Campbell et al. claim it is. As a result, I do not think that the usefulness of the analysis of electoral history which Campbell et al. conduct is diminished by my criticisms; however, those criticisms suggest that the authors may have incorrectly described the standards in terms of which they compare different elections.

The American Voter, therefore, does make a number of important contributions to political science. Campbell et al. are unable, however, to achieve what they primarily set out to achieve: They are unable to show which political attitudes have the greatest influence on voting choices and the outcomes of elections. In this respect, their attempts to apply attitude psychology to the study of public opinion are unsuccessful, and many of their specific conclusions are unacceptable.

8. Reasons for the Shortcomings of *The American Voter*

Three Assumptions

Probably more important than the fact that the authors of *The American Voter* are not successful in their attempts to compare the influence which different attitudes have on votes are the reasons for their lack of success. These reasons illuminate certain limitations of both contemporary attitude studies and traditional notions about public opinion. It should be apparent from my discussion of the specifics of the argument of *The American Voter* that the fundamental reason Campbell et al. are unable to draw many of the conclusions about politics they claim to draw is that they make three major assumptions for which they provide no adequate justification: that what I call "enduring" attitudes, those attitudes which are held for very long periods of time, must have a stronger influence on votes than other attitudes have; that only widely held attitudes can have a major effect on the outcomes of elections; and that the answers to free-response questions which they record are expressions of a few broad policy attitudes instead of a greater number of specific issue attitudes.

The first assumption is found in the analysis of party preference that Campbell et al. conduct (see Chapter 6 and "Party Preference" in Chapter 4). They believe that because party preference is more enduring than other attitudes, it must have a stronger influence on votes. As a result, they assume that their findings about party preference can be explained only in one way, whereas those findings can in fact be explained in other ways as well. The second assumption is found in the analysis of the 16 issue attitudes that Campbell et al. conduct (see "Issue Attitudes" in Chapter 4 and "The Argument Presented" in Chapter 5). They assume that because these issue attitudes are not widely held, they cannot have a major influence on the outcomes of elections. As a result, they do not believe it is necessary to apply to the 16 issue attitudes the techniques they use to determine the relationship between the six partisan attitudes and votes. The third assumption is found in the analysis of the six partisan attitudes that the authors conduct (see "Six Partisan Attitudes" in Chapter 4 and pp. 91–95). Because Campbell et al. believe that answers to free-response questions reflect broad policy attitudes rather than specific issue attitudes, they do not interpret their analyses of attitudes toward foreign and domestic issues as analyses of specific issue attitudes. For the same reason, they do not include a measure of the strength of each opinion expressed by members of the public in their analysis of the effect that attitudes toward foreign and domestic issues have on votes.

I have shown that Campbell et al. do not provide an adequate justification for any of their three assumptions. Thus their findings about party preference are inconclusive because they fail to consider alternative interpretations of the data they collect about party preference; their findings about the 16 issue attitudes are inconclusive because they do not use adequate techniques to analyze the relationship between issue attitudes and votes; and their analyses of the relationship between broad policy attitudes and votes do not indicate the influence of issue attitudes on votes because those analyses do not include a measure of the strength of issue attitudes.

In accounting for the shortcomings of the argument of *The American Voter,* it is tempting to say simply that Campbell et al. are mistaken in certain of their assumptions and end on that note. Because of the importance of their work, however, it is valuable to consider the possible reasons they make these mistaken assumptions. This is fairly easy to do in the case of their assumption that very enduring attitudes must have a stronger influence on voting choices and the outcomes of elections than less enduring attitudes. In Chapter 6 I showed that Campbell et al. explain carefully why they make this assumption, and I also showed that their explanation neglects certain possible relationships between very enduring and less enduring attitudes. I elaborated on possible additional reasons for their interest in enduring attitudes in Chapter 7. Nothing more needs to be said here about this part of their argument.

It is more difficult to explain and criticize the reasons Campbell et al. make the other two assumptions. As pointed out, they do not tell us why they believe that only widely held attitudes can have a major effect on voting choices and the outcomes of elections or why they believe that the answers to free-response questions which they record must be expressions of a few broad policy attitudes. As a result, any discussion of their reasoning on these points is bound to be in large part speculative. However, if we consider some of the major objectives the authors of *The American Voter* set for themselves, one possible explanation is strongly suggested.

In the preceding chapters I have said that two of the authors' major objectives are to explain the outcomes of particular elections by explaining the voting choices of members of the public and to evaluate certain aspects of traditional theories of public opinion. I have also said that they have limited success in achieving these objectives. If I am correct about these points, one possible reason Campbell et al. may have made the two assumptions which I contend are problematical is that this makes it far easier than it would otherwise be to reach the objectives just mentioned. Indeed, both of these assumptions make a great deal of sense within the context of each of their objectives. To show that this is true, the relationship between each objective and the two assumptions will be considered separately.

Explaining Electoral Outcomes

By assuming that only widely held attitudes have a strong influence on votes and electoral outcomes and that answers to free-response questions are expressions of broad policy attitudes, Campbell et al. make their task of explaining the outcomes of elections by identifying motives for votes much easier than it might be otherwise. There are good reasons why they should attempt to simplify their task by making these particular assumptions. To understand why, however, we must consider a serious difficulty that any attempts to explain the outcomes of elections in terms of individual attitudes face.

Problems of Psychological Explanations in Politics.   There are reasons to believe that, to some degree, a number of attitudes have an influence on the outcomes of elections. Researchers who use the technique of interviewing a small number of individuals in great detail about their views on politics have generally found that attitudes toward a variety of political objects (e.g., parties, candidates, and issues), as well as toward a variety of objects which are, strictly speaking, nonpolitical (e.g., an individual's job or family), influence political behavior.[1] These researchers have also shown that to understand the significance for political behavior of many attitudes, it is necessary to understand their relationship to such other aspects of an individual's personality as his goals, values, and temperament and that it is therefore necessary to gather a great deal of information about his general psychological makeup. Campbell et al. and the authors of other studies which survey the attitudes of large numbers of people also sometimes say that a number of psychological factors influence votes. This is implicit in the funnel of causality model Campbell et al. use to establish the context of their analysis. Moreover, they say that party preference, 6 broad partisan attitudes, and attitudes toward 16 issues may have at least some influence on voting choices, and they acknowledge that attitudes toward a variety of nonpolitical objects may also be influential (see Chapter 4).

If it is true that a number of psychological factors have some influence on the voting choices of the average individual, however, it would be a truly prodigious task to formulate a thorough explanation of the outcome of an election in terms of individual psychology. Millions of people vote in each election, and many psychological characteristics of each individual would have to be measured to determine why one candidate received the votes of a majority of the public. Of course, a number of these characteristics typify more than one person, and it would therefore be unnecessary to measure as many characteristics as there are voters. Moreover, it would be possible to simplify the task of explaining the outcomes of elections by studying the votes of representative samples of about 1,000 people rather than studying all voters. Nevertheless, the task of explaining the outcomes of elections by considering all the psychological factors that influence votes to some degree would still be prodigious.

The American Voter and Psychological Explanations.   The authors of attitude studies of public opinion do not, of course, study all the psychological characteristics that might influence the outcomes of elections. At the most, they study a dozen attitudes and a few other psychological factors. This is partly because they lack the resources to measure a greater number of characteristics and analyze the resulting data. Also, the result of such an analysis would have to be so long a recitation of the attitudes that influence votes and would contain so many qualifications about how they are related to each other and to other psychological traits that it would be difficult to comprehend. For both these reasons, there are strong pressures on the authors of attitude studies of public opinion to investigate only some, rather than all, the individual psychological factors that influence votes and the outcomes of elections. Moreover, Campbell et al. acknowledge the necessity of limiting the factors that will be used to explain votes and the outcomes of elections when they discuss their work in terms of the funnel of causality model. It will be remembered that they claim to study mainly a cross section of the funnel rather than the factors above or below the cross section which also influence votes.

However, at least one important consideration limits the way in which the authors of attitude studies of public opinion can focus on certain attitudes. This consideration is that if they are to explain the outcomes of elections, they must include enough attitudes in their analyses to explain the votes of most members of the public. For example, they could not limit their attention to only one attitude that determines the votes of only half the public; if they did this, the votes of the rest of the public would be unexplained.

Two strong pressures, therefore, are exerted on students of politics who wish to explain the outcomes of elections in terms of individual attitudes: a pressure to consider fairly few psychological characteristics; and a pressure to consider enough psychological characteristics to explain the votes of most members of the public. A logical reaction to these two pressures is to pay primary attention to widely held attitudes. In this way it is possible to explain the votes of large numbers of people in terms of the same attitude instead of several attitudes.

An imaginary example may make it clearer why the authors of attitude studies might wish to focus on widely held attitudes. Suppose they found that half the members of the public hold a strong attitude toward one or the other of the candidates in a particular election and that almost everyone who holds such an attitude votes in accordance with it. On the basis of this evidence, the authors could say that candidate preference determines the votes of half the public. This might be an incomplete explanation of votes because issue attitudes, for example, might determine candidate preference. In that case, a more complete explanation would describe the relationships among attitudes, candidate preference, and votes. Nevertheless, if we accept that the authors of attitude studies cannot consider all the psychological factors that influence voting choices, incomplete explanations are to be expected. Moreover, although an explanation of voting behavior in terms of candidate preference might be incomplete, it would certainly be more economical than an explanation solely in terms of issue attitudes or of both issue attitudes and candidate preference. The last kind of explanation would obviously be less economical than an explanation in terms of candidate preference alone because it would require an investigation of the relationship between several attitudes and votes, not just an investigation of the relationship between one attitude and votes. An explanation solely in terms of issue attitudes would also be less economical than an explanation in terms of candidate preference because only a few members of the public hold any one issue attitude. As a result, it would be necessary to consider a number of issue attitudes to explain the same number of votes that could be explained by candidate preference.

If, therefore, the authors of attitude studies are limited in the number of attitudes they can investigate, they could explain the votes of the same number of people with the same degree of completeness (in the sense that each vote would be explained by one attitude in either case) by relying on candidate preference as by relying on issue attitudes; but they could explain those votes more economically if they formulated their explanations in terms of candidate preference instead of issue attitudes. Moreover, the authors of attitude studies would probably be well advised to explain voting choices in terms of candidate preference alone, rather than attempt to increase the completeness of their explanations by explaining those choices in terms of both issue attitudes and candidate preferences. By investigating issue attitudes, they would greatly increase the number of attitudes they would have to consider. In addition, incompleteness of explanation is to be expected in attitude studies, and the authors might not make their explanations much more complete if they considered issue attitudes in addition to party preference. This would be the case if issue attitudes were determined by party preference and many nonpolitical attitudes. In this case, even though the authors would greatly increase the number of attitudes in their explanations by considering public views about issues, they would still not include most of the attitudes that have a bearing on votes. As a result, they would achieve only a marginal increase in the completeness of explanation in return for a great increase in the number of attitudes considered.

Assuming, therefore, that the authors face strong pressures for economy as well as strong pressures to explain the votes of all members of the public, it would make sense for them to accept that their analyses must be fairly incomplete and to focus on the smallest number of widely held attitudes which will explain the votes of almost all members of the public. This is, of course, what Campbell et al. do, both in their analysis of party preference and in their analysis of the six partisan attitudes. In the former analysis, they focus on one attitude that is held by most members of the public and which predicts the votes of almost everyone who holds it. In their analysis of the six partisan attitudes, they show that each of these widely held attitudes enables them to explain the votes of individuals whose votes were not explained by the others and that, taken together, the six partisan attitudes enable them to explain the votes of most members of the public.[2] In their analyses of both party preference and the six partisan attitudes, Campbell et al. could probably explain the outcomes of elections more fully if they considered more attitudes; but they could not explain more votes. In other words, by analyzing the six partisan attitudes, they are able to explain the votes of most members of the public; if they also analyzed a number of issue attitudes, they could only further explain votes that they have already partly explained in terms of the six partisan attitudes. By concentrating on the smallest number of widely held attitudes that will explain the votes of most members of the public, therefore, Campbell et al. are able to provide at least a minimal explanation of the outcomes of elections; they are also able to reduce their task of analyzing elections in terms of attitudes to manageable proportions.

Why Campbell et al. Make Problematic Assumptions.   Given the advantages of confining an explanation of the outcomes of elections to a few widely held attitudes, we can see why Campbell et al. might make two of the assumptions that I contend are problematic. To begin with, we can see why they might assume that because party preference and the six partisan attitudes are more widely held than issue attitudes, they have a stronger influence on the outcomes of elections. I said earlier that it is certainly true that both party preference and any one of the six partisan attitudes have a stronger influence on the outcomes of elections than any one issue attitude has in the sense that party preference and each of the partisan attitudes probably influence the votes of more people than any one issue attitude does (see pp. 84–85). I also pointed out, however, that the strength of the influence which an attitude exerts on votes in this sense is not important for determining whether issue attitudes collectively have a stronger or weaker influence on the outcomes of elections than party preference and the six partisan attitudes have. Nevertheless, if Campbell et al. see their task as explaining the outcomes of elections by identifying the smallest number of widely held attitudes that will explain the votes of most people to some degree, it is precisely the strength of different attitudes, in the sense of how many people are influenced by them, which is most important; it is the attitudes that are strongest in this sense which are most useful for explaining the outcomes of elections. If they set out to determine what fairly small set of attitudes can be used to explain the outcomes of elections, therefore, it makes good sense for Campbell et al. to say that because party preference and the six partisan attitudes are more widely held than issue attitudes, they have a stronger influence on the outcomes of elections.

For the same reason just discussed, it is also sensible for Campbell et al. to assume that the answers to free-response questions which they record are expressions of a few broad policy attitudes rather than many specific issue attitudes. I pointed out in Chapter 5 that on the basis of the evidence they present, it is possible that either interpretation of answers to free-response questions is correct, and I suggested that evidence which would enable them to choose between the two interpretations might be difficult to find. Given this situation, it makes sense for Campbell et al. to interpret answers to free-response questions as expressions of broad policy attitudes because this enables them to explain the outcomes of elections in terms of a fairly small number of attitudes. If, however, they were to interpret these opinions as expressions of issue attitudes, they would have to explain the outcomes of elections in terms of a much greater number of attitudes; in addition, they would have to gather more data to determine the strength of each attitude.

Given the strong pressures to explain the outcomes of elections in terms of as few attitudes as possible, it makes a great deal of sense for Campbell et al. to make at least two of their assumptions. I have shown that analyses based on these assumptions enable the authors to draw many worthwhile conclusions about politics; thus we can conclude that the assumptions are valuable, or at least not harmful, in certain parts of attitude studies. I have also shown, however, that the assumptions that only widely held attitudes have a major influence on the outcomes of elections and that answers to free-response questions must be expressions of broad policy attitudes prevent Campbell et al. from drawing one of the major conclusions they claim to draw: that issue attitudes do not exert a strong influence on the outcomes of elections. If they wish to draw meaningful comparisons between the influence of issue attitudes and the influence of other attitudes on votes, Campbell et al. must consider the relationship between issue attitudes and votes as carefully as they consider the relationship between other kinds of attitudes and votes. This means that they cannot explain the political behavior of members of the public by considering only how strong an influence widely held attitudes have on their voting choices. They must also consider the relationship between numerous less widely held attitudes and votes. This may be difficult for the authors to accomplish, but it is necessary if they wish to draw conclusions about whether issue attitudes have a strong influence on the outcomes of elections.

To recapitulate, it may be that Campbell et al. make two of the assumptions which I contend are problematical because there are strong pressures on them to focus on only a few widely held attitudes and because those assumptions enable them to adopt this focus. Moreover, in their analyses of issue attitudes, Campbell et al. may assume that only widely held attitudes have a major influence on votes and that answers to free-response questions are expressions of broad policy attitudes because they believe incorrectly that if these assumptions are useful in certain parts of their work, they must be useful in other parts as well.

Living with the Past

The second major task the authors of *The American Voter* set for themselves is to criticize certain traditional notions about public opinion, particularly the mandate theory of elections in its crude form. This task, like the task of identifying the attitudes which influence the outcomes of particular elections, is made much easier by the assumptions that only widely held attitudes have a major influence on votes and that answers to free-response questions are expressions of broad policy attitudes. As already pointed out, both assumptions enable Campbell et al. to focus their attention on a few widely held attitudes, and it was the influence of widely held attitudes on votes that was of primary interest to traditional theorists. I showed in Chapter 1 that traditional theorists devoted most of their attention to cases in which they believed the general public of a particular nation-state formed an issue public about some matter. They constantly stressed the uniformity of public opinion, and they believed that it exerts it maximum influence on government when it is both widely held and uniform. Admittedly there are passages in the works of Tocqueville, Bryce, and other theorists which suggest that they realized that most members of the public do not hold opinions on many important issues. Nevertheless, it was primarily mass opinion, the opinion of all or most members of the public about a particular issue, that traditional theorists considered important.

By focusing on mass opinion, therefore, Campbell et al. perpetuate one aspect of the tradition of theorizing about public opinion that began almost 200 years ago. Their criticism of that tradition is that older theorists incorrectly identified the objects of mass opinion, not that they were wrong to focus primarily on that sort of opinion. In other words, they argue that mass opinion consists of attitudes toward candidates and parties, rather than issues; they do not argue that focusing on mass opinion may provide only an incomplete explanation of the relationship between public views and electoral outcomes. Thus Campbell et al. are able to offer a partial criticism of traditional discussions of public opinion while still operating within the confines of some of the fundamental assumptions on which those discussions were based. This is important because, as pointed out earlier, Campbell et al. claim that one of their major accomplishments is to use scientific techniques to record and analyze public opinion as it has traditionally been understood. Since traditional theorists understood public opinion as mass opinion, it is not surprising that Campbell et al. should not question their assumption that most attention should be devoted to mass opinion. By focusing on it, they are able to level one pertinent criticism at traditional theories without having to mount a radical critique of those theories.

Although it may be prudent for Campbell et al. to focus on a few widely held attitudes in their discussion of traditional theories of public opinion, we can also say that by adopting this focus they may well be perpetuating a serious difficulty contained in those theories. I have already shown that modern studies of public opinion provide no evidence which shows that only widely held attitudes have a major influence on the outcomes of elections (see Chapter 5, "The Argument Presented"). I have also criticized the authors of attitude studies for failing to explore the significance of attitudes held by fairly small issue publics. These same criticisms can be directed at the authors of traditional public opinion theories. Unless we assume that the interests of the American public have become progressively less uniform over the years, there is a strong possibility that traditional public opinion theorists present a misleading picture of the relationship between public opinion and government. They usually portray the public as a monolithic "majority" comprised of individuals who share the same information and concerns and who decide the outcomes of elections on the basis of those interests and concerns (see pp. 4–7). Because neither they nor modern students of public opinion have been able to show that only widely held attitudes influence the outcomes of elections, however, it is possible that it would be more accurate to portray the public as comprised of a great number of attention groups of different sizes. Each individual would, therefore, share some of the information and concerns that influence his vote with a large number of other individuals, and he would share other interests and concerns which influence his vote with only a small number of other individuals.

Depending on which of these pictures of the American public we believe is correct, we may draw different conclusions about many aspects of the American political system. This has been shown to be true in my discussion of the conclusions drawn by the authors of *The American Voter* (see pp. 139–45). That discussion shows that if the authors of contemporary studies of public opinion assume that mass opinion influences the outcomes of elections at least partly because traditional theorists make that assumption, then the ideas of traditional theorists may be responsible for major shortcomings in contemporary studies of politics.

It would be wrong, however, to be too strongly critical of traditional theorists for focusing on mass opinion or of the authors of attitude studies for following in their footsteps without considering why Tocqueville, Bryce, and others might have believed that mass opinion influences the outcomes of elections. They said that mass opinion toward issues influences most voting choices, and they claimed to have discovered this as a result of observations of the workings of the American political system. But contemporary studies have shown that opinions toward issues are not often widely held; so the simplest explanation of why traditional theorists concluded that mass opinion determines the outcomes of elections would seemingly be that their observations were not accurate. It is possible that they were acquainted with only a sector of American society in which most people held views about major political issues and that they assumed incorrectly that other sectors of society had the same high level of political interest. It is also possible that traditional theorists attached too much significance to occasional cases in which most members of the public do hold views on the same subject. Wars, economic crises, or political scandals may indeed be the objects of mass opinion from time to time, and traditional theorists often cite opinions about these kinds of objects in discussions of public opinion.

Finally, it is possible that traditional theorists, like the authors of attitude studies, may simply have found it more convenient to discuss public opinion in terms of a few widely held opinions, rather than many attitudes which are not widely held.

These three explanations of why traditional theorists focused on mass opinion are fairly simple, but they may be correct. In addition, however, there are more complex reasons why Tocqueville, Bryce, and others might have assumed that in America widely held opinions determine the outcomes of elections. To begin with, this conclusion is consistent with many of their other conclusions about the United States. Their observations about the equality of American social and economic conditions, the high level of political participation compared to Europe, and the importance of the tyranny of the majority all suggest that in the United States most people will be concerned with the same issues and the majority of the public will often hold the same views. In other words, if—as traditional public opinion theorists suggest—there are no great class differences in America, if most people have a high degree of interest in politics, and if the tyranny of the majority homogenizes their views, we would expect that a truly mass opinion would exist on many important issues and that views on those issues would have an important influence on the outcomes of elections. The assumption that mass opinion is an important force in the American political system, therefore, may simply be an inference drawn from certain general characteristics of the American public, or an exaggeration made to emphasize those characteristics, rather than a conclusion based on careful observation of American politics.

Traditional public opinion theorists may have focused on mass opinion also because they were concerned with how elections enable members of the public to force government to adopt policies consistent with their opinions. It is easy to assume that an election will lead government to adopt a certain policy if a majority of the voters favor that policy. If only a small percentage of the public holds opinions about a certain policy, members of government will not win an election because they adopt that policy and will not lose an election because they oppose it. If, however, a majority of the public favors a policy, and if members of the majority are prepared to vote on the basis of their preference, government will be compelled to act in accordance with public wishes or a new government that will act in accordance with those wishes will be elected. As a result, it may seem logical to assume that if one wishes to discuss the public views which actually influence government decisions, one should concentrate on widely held opinions. I pointed out in Chapter 1 that traditional theorists were extremely interested in rule by public opinion, the influence of public views on government. Perhaps, therefore, they focused most of their attention on mass opinion because they believed that only widely held opinions could influence government decisions.

There are, therefore, a number of reasons why traditional public opinion theorists focused their attention on widely held opinions. All these reasons are, however, unsatisfactory. To begin with, it is wrong to assume that only widely held opinions can influence government decisions. Even if most issues are of concern to only small publics, members of government may still have to honor some public wishes if they are to maintain their hold on power—although they may exercise some discretion in deciding which public wishes they will honor. As a result, traditional theorists would be wrong to focus on widely held opinions because they assume these are the only kinds of opinion that can influence government decisions. In addition, while traditional theorists may be able to say that certain characteristics of the American political and social systems create greater uniformities of interests and points of view than found in other countries, the evidence presented by the authors of attitude studies refutes their claim that a majority of the public holds views about most government policies. Therefore it is misleading for the authors of traditional studies to claim that the outcomes of elections are determined by mass opinion about government policies simply because they wish to emphasize certain characteristics of American politics and society. Finally, it would obviously be wrong for the authors of traditional studies to claim that mass opinion determines the outcomes of elections because they had been exposed to a highly politicized sector of American society, because they place undue emphasis on a few unusual cases, or because they find it easier to discuss a few opinions at a time.

In short, like the authors of attitude studies, traditional public opinion theorists present no good reasons for assuming that mass opinion exerts a stronger influence on the outcomes of elections than the opinions of a variety of small issue publics. By focusing on mass opinion, the authors of attitude studies may make their task of discussing traditional theories of public opinion much easier. But they are also perpetuating a view of the nature of public opinion and of its relationship to government that neither they nor traditional theorists have shown to be correct.

The Context of Assumptions about Public Opinion

In the preceding paragraphs I suggested some reasons why the authors of *The American Voter* might assume that only widely held attitudes have a strong influence on voting choices and that answers to free-response questions must be expressions of broad policy attitudes. Both of these assumptions make sense within the context of some of the most important objectives that Campbell et al. establish for themselves. Un-fortunately, however, when they set out to explain the outcomes of elections and criticize traditional theories of public opinion, they are setting out to conduct a variety of analyses. Some of these are facilitated by the assumptions discussed here. For example, by focusing attention on widely held attitudes, these assumptions make it possible to formu-late at least a minimal explanation of the outcomes of elections with a minimal expenditure of resources; these assumptions also make it possi-ble to criticize the mandate theory of elections within the context of traditional theories of public opinion.

The assumptions which I have said are problematic stand in the way of other kinds of analysis that Campbell and his associates wish to conduct, however. In particular, they make it difficult to determine how strong an influence issue attitudes have on voting choices and the out-comes of elections. Regrettably, Campbell et al. attach greater significance to the analyses that are hindered by the assumptions I have discussed than to those which are facilitated. This makes it hard to understand why they make these assumptions, and the authors them-selves do not provide an explanation. In the absence of such an explana-tion, however, it is reasonable to conclude, for the reasons I have out-lined, that a combination of pressures for economy of explanation plus the strength of the precedent set by traditional theories of public opinion lead Campbell et al. to believe that assumptions which are useful in certain of their analyses are useful in others as well.

Summary and a Final Objection

Part II has examined the claim made by authors of contemporary studies of public opinion that they are able to use attitude psychology to identify motives for votes. This claim is important because many of the conclu-sions about politics drawn by these authors are based on the assumption that they can determine which attitudes influence voting choices and the outcomes of elections. The claim is important also because traditional political theorists believed that public opinion is significant primarily because it performs these functions. As a result, modern social scientists claim that by identifying motives for votes they are able to both continue and improve on the tradition of analyzing public opinion which is now almost 200 years old.

Because the claim that authors of attitude studies can identify motives for votes is of great importance, it is also important that I have shown that the authors of *The American Voter* are wrong in making this claim. I have summarized my objections to their work by saying that they make three important assumptions for which they do not provide adequate support. Another way to summarize my argument is to say that the findings Campbell et al. present are inconclusive. They claim that their findings show that issue attitudes do not have a strong influence on voting choices and the outcomes of elections and that party preference determines issue attitudes and votes. Admittedly, much of the evidence they present is consistent with these hypotheses, but it is also consistent with certain alternative hypotheses. Findings about the 16 issue attitudes and about answers to free-response questions are consistent with the hypothesis that, collectively, issue attitudes have a strong effect on votes and electoral outcomes; findings about party preference are consistent with the hypothesis that party preference may be determined by information flow and issue attitudes. Because Campbell et al. fail to present evidence that enables us to choose between these alternative hypotheses and the hypotheses they believe are supported by their work, I have said they fail to show which attitudes determine voting choices and the outcomes of elections.

I am not, therefore, arguing that the conclusions Campbell et al. draw are necessarily incorrect. Rather, I am arguing that their work is inconclusive because it does not show whether issue attitudes have little influence on votes and electoral outcomes and party preference is the major determinant of issue attitudes and votes or whether issue attitudes are major determinants of votes and electoral outcomes and party preference is determined by information flow and issue attitudes. In addition, I am not arguing that Campbell et al. fail to consider the alternative hypotheses I have outlined. In fact, they mention those hypotheses and seem to believe they have refuted them. My argument is, rather, that the authors do not *adequately* consider the alternative hypotheses because they do not present evidence which enables us to determine whether the alternatives are correct.

Someone might object, however, that this is not a fair criticism of *The American Voter*. The objector might say that we cannot expect social scientists to consider fully all the alternative hypotheses which might be consistent with their findings; we can only expect them to present findings that are consistent with certain important hypotheses they are exploring. The objector might conclude that it is certainly valid for social scientists to set out to build support for a particular point of view, rather than contrast different points of view.

While I agree it is valid to collect findings that build support for certain points of view, I do not think such findings significantly further our understanding of social phenomena if they are also consistent with major conflicting points of view. As a result, I do not think it is unreasonable to demand that one of the major objectives of social scientists in designing their studies should be to insure that their findings will enable them to choose between important alternative hypotheses about the phenomena with which they are concerned.

These general observations are applicable to the argument of *The American Voter* because the hypotheses that issue attitudes might influence votes and electoral outcomes and that party preference might be determined by information flow and issue attitudes are not my inventions. Rather, they are important, likely, and well-recognized explanations of certain phenomena that have a direct bearing on the questions Campbell et al. address. If we accept these explanations rather than the explanations Campbell and his associates offer, we will have to say that many of their conclusions are incorrect. Therefore it is reasonable to argue that because Campbell et al. do not present findings that enable us to distinguish between the alternative hypotheses I have outlined and the hypotheses they believe are correct, their work can be considered inconclusive and seriously flawed.

In this part I have devoted almost all my attention to the argument of *The American Voter*. Although I have not attempted to show that the criticisms I have leveled at that argument are applicable to other studies of public opinion, I believe they are. I believe my conclusions regarding *The American Voter* can be extended to show that the authors of most attitude studies of public opinion are wrong in making the first claim I have said is of major importance in the work of Campbell et al.: the claim that they can identify motives for votes.

III. Rule by Public Opinion

Part III examines the second major claim made by the authors of attitude studies of public opinion: that they have successfully used attitude psychology to investigate the way public opinion influences government decisions. This claim differs from the claim I examined in Part II in three important respects.

First, the two claims refer to the effect of public opinion on different aspects of the political process. In Part II I considered whether the authors of attitude studies are successful in explaining the influence of public opinion on the outcomes of elections. In this part I consider whether they are successful in explaining the influence of public opinion on major policy decisions made by members of government.

Second, the research focus suggested by each of the two claims is different. By ''research focus'' I mean the phenomena studied, the techniques and theories used, and the data collected. In Part II I showed that to study the influence of public opinion on elections, the authors of attitude studies focus primarily on investigating the psychological characteristics of members of the general public. In this part I show that to study the influence of public opinion on government decision making, they must focus less on individual psychology and more on the social and political processes which make that influence possible.

Third, the two claims may well refer to the influence of different sets of attitudes on the political process. This difference requires somewhat more explanation than the other two differences mentioned. As pointed out in previous chapters, most students of public opinion believe that members of government act in accordance with public opinion primarily because they wish to maintain their public office. According to this theory, if a great many members of the public favor a certain policy and if their preferences are likely to influence their votes, members of government will act in accordance with those preferences; but if attitudes toward a certain policy are unlikely to influence votes, members of government will have no reason to act in accordance with those attitudes. As a result, we might expect that the attitudes which influence government decisions will be the same attitudes as those which motivate the votes of a large sector of the public in the sense that they will be public attitudes toward the same objects.

There are two reasons why this might not be the case, however. First, members of government may not know what attitudes will motivate voting choices. Three years before an election or even at election time, they may not know whether their actions on a particular matter will be quickly forgotten by the public or will become a major political issue in the minds of many. Indeed, the authors of attitude studies have been unable to identify motives for votes by using sophisticated scientific methods, and it certainly would be difficult for politicians, working with much cruder tools, to do so. As a result, it seems likely that members of government will sometimes take actions they believe are in accordance with public attitudes when in fact those attitudes do not influence the votes of a substantial number of members of the public; it also seems likely that they will sometimes fail to heed public opinion when in fact their failure will cost them votes. Second, the authors of many attitude studies believe that the votes of most members of the public are more heavily influenced by attitudes toward parties and candidates than by attitudes toward issues. I have argued that they have not shown this conclusively, although they are possibly correct. If they are correct, the attitudes that motivate voting choices must be different from those which influence government policy decisions because attitudes of the latter kind must be attitudes toward policies, whereas—according to the authors of attitude studies—attitudes of the former kind are not.

In short, when the authors of attitude studies claim they can investigate the influence of public opinion on government, they may be claiming to study the influence of a different set of attitudes than when they say they can identify motives for votes. Certainly they are studying the influence of attitudes on a different aspect of the political process and are adopting a different research focus. As a result, the claim I examine in this part is substantially different from the claim I examined in the preceding part. Because of these differences, it is quite possible that the former claim examined in Part III may be justified, even though I have argued that the claim examined in Part II is not.

Seen in historical perspective, the claim that authors of attitude studies can explain how public opinion influences government decisions is highly significant. As pointed out in Chapter 1, traditional public opinion theorists devoted a great deal of attention to rule by public opinion, or the influence of popular views on government. It was primarily because they believed that public opinion "rules" in certain nations that they considered it important. Moreover, they believed that rule by public opinion was a political and social process which was more fully developed in the United States than in any other country and that, by explaining how it operates, they could contribute to a better understanding of many aspects of the American political system. Like many other observations about public opinion made by traditional theorists, however, their observations about whether and how public opinion influences government decisions are open to question. The evidence on which they base their conclusions consists primarily of informal interviews with a few people who may or may not have been representative of the American public and of informal observations of the processes of government decision making.

If the authors of attitude studies could use the tools of social science research to show conclusively that public opinion rules in the United States, to identify the opinions which influence government in particular cases, and to draw general conclusions about the nature of the influence process, they could add substantially to the body of knowledge about both rule by public opinion and the American political system. Broadly speaking, these are the objectives that the authors of attitude studies do pursue. Illuminating rule by public opinion is a more important objective for the authors of some studies than for the authors of other studies, however. At one extreme, the authors of *The American Voter* devote most of their attention to identifying motives for votes. For the most part, their work can be seen as an investigation of political psychology. Although they indicate that their findings are important also because many of the attitudes they record influence government decisions, they devote little attention to determining which attitudes have this effect or to investigating the characteristics of the political and social systems that, to use Key's word, "link" public opinion to the policymaking process.[1] At the opposite extreme, Key himself writes that "the properties of opinion, as well as its distribution have no great political significance unless they bear on the processes of government."[2] Investigating the "linkage" process is one of his major objectives, and he devotes over a third of *Public Opinion and American Democracy* to that task.

Because the notion that attitude psychology can be used to explain the influence of public opinion on government is developed far better by Key than by many other contemporary researchers, most of Part III is devoted to his work. However, considerable attention is also devoted to a study by Miller and Stokes that in many ways complements and expands on Key's ideas. In Chapter 9 Key's description of the process by which public opinion is related to government decision making and his ideas about how attitude studies can illuminate that process are examined. In Chapter 10 certain of his notions are criticized. In Chapter 11 it is shown that my criticisms of those notions can be extended to traditional theories about public opinion, and the reasons Key and traditional theorists may have adopted certain assumptions I believe are problematic are considered.

9. Key's Model

When he writes of the influence of public opinion on government, Key generally refers to the influence of the attitudes of a majority of the public holding views about some particular political object. Admittedly, he says that "intense minorites" may influence government from time to time, but he seems to believe that they play a role in policymaking less frequently than majorities do.[1] In any event, most of Key's references are to the influence of majority views, so only his ideas about this form of rule by public opinion will be considered here.

Outline of the Model

Key describes two processes by which majority opinion influences government decisions. Although he does not distinguish clearly between these two processes, they differ in many important respects; therefore they will be outlined separately. I call the first process Key describes "the strong form of rule by public opinion." Key refers to this process as a system of "communication and feedback."[2] In its essentials, the process is fairly simple. On any given matter about which government can take action, members of government and other political leaders develop policies. If the matter is of importance, these alternative policies become known to ordinary citizens through the press and other means of communication from political leaders to the general public. Usually government members are unwilling to take actions that are not favored by a majority of the public because they wish to retain political power and feel a moral obligation to honor public wishes. As a result, after they and other political leaders have made public the policies under consideration, members of government do not take action until it is apparent that one policy has been accepted by a majority of the public holding opinions about the matter in question.

Moreover, Key points out that members of government usually look for the support of more than a simple majority of the public on important issues. He does not believe there is any magic percentage of popular approval that will galvanize government into action. But he does believe that, broadly speaking, the stronger the public endorsement for a particular policy is, the more likely government is to implement that policy. Thus he writes that government is most likely to act when public opinion forms a "permissive consensus" about some matter, that is, when almost all members of the public approve of a certain policy. He also writes that the more intense the views of the majority are, the more likely government is to heed them.[3]

Key believes that members of government may not always await a permissive consensus, however. He writes, "How he [the member of government] behaves depends to a degree upon his conception of his role. His conception of his duty may lead him to bow to constituency opinion or to vote against it on occasion."[4] Members of government might disregard a permissive consensus because they believe most members of the public favor a policy that would harm the nation. Alternatively, members of government may believe they must take action immediately on certain matters; as a result, they may not await broad public approval of their ideas or may not submit those ideas to the public at all. Nevertheless, Key believes that the approval of policies by a permissive consensus is an important consideration in American public policymaking often enough for us to say that in many cases rule by public opinion is a reality.

The efficacy of the process of rule by public opinion that Key describes depends, of course, on the ability of government to receive correct information about the distribution of public opinion on a given matter. Key believes there are many ways members of government gain information of this sort. He mentions, in particular, that information may come from the press and television, spokesmen for such organized groups as unions or professional associations, articulate members of such unorganized groups as ethnic groups, letters and petitions sent by members of the general public, and direct contacts with constituents.[5] Key does not believe that members of government rely entirely on any one of these sources of information. Rather, he believes that by using intuition about how different sectors of the public are likely to react to a particular matter, and by drawing on experience with the biases of different sources, members of government are able to combine many sorts of information into a fairly reliable picture of the distribution of public opinion.[6]

Although he says that members of government form their ideas about the distribution of public opinion by consulting many different sources, Key believes that they rely mainly on information from members of the public who are, in some sense, official or unofficial spokesmen for certain sectors of society.[7] These are people with whom members of government have fairly frequent contact, such as journalists or leaders of organized groups, rather than ordinary members of the public, most of whom contact members of government only occasionally through letters and petitions.[8] Thus, like traditional theorists, Key believes that most of government's information about public opinion comes from certain elite sectors of society who are, so to speak, "in the business" of transmitting information to government. Also like traditional theorists, he believes that the information gained from these sectors is fairly reliable in the sense that members of government can judge accurately the distribution of public opinion on an issue by listening to elite opinion.

The second process by which Key believes majority opinion influences government decisions is what I call "the weak form of rule by public opinion." Put simply, Key believes that members of government sometimes pay no attention to the feedback they receive from the general public.[9] They act on the basis of their personal views of what is "right" or "in the interest of " their constituents. Nevertheless, Key believes that the actions of members of government often correspond with the views of a majority of their constituents because at election time members of the public usually select candidates whose general views about politics are similar to their own and who are, as a result, likely to form the same views about specific policies. Thus, referring to members of Congress, he writes, "Most of them are but extensions of their constituents; they have grown up with them and share their interests and aspirations. On many matters they need not consult the will of their supporters, for they embody it."[10] We can imagine, for example, that the voters in a farming district will send a farmer to Congress and that the voters in a suburban district will elect a fellow suburbanite. The people elected will have shared for years many of the day-to-day experiences of their constituents and, as a result, will be likely to react in the same way most of their constituents do to many issues. Moreover, we can imagine that on election day the voters ask themselves which of the candidates shares their general views about foreign affairs, housing, welfare, and other broad policy issues. If they accurately appraise the candidates or if the candidates are sensitive to the nature of their popular mandate, the voters, in effect, will have sent to Congress someone who on most, although not all, issues is "programmed" to make judgments in the way they would make them—even if he does not try to act in accordance with their views.

The differences between the strong and weak forms of rule by public opinion are obviously great, and in some respects they parallel the differences between Burke's notion of representation by a "delegate" and his notion of "virtual representation." Because Burke's distinction between these two kinds of representation has been discussed thoroughly many times, it will not be elaborated here.[11] However, if we accept that the strong and weak forms of rule by public opinion do, in fact, differ in many of the same ways that representation by a delegate and virtual representation differ, we may wonder whether the weak form of rule by public opinion should be considered a process that brings about the influence of public opinion on government at all. Certainly when Burke mentions the influence of public opinion on government, he is referring to a delegate system of representation and contrasting it with virtual representation. Although he thinks that virtual representation may lead to a correspondence of views between legislators and their constituents in some cases, he does not think this is the inevitable result of that system or the basis on which it should be justified.[12]

Moreover, when we say that someone is influenced by someone else's views we at least mean to imply that the person influenced is aware of the other person's views and that, if he were not aware of those views, he would act differently. It seems odd, therefore, for Key to suggest that public views on particular policies influence members of government who are either not aware of the views or would take the same actions regardless of what the views were. In addition, Key suggests that in the weak form of rule by public opinion, the influence of public opinion on government actions is exerted at election time.[13] Surely, there are many issues that arise during the course of a representative's term about which neither he nor his constituents held opinions when they met at the polls at the beginning of that term. Therefore Key cannot claim that at election time the views of the general public on particular issues influence subsequent government actions on many issues. Either the influence of public opinion on government actions is not only exerted at election time or it is not public views about particular issues that influence government actions in all cases.

It would seem better for Key to say that the weak form of rule by public opinion is a process by which broad political views held by members of the public exert an influence over the general directions of policymaking (or, simply, that it is a process which often brings about a correspondence of public views and government actions on particular policies), rather than to say it is a process by which public views on particular issues influence government actions on those issues. Nevertheless, both Key and other students of public opinion suggest that the weak form of rule by public opinion, like the strong form, is a process by which public views on particular issues influence government decisions. But because this is not an important point for my consideration of his model of rule by public opinion, I will not insist on another formulation.[14] It is sufficient for my purposes to note the distinction between the strong and weak forms of rule by public opinion and to note that Key believes that, taken together, these two processes account for the influence of public opinion on government in the United States.

Two Major Features of the Model

The Public Veto.   Although Key's model of rule by public opinion is fairly simple in its essentials, it has two important characteristics that should be noted. The first is that in Key's model government initiates policies and members of the public, by approving or opposing them, exercise a sort of veto power over government actions. The result of this is that government actions correspond to public opinion. It is important to realize, however, that the process Key describes differs from three other processes which might bring about a correspondence between government actions and public views.

First, the process Key describes differs from a process in which members of the public initiate ideas about public policy and impose those ideas on government. Traditional public opinion theorists sometimes suggested that ideas for government policies spring spontaneously from the general public. In Key's model, however, widespread public opinion is not formed on an issue until government or members of the opposition propose some policy to deal with the issue. Although Key admits that members of the elite and of the general public may sometimes suggest policies to government, he pays little attention to this function of the elite and the public.[15]

A second process that differs from the one Key describes, and which would bring about a correspondence between public opinion and government actions, is a process in which members of government develop a policy, decide to implement it, wait for a period of time before implementing it, and use that period of time to convince the general public to adopt their point of view. There is a great deal of evidence, some of which Key discusses, that members of government often do decide to take certain actions before members of the general public have had an opportunity to express their opinions about those actions; there is also evidence that they are often successful in convincing members of the public that their point of view is correct.[16] In addition, there are findings which suggest that after government has implemented a policy most members of the public eventually come to approve of it, regardless of whether most of them approved of it before it was implemented.[17] This does not always occur, but some studies suggest it may occur fairly frequently.

Thus a third process that might bring about a correspondence between government actions and public opinion would be a process in which members of government decide that certain actions should be taken, take those actions regardless of public views, and then attempt to convince members of the public to approve what they have done.

When he discusses rule by public opinion, however, Key is not referring to any of the processes just discussed, and it is particularly important to note that he is not talking about the second and third processes. He says he is interested in the influence of public opinion on government, not the influence of government on public opinion. Thus he focuses on cases in which government actions come to correspond with public opinion because government members are influenced by the public before they decide what actions they should take, not because government members convince the public that the policies they approve are correct after they have decided to implement them, or even after they have put the policies into effect. In other words, Key is interested in cases in which government responds to public wishes rather than cases in which government manufactures those wishes. He distinguishes clearly between these two kinds of cases by calling the influence of public opinion on government ''rule *by* public opinion'' and the influence of government on public opinion ''rule *of* public opinion.''[18]

The processes of rule by public opinion that Key discusses are, therefore, a middle ground between a radical democratic process in which government actions correspond with public opinion because the people conceive policies and impose them on government and an authoritarian process in which government conceives policies and manipulates public opinion to fit them. Traditional public opinion theorists often despaired of American democracy: They feared that rule by public opinion could degenerate into the former kind of process or they feared it would be discredited due to its inefficiencies and would be supplanted by the latter kind of process. Key believes that one of the strengths of American democracy is that it combines the ability of experienced political leaders to devise and initiate policies with a respect for public views about whether those policies should be implemented.

The Public Versus the Elite.   The second important characteristic of the processes of rule by public opinion which Key describes is that he is concerned with the influence of mass opinion on government rather than the influence of elite opinion. He does believe that government gains most of its information about public opinion from members of the elite and has no reliable way of surveying the mass public on most issues. However, Key does not believe that the influence process he describes is one by which an isolated elite imposes views different from those of the mass public on government. Rather, he sees the elite as transmitters of the opinions of the mass public.[19] Key admits that elite leaders do not always express the views of a majority of the people they speak for. He believes, however, that on any given issue, most elite leaders are fairly accurate transmitters of public views. As a result, members of government can probably form a fairly accurate impression of the distribution of opinion on most issues by considering the views of several elite leaders. Thus, according to Key, the end product of the influence process is that government actions correspond with the opinions held by a majority of the mass public, rather than with a set of elite opinions which differ from the views of a majority of the mass public.

Key does not offer a clear explanation of why elite members transmit mass opinion. But, for the same sorts of reasons that Key says government officials are responsive to the views of the people they represent, we can theorize that the elite are probably responsive to the views of groups for which they speak. For example, certain members of the elite, like members of government, are responsible to certain well-defined constituencies for the statements they make; members of the elite may also believe they have a moral responsibility to their constituents to transmit their views accurately. Thus a union leader may lose his job if he lobbies for measures which displease the majority of his constituents, or he may simply have a strong conviction that it would be wrong for him to make statements on behalf of union members which they would not approve. In addition, it seems likely that elite members often have many of the same characteristics their constituents have; as a result, even if the leaders express their personal points of view without regard for what their constituents think, they will often be expressing positions that correspond to those held by a majority of the members of the groups they represent. For example, a spokesman for a farmers' organization may be a farmer himself. Thus his views may correspond naturally with those of a majority of his constituents on such issues as farm subsidies or the regulation of shipping rates. It is also possible that similarities of interests and outlooks between members of the elite and certain members of the general public may lead spokesmen for groups which are not well organized to express the views of the majority of their group. For example, a black spokesman may accurately express the views of a majority of blacks on many issues because he approaches those issues from a perspective shared by most members of his race.

Neither similarities of interests and outlooks nor formal accountability to a constituency, however, can explain why public opinion is transmitted accurately by one of the elite groups that Key and other students of politics consider most important in bringing about rule by public opinion: journalists.[20] Of course, newspaper journalists probably share many of the interests and outlooks typical of the regions where they live, and unless the views they express are, on the whole, agreeable to their readers, their circulation rates may drop. We might imagine that for both these reasons journalists would express majority opinions in their editorials and that they might inject personal judgments consistent with majority opinions into their reporting of news stories.

However, recent studies have shown that journalists as a group differ significantly in socioeconomic status, political outlook, and education from most members of the publics they serve.[21] Moreover, most American cities are served by only one or two newspapers; in those cities, therefore, members of the public do not have a strong economic sanction over journalists with whom they disagree. Finally, a study of newspaper editorials has shown that many American cities are served by papers which regularly support government policies not favored by a majority of their readers.[22]

A complicating factor in considering journalists as transmitters of public opinion is that television news has replaced newspapers as the major source of information for most Americans.[23] In many localities television news shows are more competitive than are newspapers. Even so, it is hard to argue that television newscasters as individuals are representative of the publics they serve for the same reasons that it is difficult to argue that newspaper journalists are representative. Moreover, recent studies suggest that the editorial judgments expressed by television newsmen and the biases in their reporting often differ substantially from the opinions of a majority of the public.[24]

As a result, if we are to believe that either newspaper or television journalists play an important role in the process of rule by public opinion by accurately transmitting public views, we must believe that this is due, at least in part, to factors other than popular sanctions on the journalism profession or similarities between the interests and outlooks of journalists and those of the general public. In addition, it would seem that if journalists accurately transmit public views, they do so by some means other than editorializing or injecting personal opinions into news coverage.

Despite the importance he attaches to the news media, Key does not explain exactly how or why they express public opinion. One possible way to explain the role of the media in rule by public opinion is to say that journalists transmit public views primarily by reporting accurately the statements which other elite group members make about major public issues. For example, if the issue were whether to raise the minimum wage, a newspaper might report that union leaders express support for the measure, that industrial leaders oppose it, and that consumer advocates side with the industrialists. Collectively, these reports could be considered an accurate picture of public opinion. If we think that journalists transmit public views primarily by reporting the statements of other elite members, we could still consider them accurate transmitters even if the editorials they write or the personal judgments they inject into news stories are inconsistent with the views of a majority of the public. Moreover, if we adopt this point of view, it does not matter whether journalists as individuals share the interests and outlooks of the general public or whether they feel they must convey a point of view similar to that of most of their readers or viewers. As long as journalists feel a professional commitment to accurate and comprehensive reporting, they will be reliable transmitters of public opinion.

As already pointed out, Key does not come to grips with the problems of identifying how and why journalists transmit public opinion. However, he does at least make the general point that the reasons members of elites of all sorts express public views and the means by which those views are expressed differ because of the ways in which different elites are related to the general public.[25] Thus it would be consistent with his general ideas about the relationship between the elite and the public to say that, whereas many elite members express public views because they are responsible to certain constituencies or share the interests and outlooks of those constituencies, journalists express public views because they have a commitment to report the statements of other elite members. It is partly because of differences in the ways members of the elite are related to the general public that Key does not believe members of government should regard any one source of information about public opinion as entirely accurate. Nevertheless, he says that members of government do generally consider several sources of information; as a result, he believes they are fairly well informed about the distribution of public opinion on most issues. Key contends, therefore, that in the United States the views of the general public, rather than elite views which differ from them, influence government decisions.

Key's Model and Attitude Studies

In its essentials Key's model of rule by public opinion is accepted by the authors of most attitude studies that deal with the influence of public opinion on government.[26] From what has been said in previous chapters about the nature of attitude studies, it should be easy to see how Key and other political scientists use attitude psychology to investigate rule by public opinion within the framework of this model. As pointed out, Key and others believe that the distribution of public views on major issues influences government decisions through two processes: the strong and weak forms of rule by public opinion. Because the techniques of attitude studies can be used to record the distribution of mass opinion on major issues, political scientists believe that these techniques enable them to identify the public's input into the processes just mentioned. In Key's words, attitude psychology makes it possible to identify "the opinions which government finds it prudent to heed."[27]

As a result, political scientists claim that the techniques of attitude psychology enable them to conduct the three kinds of research on rule by public opinion. First, they believe that it is possible to use attitude psychology to determine whether public opinion does, in fact, influence government decisions. Second, they believe that by using data about public attitudes together with data about other elements of the processes of influence, it is possible to determine how those processes operate and, in particular, why they are effective in some cases but not in others. Third, they believe that findings about how rule by public opinion operates in the United States should shed light on many aspects of the American political system. Most attitude studies that deal with rule by public opinion are aimed at one or more of these three research objectives. In the following chapters, how these studies have been conducted and how successful they have been are considered in more detail.

10. Criticisms of Studies of Rule by Public Opinion

Essentials of My Criticisms

I have three criticisms of the application of attitude psychology to the investigation of rule by public opinion. First, although the authors of attitude studies sometimes say that government actions may come to correspond with public opinion because members of government influence the views of the public, as well as because the public influences government decisions, they do not generally give the former process adequate attention in their research. They almost invariably assume that the correspondences between government actions and public views which they discover are due to the influence of public opinion on government; they rarely attempt to determine whether those correspondences might be due to the influence of government on public opinion. As a result, many of their findings are inconclusive.

My second criticism of attitude studies of rule by public opinion is that the authors of these studies do not consider the role of the elite carefully enough. They assume that insofar as members of the elite play a role in the processes which cause government actions to correspond to majority opinion, they must do so by transmitting public views to government. As a result, the authors neglect the possibility that correspondences between government actions and mass opinion might be due, at least in part, to the influence of the elite on mass opinion and government decisions rather than to a process whereby elite members convey public views to government. Unfortunately, however, the authors do not present any evidence which shows that elite members are solely or even primarily transmitters of mass opinion. In fact, they gather practically no data about the elite at all. Their neglect of the role of the elite is another reason why many of their findings are inconclusive.

Before going on to my third criticism of attitude studies of rule by public opinion, it is valuable to expand on the second criticism by mentioning a few examples of the kinds of evidence about the elite that the authors of these studies do not gather. This will make it much easier to pursue my argument in subsequent pages.

Examining the Elite. To begin with, in a comprehensive survey of research on mass communications, Weiss points out that there have been practically no studies which enable us to determine how members of the elite gain information about public opinion or how accurate their perceptions of public attitudes are.[1] The studies of journalists mentioned in Chapter 9 come the closest to providing a clear picture of the relationship between elite members and the sectors of society for which they claim to be spokesmen. If we turn our attention to, for example, union leaders, presidents of professional societies, lobbyists, or spokesmen for unorganized groups, most of the available information is fragmentary and often anecdotal. We can find information about particular cases in which leaders did or did not express the majority opinions of the groups they claimed to represent; but these, together with informal reports of people familiar with the ways in which public spokesmen behave, suggest only the general conclusion that sometimes leaders are accurate transmitters of public opinion and sometimes they are not.[2] We do not know, and the authors of most attitude studies have not attempted to discover, exactly how frequently the statements of elite members correspond with public opinion, what factors lead elite members to express public opinion in some cases and prevent them from expressing it in other cases, what factors influence the perceptions that elite members form about public opinion, or a variety of other things which would illuminate the role of the elite in rule by public opinion.

The only substantial body of research on the relationship of the elite to the mass public deals with the influence of elite opinion on mass opinion rather than the influence of mass opinion on elite opinion.[3] We know that, ultimately, most people get their information and many of their opinions about public affairs from local opinion leaders; we know also that these leaders are more aware than the average member of the public of the views held by elite members who are nationally or regionally prominent. These findings suggest that, if for no other reason, elite leaders may express mass opinion because they form it by influencing local opinion leaders who, in turn, influence the mass public.

On the other hand, the available evidence does not show whether the elite leaders who form mass opinion are generally the same as those whose views government leaders rely on in judging what positions members of the public favor. For example, studies of the press show that members of government often believe that the views expressed by journalists reflect public opinion; these studies suggest further that journalists may have a role in forming some of the broad political attitudes held by members of the public, such as attitudes toward isolationism in foreign affairs or federal involvement in social welfare activities. These studies also suggest that the information reported by the press may be among the factors which influence the "frames of reference" that lead members of the public to consider some issues very important and other issues less important. These sample studies indicate, however, that journalists probably do not shape public attitudes toward particular issues or candidates.[4]

Thus, although members of government may believe that the opinions expressed by the press reflect public opinion because journalists both form that opinion and express it in their writing, it is not clear that journalists are in fact able to transmit public views because they perform this dual function. On balance, one might suspect that elite opinions correspond with mass opinion both because members of the public influence the elite and because they are influenced by the elite. But there is little evidence about how these two processes are related to each other, and there are few findings which show that either, in fact, causes members of the elite to present accurate versions of public opinion to government in particular cases.

Just as we know too little about the relationship of the elite to the general public, we know too little about the relationship of the elite to government. This relationship must obviously be complex. Although some elite members claim to speak for the general public, others claim to speak only for certain sectors of it. Members of government probably cannot be exposed to all the public spokesmen who express points of view on important issues. Determining the distribution of mass opinion on the basis of statements made by members of the elite must be a formidable task for members of government because there is no assurance that the elite leaders to whom they are exposed represent all sectors of the public, rather than a few sectors composed of people whose views are not representative of the views of the general public.

Moreover, members of government face other difficulties in attempting to determine what policies are favored by a majority of the public on the basis of statements made by members of the elite. To begin with, it may be that most elite leaders to whom government officials are exposed do not transmit accurately the views of their constituents on at least some occasions. Government officials may have no good way of finding out which elite leaders do and which do not express the views of their constituents on any given occasion, and this will surely make it difficult for them to determine the distribution of mass opinion. In addition, it is often hard to define exactly what constituencies elite members speak for. Does a newspaper editor, for example, speak for everyone in his city, for only the readers of his newspaper, or for only the people who agree with him? If the test of "speaking for" a group is expressing the opinion of a majority of its members, newspaper editors probably speak for different publics at different times; members of government may have no way of knowing which public editors are speaking for at any particular time. Finally, however we define their constituencies, it is clear that elite leaders speak for sectors of society of different sizes, and their statements will often be endorsed by different percentages of their constituents. As a result, members of government may find it difficult to estimate how many people share the views of any elite leader or to compare the sizes of the groups of people who share the views of different elite leaders.

Faced with these characteristics of elite opinion, a government member certainly cannot ascertain which position on an issue is endorsed by a majority of the general public simply by determining which position is endorsed by a majority of the elite members with whom he has contact. How, then, do members of government ascertain mass opinion? Key says simply that they use their "intuition," without explaining exactly what this means.[5] We can imagine that after many years of experience politicians might develop rules of thumb which enable them to seek out elite members who speak for a cross section of the general public. No one, however, has investigated carefully what these rules of thumb are, whether they are reliable, what elite members government officials turn to for information about public opinion, or how government officials interact with those elite members. We know from the reports of people who are familiar with public policymaking that members of the elite play an important role in government decisions in ways which range from corrupting government members to providing them with factual information about issues.[6] What we lack is a comprehensive picture of how these different functions of the elite are related to each other and to the role of the elite as transmitters of mass opinion.

There are, therefore, many different kinds of information about the relationship of the elite to both the general public and the government that the authors of attitude studies fail to gather. They present us with little direct evidence about whether members of the elite do in fact transmit mass opinion or how members of government interpret the elite opinions they hear. However, in the following pages I am not too concerned with the specific kinds of information the authors of attitude studies fail to present. I am more concerned with the fact that, in general, they base their conclusions about rule by public opinion on a great deal of evidence about the two ends of the influence process—government and the public—but on little evidence about the middle of that process—the elite.

Third Criticism.   My third major criticism of attitude studies of rule by public opinion is that the authors do not consider adequately processes by which limited sectors of the public might inflence government decisions or processes by which the mass public might inflence the ways in which those decisions are made without causing government actions to correspond to majority wishes. In studies of rule by public opinion, political scientists are concerned almost exclusively with processes by which government actions and majority wishes might be made to correspond. This focus is not problematic in many aspects of attitude studies; but it is argued later that by failing to consider other ways in which public opinion might influence government, the authors of the studies with which I am concerned run the risk of presenting a misleading picture of the American political system.

Having outlined the three major shortcomings of attitude studies of rule by public opinion, I shall now show that these shortcomings prevent the authors of these studies from fully achieving the three major research objectives mentioned in Chapter 9: to determine whether public opinion inflences government decisions, to show how the influence process operates, and to shed light on the operations of the American political system. The first objective will be considered in this chapter, and the second two will be considered in the next chapter.

Determining Whether Public Opinion Influences Government Decisions

The Evidence Presented.   Even if the authors of attitude studies are not able to achieve any of their other objectives, we might expect that they would be able to determine whether rule by public opinion in fact occurs. After all, they are able to record the distribution of mass opinion about particular issues, and they can easily gather information about government actions and attitudes. With these data, we might think it would be possible to determine whether public opinion influences government decisions or if rule by public opinion is simply a myth.

The fact is that attempts to draw general conclusions about whether public opinion influences government decisions are disappointing, and attempts to show that public opinion influences government decisions in particular cases are also unsatisfactory. For example, although large parts of his book are based on the assumption that public views are an important factor in government decisions, Key presents no firm evidence to show this is the case. He instead relies on largely unsubstantiated anecdotes, and in this respect his work is typical of many other studies of rule by public opinion. He points out, for example, that Roosevelt was unwilling to enter World War II until a popular consensus in favor of war was formed after the Pearl Harbor attack; he also points out that Roosevelt was dissuaded from "packing" the U.S. Supreme Court by a hostile public opinion, despite his attempts to convince the public of the wisdom of his plan.[7] These episodes are suggestive, but they are hardly conclusive. One may wonder whether Roosevelt would have entered World War II after American forces were attacked regardless of public sentiments and whether it was in fact the hostility of mass opinion, rather than the opposition of major party leaders, that prevented him from pursuing his court-packing plan. In short, it cannot be shown convincingly that rule by public opinion occurs simply by showing that government actions correspond with public opinion in a few particular cases. These correspondences may be due to chance or some other factors. To show that government is influenced by public opinion, evidence other than the anecdotes which Key and the authors of many other discussions of rule by public opinion use as the basis for their analyses must be sought.

The Miller and Stokes Study.   Probably the most sophisticated attempt to show that public opinion influences government decisions is a study by Miller and Stokes which deals with the relationships between members of Congress and their constituents.[8] In 1958 Miller and Stokes recorded the attitudes on major political issues held by samples of the constituents of over 100 congressmen. For purposes of analysis, they divided these attitudes into three types: social welfare, foreign policy, and civil rights attitudes. The authors also interviewed the congressmen who represented each of the districts in which constituents had been interviewed. They recorded each congressman's personal attitudes on the issues about which members of the public had been interviewed; they also recorded each congressman's roll-call voting record on the issues and his perceptions of what attitudes a majority of his constituents held.

To determine whether public opinion influences government decisions (in this case, roll-call voting), Miller and Stokes correlated the votes of congressmen with the attitudes of the majority of their constituents. They tell us that a correlation of 0 would show that, on the whole, there was only a chance relationship between congressional votes and public attitudes.[9] A positive correlation, on the other hand, would show that congressional votes corresponded to public attitudes with a frequency greater than chance. This, the authors tell us, would indicate that there is some factor which causes congressmen to tend to vote in accordance with the views of a majority of their constituents. A negative correlation would indicate that congressional votes corresponded to public attitudes with a frequency less than chance. This would show that there is some factor which causes congressmen to tend to vote in a way inconsistent with the views of a majority of their constituents.

Miller and Stokes found that the correlations between congressional votes and public attitudes were positive, although not uniformly high. The correlation for social welfare issues was .40; for foreign policy issues, .20; and for civil rights issues, .65.[10] The authors do not immediately assume that these correlations show that rule by public opinion occurs, however.

They say that such relationships between constituency attitudes and public policy decisions may be due to "other causes," although they do not specify what these causes might be.[11] Nevertheless, at least one set of possible causes is suggested by my criticisms of attitude studies. It might be that correlations between government decisions and popular attitudes are due to the influence of government members on members of the public or to the influence of members of the elite on both the general public and government. Miller and Stokes are right, therefore, not to jump to the conclusion that the correlations just mentioned show the effects of rule by public opinion.

To find a way of determining whether public opinion, to use their word, "controls" government decisions, Miller and Stokes turn to the model of rule by public opinion which I discussed earlier (see pp. 164–67); that is, they say that public opinion can influence government decisions as a result of two processes, which correspond to what I have called the strong and weak forms of rule by public opinion.[12] They illustrate these processes by using a diagram similar to Figure 10.1.[13] The dashed line with arrows running from left to right in the middle of the diagram symbolizes the correlations between public attitudes and government actions that are to be explained. The two processes that Miller and Stokes believe explain these correlations are indicated by the solid lines with arrows at the bottom of the diagram and the dashed lines with arrows at the top of the diagram. In the first process, the one indicated by the solid lines, members of government act in accordance with public attitudes because they realize what a majority of their constituents want and because they feel obliged to act in accordance with public wishes. To put this in the language Miller and Stokes use, one can say that congressmen form accurate perceptions of constituency attitudes and act in accordance with those perceptions. In the second process, the one indicated by the short dashes, members of the public elect government members whose personal attitudes correspond with their own attitudes, and members of government act in accordance with their personal attitudes. To put this in the language used by Miller and Stokes, congressional attitudes correspond to public attitudes and members of Congress act in accordance with their personal attitudes. Miller and Stokes conclude, therefore, that two conditions must be fulfilled if public opinion is to control government decisions. They state these conditions as follows:

> *First,* the Representative's votes in the House must agree substantially with his own policy views or his perceptions of his district's views, and not be determined entirely by other influences to which the Congressman is exposed; and, *second,* the attitudes or perceptions

governing the Representative's acts must correspond, at least imper-
fectly, to the district's actual opinions.[14]

Miller and Stokes assume that if they can show these two conditions are
fulfilled, they will have shown that government is in fact influenced by
public opinion, and they set out to accomplish this task.

Figure 10.1. The strong and weak forms of rule by public opinion. (Adapted from Warren
E. Miller and Donald E. Stokes, "Constituency Influence in Congress," in Angus Camp-
bell, Philip E. Converse, Warren E. Miller, and Donald E. Stokes, *Elections and the
Political Order* [New York: Wiley, 1966], p. 361.)

By a series of correlations, Miller and Stokes attempt to assess
whether their two conditions for rule by public opinion are achieved.
First, they correlate congressional perceptions of constituency attitudes
and congressional attitudes with congressional votes. They find that if

congressional perceptions and congressional attitudes are taken together, their correlation with congressional votes is .67 for social welfare
issues, .56 for foreign policy issues, and .86 for civil rights issues.[15]
These correlations lead the authors to believe that the personal attitudes
of congressmen and their perceptions of constituency attitudes must
account for most of their votes. In addition, they find that for social
welfare and foreign policy issues, correlations between congressional
attitudes and congressional votes are much higher than correlations between congressional perceptions of constituency attitudes and congressional votes.[16] In the case of civil rights issues, however, they find that
the correlations between congressional perceptions of constituency attitudes and congressional votes are higher than correlations between congressional attitudes and congressional votes. This leads them to conclude that votes on social welfare and foreign policy issues must have
been influenced by the personal attitudes of congressmen, whereas votes
on civil rights issues must have been influenced by their perceptions of
the attitudes of their constituents.

These findings could, of course, simply show that congressmen act in
accordance with their personal views or their mistaken ideas about the
views of their constituents—not that they are actually "controlled" by
the general public. To investigate whether there is any constituency
"control" exercised over congressional voting, Miller and Stokes examine two separate sets of correlations consisting of two correlations each.
First, they examine the correlations between constituency attitudes and
congressional attitudes, and between congressional attitudes and congressional votes. Second, they examine the correlations between constituency attitudes and congressional perceptions of constituency attitudes, and between those perceptions and congressional votes. In effect,
therefore, they examine separately the correlations that correspond to
the short dashes and solid lines, respectively, in Figure 10.1.

Miller and Stokes find that all these correlations are positive, ranging
from a low of .17 for correlations between constituency attitudes on
social welfare issues and congressional perceptions of those attitudes, to
a high of .74 for correlations between constituency attitudes on civil
rights issues and congressional perceptions of those attitudes.[17] Because
all these correlations are positive, and in some cases quite high, the
authors conclude that the two sets of correlations they examine correspond to two causal "paths" linking constituency attitudes to congressional votes.[18] In other words, they conclude that because there is a
positive correlation between constituency attitudes and congressional
attitudes, constituency attitudes must influence congressional attitudes
in some way. Moreover, because there is a positive correlation between
congressional attitudes and congressional votes, congressional attitudes

must influence congressional votes. As a result, they conclude that constituency attitudes must sometimes influence congressional votes by influencing congressional attitudes. Through a similar process of reasoning, Miller and Stokes conclude that constituency attitudes must sometimes influence congressional votes because congressmen form correct perceptions of the views of their constituents and act in accordance with public wishes. They conclude, therefore, that they have shown that public opinion does in fact influence government decision making through the strong and weak forms of rule by public opinion.

An Alternative to Miller and Stokes.   The difficulty with the argument just outlined should be apparent from my general criticisms of attitude studies of rule by public opinion. It is the same difficulty Miller and Stokes would have faced if they had simply rested their case on evidence about correlations between public opinion and government decisions. The correlations between popular attitudes, government perceptions of those attitudes, and government actions and between popular attitudes, government attitudes, and government actions which Miller and Stokes report are just as consistent with the hypothesis that members of government (perhaps working together with members of the elite) form popular attitudes as they are with the hypothesis that public opinion influences government actions.

We can see this by examining, first, the findings which Miller and Stokes believe show that public views influence government through the operation of the weak form of rule by public opinion. Correlations between constituency attitudes and congressional attitudes can be explained by saying that personal attitudes held by members of government are influenced by public attitudes, as Miller and Stokes claim. Alternatively, these correlations can be explained by saying that members of government influence the attitudes of the public. Likewise, correlations between congressional attitudes and congressional votes can be explained by saying that members of government act in accordance with personal attitudes which were influenced by members of the public; but these correlations can also be explained by saying that members of government act in accordance with personal attitudes which members of the public do not influence. Thus we can conclude that findings that constituency attitudes correlate with congressional attitudes and that congressional attitudes correlate with congressional votes are consistent with the hypothesis that public attitudes influence government attitudes which in turn influence votes, as Miller and Stokes claim. These same findings, however, are also consistent with the hypothesis that members of government and their friends in the elite attempt to convince members of the public to adopt their personal attitudes; that they often succeed;

and that, regardless of whether they succeed, they act on the basis of their personal attitudes. As a result, the findings which Miller and Stokes assume show that public views influence government through the weak form of rule by public opinion might also show that government influences public opinion.

If we look at the findings which Miller and Stokes believe show that public views influence government through the strong form of rule by public opinion, we can draw conclusions similar to those just outlined. Correlations between constituency attitudes and congressional perceptions of those attitudes can be explained by saying that members of government form accurate ideas about what policies most members of the public favor by talking with members of the elite and, occasionally, with ordinary citizens. This is the way Miller and Stokes interpret these correlations. Alternatively, however, the same correlations can be explained by saying that members of government attempt to convince members of the public to adopt their personal attitudes; that they often succeed; that they often assume they have succeeded; and that, as a result, they correctly assume that members of the public share their personal attitudes. Thus government perceptions of public attitudes would often be accurate even if members of government received no accurate information about public views from members of the elite or anyone else.

Likewise, correlations between congressional perceptions of constituency attitudes and congressional votes can be explained by saying that members of government often vote for certain policies because they believe members of the public favor those policies. Alternatively, these correlations can be explained by saying that members of government often assume that members of the public share their personal attitudes and that they act on their personal attitudes in most cases. Thus we can conclude that findings that constituency attitudes correlate with congressional perceptions of constituency attitudes and that those perceptions correlate with congressional votes are consistent with the hypothesis that members of government have ways of finding out what policies most members of the public favor and vote for certain policies because they believe that most members of the public favor them, as Miller and Stokes claim. These same findings, however, are consistent with the hypothesis that without having any reliable way of ascertaining majority wishes, members of government attempt to convince members of the public to adopt their personal attitudes; that they often succeed; that they often assume they have succeeded; that they, therefore, assume that members of the public share their personal attitudes; and that they generally act on the basis of their personal attitudes.

My alternative explanation of the findings which Miller and Stokes explain in terms of the strong form of rule by public opinion would obviously be more plausible if there were high correlations between government attitudes and government perceptions of public attitudes. Such correlations could be interpreted as evidence that members of government assume that members of the public hold the same attitudes they do. Admittedly, however, such correlations could also be interpreted as evidence that the personal attitudes held by members of government are influenced by their perceptions of the attitudes which members of the public hold. Miller and Stokes do not report correlations between government attitudes and government perceptions of constituency attitudes for social welfare and foreign policy issues, but they do report that for civil rights issues the correlation is .64.[19] This finding indicates that members of government either adopt public attitudes on civil rights issues or assume that members of the public share their attitudes fairly often. Therefore, just as it is possible that the correlations between constituency attitudes, congressional attitudes, and congressional actions which Miller and Stokes report may be due to the influence of government on public opinion or to the weak form of rule by public opinion, so the correlations between constituency attitudes, congressional perceptions of those attitudes, and congressional votes which they report may be due to the influence of government on the public or to the strong form of rule by public opinion.

Criticism of the Alternative Explanation.   Having outlined these two explanations of the findings Miller and Stokes report, I admit that the second explanation (that correlations between constituency attitudes, congressional perceptions of those attitudes, and congressional votes may be due to the influence of government on public opinion) can be subjected to at least one criticism. Someone might say that if we accept this explanation, it is hard to understand one of the findings about civil rights issues which Miller and Stokes report. They show that the correlation between government attitudes and government actions on civil rights issues is lower than the correlation between government perceptions of public opinion and government actions on these issues.[20]

A critic of my explanation might argue that this finding is problematic. To begin with, he might recall that I have assumed that the reason government perceptions of public attitudes correlate highly with government actions might be that members of government generally act in accordance with their personal attitudes and often assume that members of the public share those attitudes. My critic might admit that if this is true, it is possible that government perceptions of public attitudes could have the same correlations with government actions that government attitudes do. This would occur, for example, if members of government always assume that members of the public share their attitudes. In this case, whenever they act in accordance with their personal attitudes, they would be acting in accordance with their perceptions of public attitudes. Moreover, my critic might admit that according to my assumptions, it is possible that the correlation between government perceptions of public attitudes and government actions could be lower than the correlation between government attitudes and government actions. This would occur if members of government sometimes, but not always, assume that members of the public share their attitudes. If this occurred they would sometimes, but not always, be acting in accordance with public attitudes when they acted in accordance with their personal attitudes. My critic might insist, however, that if my assumptions are correct, the correlation between government attitudes and government actions could never be lower than the correlation between government perceptions of public attitudes and government actions. Yet, he might say, this is what we find in the case of civil rights issues. My critic might insist, therefore, that my explanation of the findings reported by Miller and Stokes cannot be correct. (A similar objection could be raised with regard to the correlations between public attitudes and government attitudes and between public attitudes and government perceptions of those attitudes on civil rights issues, as reported by Miller and Stokes. Because that objection follows essentially the same lines as the objection just outlined, and because it can be answered in the same way, it will not be discussed in detail.)

One answer to this objection is that even if it is supported by the findings about civil rights issues which Miller and Stokes report, it is not supported by their findings about social welfare and foreign policy issues. The authors report that on these issues, government attitudes correlate more highly with government actions than government perceptions of public attitudes do.[21] Thus, even if my explanation is wrong with regard to civil rights issues, it still might be right with regard to social welfare and foreign policy issues.

Another answer to the objection just outlined is that the strong form of rule by public opinion may be only partially responsible for correspondences between government perceptions of public attitudes and government actions. Miller and Stokes show that the correlation between government attitudes and government actions on civil rights issues is .72.[22] This means that if members of government acted in accordance with their personal attitudes with a frequency indicated by this correlation, and if they always assumed that members of the public shared those attitudes, the correlation between government perceptions of public attitudes and government actions would also be .72. Miller and Stokes report, however, that the correlation between government perceptions of public attitudes and government actions is, in fact, .82.[23] If members of government generally act in accordance with their personal attitudes on civil rights issues, and if they always assume that members of the public share their attitudes, therefore, it is possible that this process might account for .72 of the correlation of .82 between government perceptions of public attitudes and government actions; the strong form of rule by public opinion might account for only .10 of that correlation. Thus it is possible that although public opinion does influence government actions on civil rights issues to some degree, correspondences between public attitudes and government actions are largely due to a process, such as that just described, whereby government influences public opinion.

A final answer to the objection I have been discussing is that the part of the correlation between government perceptions of constituency attitudes and government actions which is inconsistent with my hypothesis that members of government assume their constituents share their attitudes (the .10 of the correlation mentioned above) need not be explained in terms of the strong form of rule by public opinion. This part of the correlation can be explained by saying that members of the elite influence both members of the public and members of government to adopt their personal attitudes. Thus we might say that correlations between government perceptions of public attitudes and government actions on civil rights issues are partly due to the influence of government on public opinion and partly due to the influence of the elite on government and the public; but they are not due to the influence of public opinion on government, as Miller and Stokes claim. Alternatively, we could say that all the findings which Miller and Stokes report might be explained by the influence of the elite on government and the public rather than by either of the other two processes I have been discussing (rule by public opinion or the influence of government on public views). One can follow essentially the same line of argument to show that the influence of the elite might account for part of the findings reported by Miller and Stokes as one would follow to show that the influence of the elite accounts for all those findings. As a result, for the sake of brevity I will confine myself to the latter task.

The first step in understanding how the influence of the elite on public opinion and government might account for the findings which Miller and Stokes report about all the issues they study is to note that correlations between public attitudes and government attitudes might be due to the fact that members of the elite convince both members of the public and members of government to adopt their personal attitudes. In addition, correlations between public attitudes and government perceptions of those attitudes might be due to the fact that members of the elite convince members of the public to adopt their personal attitudes and at the same time convince members of government that members of the public share those attitudes. If the elite does influence the public and government in these ways, Miller and Stokes are wrong to conclude that correlations between constituency attitudes and congressional attitudes and between congressional attitudes and congressional votes are due to the weak form of rule by public opinion. Rather, they should conclude that these correlations can be explained best by saying that the personal attitudes of both members of the public and members of government are influenced by the elite and that members of government act in accordance with their personal attitudes.

Moreover, if we accept that members of the elite have the kind of influence I have outlined, Miller and Stokes are wrong to conclude that correlations between constituency attitudes and congressional perceptions of constituency attitudes and correlations between those perceptions and congressional votes are due to the strong form of rule by public opinion. Rather, they should conclude that these correlations can be explained best by saying that members of the elite convince members of the public to adopt their attitudes, that they convince members of government that members of the public have adopted those attitudes, and that members of government act in accordance with their perceptions of public attitudes. Alternatively, these same correlations can be explained by saying that members of the elite convince both members of the public and members of government to adopt their attitudes, that they convince members of government that members of the public share elite attitudes, and that members of government act in accordance with their personal attitudes.

If we accept the latter explanation, we can expect positive correlations between public attitudes and government perceptions of those attitudes because members of the elite simultaneously influence members of the public to adopt their personal attitudes and convince members of government that the public has adopted those attitudes. We can expect positive correlations between government perceptions of public attitudes and government actions because, although members of government act only on the basis of their personal attitudes, these will often be elite attitudes and members of the elite will often have convinced government that members of the public share those attitudes.

My Argument.   Despite possible objections, therefore, the findings reported by Miller and Stokes are consistent with at least three hypotheses: their hypothesis that public opinion transmitted by the elite influences government decisions and my two hypotheses that government influences public opinion and that the elite influences the opinions of government and the public. This interpretation of their work is very different from the one Miller and Stokes provide. They do not even discuss the two alternative hypotheses I have outlined. For example, although at one point they review a whole family of different patterns of influence they believe might be consistent with their findings, all of these are patterns by which public opinion might influence government.[24] None of them are patterns by which government and the elite might influence the public. In effect, therefore, Miller and Stokes neglect the possibility that influence might flow from government to members of the mass public and from members of the elite to both the public and government. They ignore the role of the elite and assume that any correspondences between government actions and public views must be due to the influence of mass opinion on government.

Even though I have placed great emphasis on my two alternative hypotheses about the relationship between public opinion and government, I am not claiming they are necessarily correct; I admit it is possible that Miller and Stokes have drawn the right conclusions from their data. Rather, my argument is that because Miller and Stokes hypothesize that correspondences between government actions and public views must be due to the influence of those views on members of government, they do not gather data which enable us to choose between that hypothesis and the hypotheses that government influences public opinion or that the opinions of both government and the public are influenced by elite members. Moreover, because their findings do not enable us to choose between these three hypotheses, they cannot claim to have shown that public opinion influences government decision making. Their findings are consistent with that hypothesis, but they are also consistent with contrary hypotheses. My argument is, therefore, that the findings about the relationship between public opinion and government which Miller and Stokes present are inconclusive. They show us that there is some relationship between public opinion and government actions, but they do not show us what the nature of that relationship is.

It would be convenient, of course, if Miller and Stokes could draw upon findings other than those they present to support their hypothesis that correlations between public opinion and government actions are due to rule by public opinion. It would be convenient, that is, if they could admit their findings are not conclusive but could claim that certain findings by the authors of other studies indicate that theirs is a more likely hypothesis than those I have suggested. Miller and Stokes could not defend their argument effectively in this way, however. I have already shown ("Essentials of My Criticisms") that contemporary social scientists provide little evidence about what role the elite plays in linking public opinion to government and little information about whether or how government influences public opinion. As a result, there is no body of evidence which shows that correlations between public opinion and government actions are probably due to the influence of public opinion on government rather than the influence of government on public opinion or the influence of the elite on both government and public opinion.

In addition to the criticism just outlined, there are two other criticisms we can level at Miller and Stokes's work. They do not only claim to show that, in general, public opinion influences government decisions. They also claim to show that public opinion on particular kinds of issues is influential and that they can determine whether the strong or weak form of rule by public opinion is mainly responsible for bringing about correspondences between public attitudes and government actions. By establishing that public opinion on particular kinds of issues, such as civil rights and foreign policy, is influential, Miller and Stokes attempt to establish that, in general, public opinion influences government. However, having shown that they cannot establish the general influence of public opinion, I have also shown that they cannot establish that particular kinds of opinion are influential. Moreover, if Miller and Stokes cannot determine how public opinion is related to government decisions, they certainly cannot claim to determine whether the strong or weak form of rule by public opinion or any other process is mainly responsible for correspondences between public views and government actions. As a result, none of the three major claims that Miller and Stokes make about their work is acceptable.

Objections.   Two general objections might be raised to my criticisms of the study by Miller and Stokes. First, as in the case of my criticisms of *The American Voter,* it might be objected that social science researchers cannot be expected to consider all the alternative hypotheses which are consistent with their findings. All they can be expected to do is to discover whether there are data that are consistent with certain important hypotheses they are exploring. My answer to this objection is the same as it was to the same objection raised in Chapter 8. Although social science researchers should not feel obliged to consider all alternative hypotheses, our understanding of social phenomena will not advance rapidly unless they consider at least the major alternative hypotheses that for some reason can be considered likely. In fact, it is not being overly demanding of researchers to say that one of their major purposes in designing studies should be to analyze data which will allow them to choose between major conflicting hypotheses and to say that, while studies not designed in this way may be interesting and worthwhile, they will be inconclusive. I do not deny either the interest or the worth of the study by Miller and Stokes. Nevertheless, many students of politics have suggested that government sometimes influences mass opinion and that members of the elite are more than mere transmitters of public views. For example, the notion that government manipulation of the news and mass-media bias affect public opinion has been with us for a long time, and it is taken seriously by thoughtful people.[25] This and other notions about how government and the elite might influence mass opinion can be regarded as major alternative hypotheses which any researchers attempting to show that rule by public opinion is a reality must consider. Because they do not consider these hypotheses, Miller and Stokes can be faulted for providing inconclusive findings about whether public opinion influences government decisions.

The second objection which might be raised to my criticisms of the study by Miller and Stokes is that the distinctions among processes by which public opinion influences government, processes by which government and the elite influence public opinion, and processes by which the elite influences both public opinion and government are not important. It might be argued that it is enough to show that there is some process by which government actions and public attitudes come to correspond. While not wishing to belittle the importance of findings about correlations between government actions and public attitudes, there are two answers to this objection.

First, the distinctions I have outlined are important because they help us understand the work of Miller and Stokes, Key, and the authors of other attitude studies. These political scientists do not set out to show simply that there is some relationship between public opinion and government. Rather, they say that they set out to discover whether public opinion "controls" government through the strong and weak forms of rule by public opinion. As pointed out in Chapter 9, when they refer to the strong and weak forms of rule by public opinion, political scientists have some fairly specific ideas about what they mean. For example, they are quite clear that they do *not* have in mind a process by which members of government present a policy to the public, members of the public adopt it, members of government have no reliable way of knowing public views, and members of government act in accordance with their personal attitudes. This is a process different from the strong or weak forms of rule by public opinion as I have described them or as students of politics usually describe them. In fact, I have tried to show that all the processes by which government and the elite might influence the public are different from rule by public opinion as political scientists understand it. Therefore the distinctions between the influence of government and the elite on public opinion and the influence of public opinion on government are important because the authors of attitude studies make it quite clear that they are attempting to show that members of the public are linked to government by the latter process, rather than simply by *some* process. Thus this distinction enables us to understand the task which the authors of attitude studies have set for themselves, and it helps us to measure their success in accomplishing that task.

My second answer to the objection that the distinction between the influence of government and the elite on public opinion and the influence of public opinion on government is unimportant is that this distinction is of great value in understanding a number of aspects of the American political process and possibly the political processes of other nations. Because this point is discussed at length in Chapter 11, it will not be expanded on here. Nevertheless, it is probably the more important reason for making the distinction I have been defending.

Alternative Approaches.   Despite the objections just reviewed, I think my criticisms of the study by Miller and Stokes are valid. If we accept this as true, however, two more questions immediately arise: If Miller and Stokes have not shown that rule by public opinion is a reality, who has? And how should we go about determining what factors link public opinion to government decision making? My answer to the first question is that no one I know of has used attitude psychology to show conclusively that public opinion influences government decisions. All the major discussions of rule by public opinion using the techniques of attitude psychology that I know of rest on anecdotal evidence of the sort Key presents, correlations of government actions and public attitudes of the sort Miller and Stokes reject, or techniques similar to those Miller and Stokes use.[26] Moreover, it has already been pointed out that other contemporary social scientists provide little information about what role the elite plays in linking public opinion to government or whether and how government influences public views. Thus the authors of attitude studies other than those I have discussed do not provide information that would enable us to determine whether correlations between public opinion and government are due to rule by public opinion or to the other processes I have mentioned. Although more satisfactory studies of the relationship between public opinion and government may exist, a search of the literature has failed to find them. My conclusion is, therefore, that at least the best known works dealing with rule by public opinion—Key's book and the article by Miller and Stokes—have failed to show that the distribution of public views does in fact have a strong influence on government decisions.

Unfortunately, I do not have a good answer to the question of how to determine what factors link public opinion to government decision making. It would, of course, be difficult to determine accurately whether and how government members influence elite members and, through them, the public, or to trace how elite members might influence the public and government members. Anecdotal information suggests that these forms of influence do occur but are extremely subtle and possibly occur over a long period of time. Moreover, it is likely that the influence of public opinion on government and the influence of government and the elite on public opinion occur at the same time. If true, the real problem is to gauge the relative strengths of these different processes, rather than show that one or the other is entirely responsible for correlations between government actions and popular attitudes.

In addition, it seems quite possible that the influence of public opinion on government and the influence of government and the elite on public opinion cannot be distinguished clearly. Perhaps the relationships between government, the elite, and the general public can best be described as a series of crosscurrents of influence. One might say that as a result of this process, everyone eventually comes to agree with almost everyone else but no one can be said to have been more influential than anyone else. Thus the life history of an issue might begin by some individual or group of individuals suggesting that it is important and conveying this idea to members of government, the public, and the elite. Next, members of all three groups would form initial opinions, and these opinions would be conveyed from each group to all the others. There would follow a process by which, through a series of steps, everyone would readjust his position to come closer to the positions of everyone else. Finally, when most people agree on some sort of compromise, government would act. If this is a correct description of the relationship between public opinion and government action, it is surely wrong to regard this simply as a process whereby the public influences government decisions (rule *by* public opinion) or a process whereby government and the elite influence the public (rule *of* public opinion). As a result, any attempts directed solely at showing that rule by public opinion is a reality would be either inconclusive or misleading. They would overlook the possibility that the influence of government and the elite on public opinion and the influence of public opinion on government and the elite are inextricably intertwined. Moreover, we could conclude that it would probably be extremely difficult to show how strong an influence public opinion has on government because it would be extremely difficult to separate its influence from all the other crosscurrents which link the public to government.

One approach to the difficulties raised by the possible interrelations between factors which may lead to correspondences between government and public views would be to follow the life histories of particular issues with great care. We might record when an issue was first discussed extensively in government circles, among selected members of the elite, and among the public. We might then record at regular time intervals what opinions, if any, members of all three sectors of society held toward the issue and their awareness of the opinions held by other sectors. We might then attempt to identify at regular intervals any changes in opinion or new opinion formation; we could correlate these developments with changes in the perceptions that each sector of society holds about other sectors and with changes in the actual opinions of other sectors. This recording process could continue until government takes action on the issue. The resulting data could be analyzed to determine how well they correspond with several possible models of the relationship between public opinion and government.

For example, if we found that government members generally formed their opinions about an issue early in its life history, that they did not change their opinions, that they subsequently acted on them, that elite members generally adopted the position held by government members as soon as they heard about it, and that members of the public generally adopted the government position as soon as they heard about it from elite members, we would have a clear-cut case of rule *of* public opinion. If, however, we found that early in the life history of an issue certain government members were indecisive or noncommittal about their positions, that members of the elite generally presented both sides of the issue, that members of the public eventually formed a majority on one side of the issue, that government members for some reason realized this and made their decision soon after they reported their realization, we would have a clear-cut case of rule *by* public opinion. Other models, including some that would give a larger role to the elite and some that would describe a system in which there are many crosscurrents of influence, could be constructed, and an attempt could be made to determine which model best described the data in particular cases.

Fully developing models of this sort and designing in detail the research strategies that would make it possible to test them would be formidable tasks. Even more formidable would be the task of gathering the mass of data that would be needed to implement a research strategy of the sort outlined. Simpler research strategies may be possible, of course. But it seems clear that if we wish to design any kind of successful strategy for illuminating the relationship between public opinion and government, we must take into account the possibility that the elite may play an active role in this relationship; we must also take into account the possibility that influence may flow from government and the elite to the general public as well as in the opposite direction.

In short, to determine whether rule by public opinion is a reality, researchers must consider all aspects of the influence process described by Key. The results of such research may or may not be clear findings about whether rule by public opinion accounts for correspondences between public views and government actions. Careful investigations may show that the crosscurrent model is closest to reality or that different models apply to different kinds of issues. Nevertheless, such research could at least show what the relationship between public opinion and government action is; as I have argued, research based on the assumption that rule by public opinion is the only possible explanation for correlations between public attitudes and government actions has not demonstrated what that relationship is.

11. Additional Considerations about Rule by Public Opinion

It was pointed out in Chapter 9 that the authors of studies of rule by public opinion do not restrict themselves to trying to show that public attitudes influence government. They also claim they can identify the mechanisms by which public opinion influences government and can contribute to a better general understanding of the American political system. Chapter 10 was devoted to showing that the authors of attitude studies cannot claim to have demonstrated that public attitudes influence government. This chapter is devoted to discussing the other two claims and to raising certain theoretical problems regarding the studies I have been discussing.

Identifying Factors That Create Rule by Public Opinion

General Criticisms.   My criticisms of the claim by authors of attitude studies that they can identify and analyze the factors which create rule by public opinion follow directly from my criticisms of their claim that they can show that public opinion influences government decisions. All of the attempts to show that rule by public opinion is a reality which have been discussed can also be regarded as attempts to show what factors bring it about. Thus anecdotes aimed at showing that public opinion influences government decisions in particular cases, studies which correlate public opinion with government decisions, and analyses such as the one conducted by Miller and Stokes can be seen as attempts to show that certain factors lead to rule by public opinion. In the case of anecdotes, many factors may be mentioned; in the case of correlations between government decisions and public views, it is generally assumed that the factors identified by Key are of major importance; and in the case of analyses such as the one conducted by Miller and Stokes, government perceptions of popular attitudes and government attitudes that correspond to public opinion are emphasized.

However, if I am correct in saying that none of these analyses is successful in determining whether public opinion influences government decisions, either in general or in particular cases, then these analyses surely cannot be successful in showing what factors cause rule by public opinion, in either general or particular cases. If, for example, Miller and Stokes cannot claim that their correlations among government actions, government perceptions of constituency attitudes, and constituency attitudes show that public opinion influences government because members of government identify and act on constituency attitudes, then they cannot claim that these correlations show that government perceptions of constituency attitudes are important factors in rule by public opinion.

In addition to the studies already discussed, however, there is another group of studies that might be regarded as analyses of how government actions come to correspond to public wishes. Each of the investigations already discussed considers several factors that might link public opinion to government decisions in an attempt to draw a comprehensive picture of the process of rule by public opinion. Each of the studies to which I am now referring considers only one or two of those factors. While the authors of these studies do not generally claim that their findings show that certain factors cause rule by public opinion, this is an interpretation which might be placed on at least some of their work. In addition, that work constitutes a large and often discussed body of research for which my conclusions about other kinds of attitude studies have implications. As a result, it is important to consider briefly the significance of studies that investigate only a few of the factors often presumed to cause rule by public opinion. For the purposes of discussion, these studies are divided into empirical and theoretical analyses.

Empirical Analyses.   Empirical analyses of factors presumed to cause rule by public opinion are attempts to show that certain factors have some of the characteristics which, according to Key and others, they must have if they are to link popular attitudes to government actions. For example, Eulau, Wahlke, Buchanan, and Ferguson attempt to determine whether members of government in fact believe they should act in accordance with public opinion, and Key attempts to determine whether members of the public in fact elect congressmen who hold political views similar to their own.[1] The analysis by Eulau et al. can be considered significant because, if we are to believe that the strong form of rule by public opinion operates in the United States, we must believe that congressmen think they should act in accordance with public views. Key's analysis is significant because, if we are to believe that the weak form of rule by public opinion operates in the United States, we must believe that members of the public elect congressmen who share their political values. Both studies show that the conditions necessary for rule by public opinion are fulfilled to some extent.

It is important to realize that the authors of the studies just mentioned do not claim that their work shows that the process of rule by public opinion is a reality or that the factors they study are parts of that process. Eulau et al., for example, do not draw any general conclusions about whether rule by public opinion links government actions to public views in the United States. They claim only to have shown that the factors they study have some, but not all, the characteristics they would have if they were among the factors which caused rule by public opinion. Although Key assumes that the factors he studies do, in fact, link public opinion to government decisions, he does not believe his analysis shows this. Rather, like Eulau et al., he believes he has provided one among several kinds of evidence which would be needed to show that the factors with which he is concerned cause rule by public opinion.

If Eulau et al., Key, and others who conduct studies similar to theirs do not show that the factors they consider link government actions to public opinion, however, my criticisms in the preceding chapters raise serious questions about what contribution their work makes to political science. I have argued that no one has determined whether rule by public opinion is a reality or what factors cause it. If this is correct, it is difficult to say exactly what the studies just mentioned show us. For example, Eulau et al. report that some congressmen believe they should act in accordance with public wishes. This is undoubtedly a valuable and interesting finding. They do not show us, however, whether congressmen accurately interpret public wishes or whether they actually act in accordance with them; that is, they do not show us whether congressional perceptions of public views are among the factors that cause rule by public opinion, and I do not think anyone has shown this. As a result, it is difficult to say whether the findings reported by Eulau et al. are simply small but important contributions to our understanding of the legislative process or whether they are the key to understanding how that process is part of an effective system of popular government. In other words, are Eulau et al. elaborating on one component of rule by public opinion, or are they simply elaborating on the psychology of congressmen?

Similar questions could be raised about other studies of factors presumed to cause rule by public opinion, and these questions can be resolved only if it can be shown whether these factors do perform the important role in political systems that they are said to perform. If we accept my argument that no one has shown conclusively that rule by public opinion is a reality or how it functions, therefore, we must conclude that it is not clear exactly what significance empirical studies of factors presumed to cause rule by public opinion have.

It might be argued, however, that the significance of empirical studies of factors presumed to cause rule by public opinion is much clearer and much greater than just suggested. In particular, one might regard Key's book, which surveys a number of such studies, as an attempt to collect a body of evidence which shows that rule by public opinion is a reality. In other words, we might argue that although no one study of this sort casts much light on whether public opinion influences government decisions, Key has been able to build a case that his model is an accurate description of the relationships between public opinion and government by collecting evidence that each of the conditions he considers necessary for rule by public opinion is, in fact, fulfilled.

Key does not make this argument, and he would be wrong to do so because the body of evidence collected by attitude studies of factors presumed to cause rule by public opinion is not complete enough to show whether those factors link government actions to public views. For example, Key does not present findings that show whether representatives who say they believe they should act in accordance with public opinion actually do so, or whether representatives who share the political values of their constituents vote in accordance with those views more often than other representatives do. Moreover, even if he were able to show these things, Key's argument would be inconclusive unless he could show that the relationships among popular attitudes, government attitudes, government perceptions of popular attitudes, and government actions which he discusses are due to the influence of public opinion on government rather than the influence of government and the elite on public opinion.

Unfortunately, Key presents no evidence that bears upon the problems just mentioned, and none of the authors of attitude studies of factors presumed to cause rule by public opinion present such evidence. Like the authors of more comprehensive studies of the relationship between public opinion and government, they rarely attempt to determine whether or to what extent government influences the formation of mass opinion, or whether or to what extent members of the elite influence the opinions of the public and government. Apparently, like the authors of more comprehensive studies, they assume that a correspondence between public opinion and government actions must be due to a flow of influence from the public to government, rather than from government to the public or from the elite to the public and government. As a result, studies of factors presumed to cause rule by public opinion have the same shortcomings that studies of rule by public opinion which are more comprehensive have. Therefore, it would be wrong to say that empirical studies of factors presumed to cause rule by public opinion are significant because, collectively, they show that this process links public views to government actions. Also, it would be wrong to say that Key has shown that rule by public opinion is a reality by gathering together a number of these studies.

Theoretical Analyses.   Like empirical analyses of factors presumed to cause rule by public opinion, theoretical analyses of those factors face serious difficulties. A good example of a theoretical analysis of this kind is Key's discussion of the distribution and intensity of opinions.[2] As mentioned earlier, Key goes to great lengths to explain how he thinks differences in the distribution and intensity of public opinion influence government decision making. He points out, among other things, that the nearer the distribution of opinions on an issue approaches a consensus, the more likely it is that government members will act in accordance with public wishes. Moreover, he says that the greater the overall intensity of public views, the greater the likelihood that government will heed those views. Key provides practically no evidence to support these contentions, however. He shows that on different issues public opinion does in fact differ in distribution and intensity, but he does not show that these variations correlate with variations in government actions or other factors. Essentially, his discussion of the distribution and intensity of public opinion is an exercise in developing a series of models that, on the basis of his general knowledge about government and the public and on the basis of certain general theories about the operations of political systems, he believes are likely to be verified by empirical investigation.

Model building of this sort faces the same fundamental difficulty faced by empirical studies of factors presumed to cause rule by public opinion: If we do not know whether the factors being discussed actually bring about the influence of public opinion on government, it is difficult to say what significance even the most thoughtful models of how they might function have for political science. It may be that the characteristics of the distribution and intensity of opinions which Key discusses are simply curiosities. This would be the case if he were wrong to assume that the distribution and intensity of opinion affect government actions. Alternatively, Key's models may be misleading. This would be the case if the factors he discusses do influence government decisions but if he incorrectly interprets how they exert this influence because he lacks any reliable information about the relationship between public opinion and government. As a result, until it has been shown that differences in the distribution and intensity of opinions do in fact correlate with differences in government decision making, the significance of models such as those constructed by Key will remain in doubt.

My Argument.   All in all, none of the three kinds of study I have been discussing—empirical and theoretical analyses of factors presumed to cause rule by public opinion and more comprehensive studies—shows conclusively how public opinion is related to government decision making. None of these kinds of study determines whether or how rule by public opinion operates in the United States.

Moreover, it is unclear whether findings about factors presumed to cause rule by public opinion contribute at all to our understanding of the relationship between public views and government. Most contemporary attempts to use attitude psychology to determine what factors cause rule by public opinion can be classified as one of the three kinds of study that have been discussed. As a result, we can conclude that the authors of attitude studies have been unsuccessful in their attempts to determine what factors link public opinion to government actions.

Contributing to a Better Understanding of the American Political System

The Objective.   Thus far my criticisms of attitude studies of rule by public opinion have focused on their first two research objectives. As pointed out earlier, however, all these studies have a third objective: to add to our general understanding of the relationship between the public and government in the United States and, therefore, to illuminate many aspects of the American political system. The authors of *The American Voter,* for example, write that they believe governmental responsiveness to public views is an essential part of a working democracy and that studies of the relationship of public opinion to government decisions should shed light on how closely and in what ways the political system of the United States approximates a democratic model.[3] One can quarrel with the notion of democracy adopted by the authors of *The American Voter;* but it is hard to quarrel with the notion that studies of the relationship between public opinion and government in the United States should be of value for many different kinds of analysis of the American political system.

If we accept that the authors of attitude studies of rule by public opinion should be able to improve our general understanding of the American political system and that they attempt to do this, their work can be criticized on two counts.

The First Problem.   As already pointed out, the authors do not explain what form rule by public opinion takes in the United States or even whether it exists. As a result, they are unclear about exactly how government, the public, and the elite are related to each other in the political system. The findings reported in attitude studies do not show, for example, which of these three sectors of society generally initiates policies, which must generally approve policies before they are adopted, or how different sectors come to share the views of the others. These and other omissions from attitude studies are problematic because there are many different ways in which government, the elite, and the public might be related in the policymaking process. Perhaps, as Key suggests, the United States is a nation with a social and political system in which government members articulate policy alternatives, await popular reactions, and then act on the basis of those reactions. This model gives a large role to the general public in public policymaking, while giving the initiative in policy formation to government and excluding the elite from any active role except the transmission of government and public views. Perhaps, however, America is a country in which an elite, consisting of a small percentage of the public, takes a major share of the responsibility for formulating policies and in which members of that elite are usually successful in getting members of government and the public to adopt their ideas. Perhaps, by contrast, America is a country in which government members initiate most policies, generally act on the basis of agreements reached among themselves, and, once they have reached these agreements, are generally successful in convincing the elite and the public that they are correct. Perhaps, finally, America is a country in which there are so many crosscurrents of influence that it makes no sense to talk of any one sector of society initiating a policy or of government and the elite influencing public opinion any more than they are influenced by it. Because the authors of attitude studies do not show whether or how public opinion influences government, they provide no basis for judging which, if any, of these descriptions of the relationship between the public, the elite, and government is correct.

This failure of attitude studies of rule by public opinion has several important consequences. To begin with, depending on which of the descriptions of the American political system we believe is correct, we may draw different conclusions about what the strong and weak points of U.S. government are. For example, if we think that America is a nation in which there are many crosscurrents of influence, we may conclude that it lacks strong political leadership and we may fear that public policy will fall to the lowest common denominator. If, on the other hand, we think that the government initiates policies and forms public opinion, we may conclude that political leadership is too strong and that some mechanism should be devised to give the people a larger role in public affairs. If we believe that members of the elite play a large role in the political system by initiating policies and convincing members of both the public and the government that their ideas are correct, and if we believe that members of the general public or their elected representatives should take the initiative in policymaking, we may conclude that political leadership has been misplaced or that the actions of the elite should at least be carefully scrutinized. In short, the way we evaluate the American political system and the aspects of it that we believe raise serious problems may depend very much on which of the descriptions of the relationship between the public and government we adopt.

In addition, our conclusions about the relationships among the American public, the government, and the elite will affect our conclusions about how other aspects of the political system do or could operate. By affecting our ideas about how at least some government decisions are made, conclusions about the relationships among the public, the government, and the elite are bound to affect our conclusions about many of the individuals, processes, and institutions that are involved in making those decisions. For example, if we believe that Key correctly describes the relationship between the public and government, we can conclude that members of Congress often attempt to honor the wishes of a majority of their constituents. As a result, we may not expect Congress to take rapid or imaginative steps in implementing new policies because it will take time for each congressman to ascertain public opinion and because a majority of the public may be reluctant to approve novel ideas. Moreover, we may expect it would be difficult to reform Congress in such a way that it could move more swiftly and imaginatively; we may also expect that the executive and judicial branches of government, which may not be as responsive to public opinion as Congress is, will have to bear the major responsibility for taking quick initiatives in public policy. If, on the other hand, we believe that congressmen generally decide among themselves what policies to adopt and that correspondences between their actions and public views occur only because the general public usually follows their leadership, we may conclude that Congress can act quickly and imaginatively, that it can be reformed to insure that it does so more often, and that the other branches of government do not necessarily enjoy a monopoly on quick and imaginative actions.

Conclusions about the relationships among the public, the government, and the elite are, therefore, important because they may affect our ideas about what the strong and weak points in the American political system are and because they may affect our ideas about how many aspects of that system function. In addition, two other reasons these conclusions are important deserve mention.

First, social science research priorities may be influenced by ideas about the relationships among different sectors of American society. For example, if we believe that members of the elite generally influence members of the public and government to adopt their opinions, we may find it less interesting than the authors of many attitude studies apparently do to ask whether members of government share the values of their constituents. We may feel that we have eliminated the possibility that shared values have an important influence on government decision making.

Second, depending on our conclusions about the relationships among the public, the government, and the elite, we may draw different conclusions about whether the political system in the United States approximates a working democracy. The authors of many attitude studies seem to regard this question as important. It is beyond the scope of my work to consider at length what models of democratic systems social scientists do or should adopt, but several possible models are discussed later in this chapter. However, it is fairly safe to say that, for example, a system in which government members generally initiate policies and then act in accordance with public views about those policies is arguably democratic; a system in which government members generally initiate policies, often convince members of the public to adopt those policies, and almost always act in accordance with their personal views—regardless of whether members of the public agree with those views—is arguably not democratic (at least with regard to day-to-day decision making). Depending on which of these models we believe is an accurate description of the American political system, or depending on whether we even believe that either is an accurate description, we may draw different conclusions about whether that system is democratic.

The first reason the authors of attitude studies of rule by public opinion have failed to illuminate the nature of the American political process is, therefore, that they fail to identify the relationships among mass opinion, the elite, and government decision making. As a result of this failure, their findings leave us in doubt about which of several processes generally typify the relationship between the public and its government, what value judgments we should make about certain aspects of the political system, what conclusions we should draw about how aspects of that system do or can operate, what many of our social science research priorities should be, and whether the United States can be considered a working democracy. These are among the principal ways in which we could expect attitude studies of rule by public opinion to illuminate the American political process. By failing on these counts, Key and other political scientists have failed in one of their major objectives.

The Second Problem.   The second reason the authors of attitude studies of rule by public opinion have failed to add to our general understanding of the American political process is that their notions of both influence and public opinion are too restricted. The major question addressed by the authors of these studies is whether members of government feel obliged to act in accordance with the opinions of a majority of the public. This is surely an important question; but the influence of majority opinion on government might not be the only form of the influence of public opinion on government that is an important part of the political system.

For example, it might be argued that whether or not members of the elite accurately gauge the distribution of opinion among their constituents, and whether or not government members accurately infer mass opinion from elite opinion and act on the opinions of a majority of the general public, it is likely that elite leaders will bring several points of view on any issue to the attention of government members. We might argue that this is true by saying that American society is so large and diverse that a majority of the members of all major social groups will rarely hold the same opinion about any given issue. If most elite leaders who speak for those groups accurately convey the opinions of a majority of their constituents to government, therefore, members of government will probably hear several views on every subject. Alternatively, if we believe that elite leaders attempt to take positions which they personally regard as right or in the interest of their constituents, we can argue that there are so many different elite leaders with so many different perceptions of what is right or in the interest of their constituents that there will be at least two sides to every story presented to government.

If we believe that either of these arguments is correct, it is possible to conclude that even if members of government are not able to determine accurately what point of view on an issue is held by a majority of the public, they will at least be under the impression that members of the public hold different points of view. We can see the possible significance of this if we recall Key's observation that members of government are more comfortable making decisions when they believe that one point of view is held by almost all members of the public than when they believe there are divisions within public opinion. If Key is correct and if, for the reasons mentioned, members of government often hear different points of view about issues expressed by people who claim to speak for the general public, we might conclude that they will often debate and attempt to reconcile these points of view. These attempts may not always result in decisions that are consistent with majority wishes. The decisions may be opposed to majority opinion, or they may be compromises with the wishes of the majority. Nevertheless, this whole process beginning with the perception by members of government that public views differ on an issue can be considered a way in which public opinion influences government, even if it is not a process by which government members are influenced to act in accordance with majority opinion. Through this process, some views held by members of the public can affect government in the sense that they may be taken into consideration in setting the agenda for government deliberations and decision making. Despite the possible importance of this form of the influence of public opinion on government, however, the authors of attitude studies of rule by public opinion do not generally discuss it. Their attention is devoted entirely to determining whether and how majority opinion influences government decisions.

A second form of the influence of public opinion on government that authors of attitude studies do not investigate is the influence of views held only by limited sectors of society. We know from many anecdotal accounts of government decision making that this influence can take many forms.[4] For example, members of government often rely heavily on lobbyists and other elite members for factual information on which to base their decisions. In addition, members of government may have loyalties to certain special interests. A congressman might feel that on issues affecting organized labor, the views of union members should be given particular weight, and he may usually expose himself to information that supports the unions' point of view. Relationships of these sorts between members of government and limited sectors of society may not cause government actions to correspond to mass opinion. However, they can be regarded as ways in which public opinion influences government decisions. It is useful to consider briefly in what sense this is true of relationships in which elite members provide government officials with information and of relationships in which government members are particularly sensitive to the wishes of certain special interest groups.

Information is a kind of influence in the sense that it often affects the decisions which the people who receive it make and in the sense that the people who present the information often present it in a biased way. Moreover, the people who provide information to government can be regarded as members of the public (in the sense that they are outside government), even if they cannot always be regarded as representatives of the mass public. If information providers are able to influence government, at least some sectors of the public have a continual input into public policymaking. Although many political commentators might not think that the influence of the elite on decisions is, by itself, an ideal form of popular government, that influence can at least create a more open form of government than would exist if government members relied entirely on their colleagues for information. Openness in government makes it possible for perspectives not held by government members to affect public policy, and this is surely an important element in popular government. (For purposes of discussion here and in the following pages, the terms "popular government" and "democracy" will be used interchangeably. Both terms refer to political systems in which members of the general public exercise some sort of control over their government.[5]) As a result, even if public opinion influences government decisions only in the sense that elite members provide information to government, it would still play a large and valuable role in the American political system.

Like the influence of information provided by the elite, the influence of special interests on government can be considered a form of the control of decision making by public opinion. This is true because members of special-interest groups are members of the public, if for no other reasons. In addition, everyone is a member of some special-interest group, and a system which insures that each group has its wishes accommodated on a reasonable number of issues which particularly concern it can surely be considered some form of popular government, even if it does not insure that government members will act in accordance with majority opinion in all cases.

Public opinion, therefore, might influence government decisions because it introduces points of view into the decision-making process that government members must reconcile, because elite members provide government members with information, and because special interests persuade government members to act in accordance with their wishes. I am not claiming that public opinion frequently influences government in these ways. Nevertheless, this is a strong possibility. As a result, it is problematic that the authors of attitude studies rarely attempt to study the agenda-setting function of public opinion, the role of elite members as providers of information, or the influence of special interests. Authors focus their attention almost exclusively on whether and how mass opinion affects government decision making. My concern is that for the purposes of understanding the relationship between public opinion and government in the United States and for the purposes of improving our general understanding of the political system, this focus is far too narrow.

We can see why the focus of attitude studies which concentrate almost exclusively on the effect of majority opinion on government might be too narrow by imagining for a moment that the authors of these studies found that majority opinion rarely has this effect. Looking at the American political system from their perspective, we might be left with the impression that the public has no influence on the day-to-day course of public policymaking. We might conclude, that is, that government members do what they want to do regardless of public wishes. Alternatively, assuming that the authors found that majority opinion does influence government decisions, we might be left with the impression that this is the only way in which public opinion has an impact on public policy. In fact, it may well be the case that public opinion has a major and continuing influence on government decisions in some of the other ways mentioned earlier. These forms of the influence of public opinion may account for many of the decisions that government members make in particular cases and many of the ways in which they go about making decisions. In short, if we believe that public opinion often does set the agenda for government deliberations, that the elite does provide valuable information to government members, and that government members are influenced by special interests, we may believe that there is some form of popular government in the United States—even if we find that majority opinion does not influence public policy. Moreover, even if we find that majority opinion does influence public policy, we may draw different conclusions about what form popular government takes, depending on whether we believe that public opinion also influences government in the other ways outlined.

By concentrating almost exclusively on rule by public opinion (i.e., the influence of majority opinion on government), therefore, the authors of attitude studies may paint an incomplete and misleading picture of many aspects of the American political system. To determine whether public opinion influences government in other ways, the authors of attitude studies would have to change their research strategies in many of the same respects they would have to change those strategies to determine whether rule by public opinion is a reality. To look at the role of certain members of the public as providers of information, they would have to examine the elite more closely than they now do. To examine the agenda-setting function of public opinion and the influence of special interests, they would have to examine carefully the relationship between the elite and government and between the elite and the general public. These research directions would represent a considerable change of emphasis for the authors of attitude studies. But if the authors were to make this change, their studies could probably make a greater contribution to improving our general understanding of the American political system.

Summary of the Argument

The major thrust of my criticisms of attitude studies of rule by public opinion in Part III has been that the authors of these studies confine their attention to a single model of the relationship between public opinion and government: a model of how the views of a majority of the mass public influences government decisions. In this model, government actions come to correspond with majority views as a result of the operation of two processes. The first process is one by which members of the public elect members of government who share their basic political values and who, as a result, generally form the same opinions about specific issues that they do. The second process is one by which members of government learn from the elite what policies a majority of the public favors and feel obliged to adopt those policies. Neither of these are processes by which government and the elite form public opinion or by which members of the elite play any role in policymaking except as transmitters of opinion. Moreover, neither of these are processes by which limited sectors of society influence government decisions. The important elements in the model to which the authors of attitude studies confine their attention are government and the mass public; accordingly, most attitude studies have focused on these two elements.

In a sense, it is not surprising that the authors of attitude studies devote a great deal of attention to the model just described. After all, it is a model of the process which traditional theorists called "rule by public opinion," and Key, Miller and Stokes, and others say they are primarily interested in that process. Nevertheless, I have shown that the authors of attitude studies concentrate on the influence of majority opinion on government to the extent that they rarely discuss at length the possibilities that government and the elite might influence public views; that members of the elite might transmit their personal opinions, rather than the opinions held by a majority of the public, to government; or that limited sectors of the public might influence government decisions. More important, they do not consider these possibilities when they analyze data about the relationship between public opinion and government. Because the authors focus so exclusively on rule by public opinion, many of their findings are inconclusive; also, these authors may provide an incomplete and misleading picture of how the American political system operates.

At this point someone might object that my conclusions in this part are inconsistent with at least one of my conclusions in Part II. There I argued that people might vote for the same party over many years because that party generally adopts policies which they favor (see Chapter 6). In this part I have argued that members of government and other political leaders might not have a good idea of popular policy preferences and might not attempt to act in accordance with those preferences. Someone might argue, therefore, that if my conclusions in this part are correct, I must have been wrong to argue in the preceding part that party preferences might be determined by issue attitudes.

In fact, I do not think there is necessarily any contradiction between my conclusions in Parts II and III. In the preceding part I argued that party loyalties might endure for many years because members of government attempt to please members of the public *or* because members of government influence public views. Thus it is possible that even if the leaders of a particular party are unaware of popular views, and even if they do not attempt to act in accordance with those views, they might succeed in convincing certain members of the public to adopt their personal policy preferences over a period of many years. As a result, members of the public might share the political attitudes of the leaders of a certain party for a long time, and they might continue to vote for that party because they shared those attitudes. Party loyalties may therefore be due to issue attitudes regardless of whether politicians attempt to please members of the public.

In addition, in this part I have not argued that students of politics are wrong to say that the strong form of rule by public opinion accounts for correspondences between popular views and government actions. Rather, I have argued that their findings about this point are inconclusive. It is therefore possible that party loyalties may persist partly because public opinion influences politicians and partly because politicians influence public opinion.

Therefore, regardless of whether influence flows from government to the public or in the opposite direction, as long as there are correspondences between public views and government pronouncements, it is possible that party loyalties might be due to the fact that members of the public support the party which articulates policies consistent with their issue attitudes.

Traditional Theories

The authors of attitude studies did not, of course, invent the model of rule by public opinion that they employ; nor were they the first students of politics to focus their discussions of the relationship between public opinion and government on that model. As pointed out, one of the processes in that model—the process I have called "the strong form of rule by public opinion"—has been a major concern of public opinion theorists since the late eighteenth century. Indeed, traditional theorists considered public opinion important primarily because they believed that mass opinion transmitted by the elite influences government decisions. Thus Bryce writes that "the mass of the citizens may be deemed as directly the supreme power in the United States as the Assembly was at Athens or Syracuse." He believes that this occurs because "administrations are quick to catch its [the public's] wishes in whatever way they may be indicated." Moreover, although Bryce says that members of government may sometimes have difficulty determining what policies members of the public favor, he contends, "Generally, however, there are indications of the probable set of opinion in the language held by moderate men and the less partisan newspapers."[6] In short, Bryce and other traditional theorists understood the strong form of rule by public opinion in much the same way that contemporary researchers do. Moreover, they too seemed to consider it extremely important. Almost all their discussions of the relationship between public opinion and government are discussions of the influence of majority opinion on government. They infrequently discussed the influence of government on mass opinion or the influence of the elite or limited sectors of society on government.

In focusing on the model of rule by public opinion, therefore, the authors of attitude studies are perpetuating a way of discussing the relationship between public opinion and government that has a long ancestry. This model is interesting in itself, and it may illuminate certain aspects of the American political process. We can thus be grateful to traditional theorists for directing the attention of contemporary researchers to the possibility that government actions and public wishes might be linked in this way. The model becomes a liability to social science researchers, however, when they follow the example of traditional theorists by devoting most of their attention to it and when, in doing so, they neglect other possible relationships between public opinion and government.

One cannot, of course, claim that the model was a liability to traditional theorists in the same way it has been a liability to contemporary researchers. Traditional theorists were not engaged in quantitative analyses of public opinion. As a result, it is not possible to argue that because they focused on rule by public opinion, their analyses of survey data were inconclusive. Nevertheless, by suggesting that discussions of the relationship between public opinion and government should be primarily discussions of rule by public opinion, traditional theorists may well have set a precedent which is responsible for many of the difficulties of attitude studies. Moreover, traditional theorists share at least one important problem with contemporary researchers: Because they devote so much attention to rule by public opinion, they may create a misleading picture of the relationship between public opinion and government in the same ways contemporary researchers do.

Why Studies of Rule by Public Opinion Fail

One perplexing thing about the way both contemporary and traditional students of politics discuss rule by public opinion is that although they focus mainly on one model of the relationship between public views and government, they sometimes make statements which suggest that the model they adopt is not necessarily an accurate or comprehensive description of that relationship. It has already been pointed out that Key and the authors of other attitude studies occasionally mention that government and the elite may sometimes influence public opinion and that members of the elite may sometimes be inaccurate transmitters of public views. These same observations can be found in traditional discussions of rule by public opinion. For example, Bryce discusses the way government and the elite influence public views, and at one point he remarks on "how little there is of that individuality in the ideas of each individual which they would have if he had formed them for himself." Moreover, at another point he says that many elite members are in fact highly partisan and not to be relied on as transmitters of public opinion. In a famous passage, which was cited in Chapter 1, he concludes, "The obvious weakness of government by opinion is the difficulty of ascertaining it."[7]

There seem to be, therefore, at least two models of the relationship between public views and government found in both contemporary and traditional discussions of rule by public opinion. According to one model, majority opinion, transmitted by the elite, has a strong influence on government decisions; according to the other model, government, the mass public, and the elite are linked by channels of imperfect communication, and each exerts an influence on the others. For some reason attention has been focused mainly on the former model. If both contemporary and traditional students of politics realized that rule by public opinion is not the only relationship between public views and government, then why has this occurred?

Students of public opinion do not attempt to answer this question, so any attempt on my part to explain it is bound to contain a large element of speculation. Nevertheless, at least four possible reasons come to mind, all of which are similar to the reasons that were discussed in explaining why the authors of *The American Voter* might make the assumptions which prevent them from identifying motives for votes (see Chapter 8).

First, the model of rule by public opinion adopted by traditional theorists and authors of contemporary attitude studies is fairly simple compared to a model which would take into account the possibilities that the elite might not perfectly transmit public views and that influence might flow from government and the elite to the general public, as well as in the opposite direction. Moreover, attempting to determine whether the latter kind of model or any one of several alternative models accurately describes the relationship between public opinion and government would be a prodigious task involving the analysis of masses of data. The complexity of this task may have discouraged both modern and traditional theorists. In other words, they may have decided to devote most of their attention to their model of rule by public opinion primarily because it is simpler to comprehend and work with than other models are and because it would be prohibitively difficult for them to determine whether their model or some other model best describes the relationship between public opinion and government.

Second, both contemporary and traditional students of public opinion may have regarded the model of rule by public opinion on which they focus as only a broad generalization of certain basic tendencies in the American political system. They may never have thought of it as a comprehensive picture of the relationship between public opinion and government. Thus they may have focused on rule by public opinion rather than on other models of the relationship between public opinion and government because they believed that government actions correspond to public opinion more often in the United States than in other countries and that this is due to social and political conditions which, if not unique to America, are at least more fully developed there than elsewhere. Students of public opinion may have believed that in contrast to rule by public opinion, the influence of government and the elite on the general public can be found in many countries as well as in the United States. Thus they may have focused most of their attention on rule by public opinion simply because they considered it one of the most interesting and distinctive characteristics of the American political system.

Third, traditional and contemporary students of public opinion may have focused on rule by public opinion because they may have believed that findings about it have a special significance in terms of normative theories of democracy in at least two different ways. For one, students of public opinion may have believed that the influence of majority opinion on government is a defining characteristic of a democratic political system. Thus they may have thought it important to determine whether rule by public opinion operates in the United States in order to discover whether the American political system is democratic and, if it is, to determine how this important component functions. In fact, as already mentioned, both Key and the authors of *The American Voter* seem to be interested in rule by public opinion partly because they wish to determine how well the United States measures up to democratic political ideals; this may have been one reason they devote so much attention to that process.

I have argued, however, that it may be wrong to say that a political system can be democratic or popular only if, in that system, majority opinion influences government actions. Admittedly, we can determine whether a political system is democratic by determining whether members of the public exert some sort of control over the state in that system; but this does not necessarily mean that rule by majority opinion should be considered the *sine qua non* of democratic government. Even in a system in which majority opinion does not influence government decisions, public opinion might affect government in certain other ways; as I have said, a system in which it exerts other kinds of influence might be considered democratic.

Of course, some theorists might argue that majoritarianism is the only acceptable form of popular government, but it is beyond the scope of this work to discuss the merits of their point of view. If we reject that point of view, however, and if we wish to determine whether a particular political system is democratic, we should probably consider other characteristics of the relationship between public opinion and government in that system in addition to whether majority opinion influences government decisions.

Indeed if we wish to determine whether a country is democratic, it may not be necessary to consider public opinion at all. I argued earlier that findings about whether rule by public opinion occurs in a political system do not necessarily show whether that system is democratic because there are other ways in which public opinion might influence government and because a system in which public opinion is influential in these ways might be considered democratic or popular. I have, however, neglected the point—mentioned in my discussion of Rousseau in Chapter 1—that popular government should not be defined in terms of the relationship between public opinion and the state at all. I have neglected this point primarily because elaborating on it would require an extensive discussion of theories of democracy. Nevertheless, some of the kinds of political theory that might support that view of popular government can be discussed briefly.

To begin with, we might say that the most important characteristic of popular government is that members of the public can hold members of government accountable for their actions at election time, rather than that members of government are influenced in any sense by public views during their terms of office. As a variation on this, we might say that the most important characteristic of democratic government is that popular views expressed in certain organized and prescribed ways, such as in elections and referenda, rather than all views which members of the public hold, are binding on government. Both these notions about democracy are expressed by many contemporary theorists.[8]

We might say that another important characteristic of popular government is that public spokesmen are able to influence government decisions. We might add, however, that to qualify as a public spokesman an individual need not express the opinions of a majority of his constituents. For example, the members of a particular group might acknowledge (either tacitly or by taking some action, such as hiring a lobbyist) that they have authorized a certain individual to advocate positions to government which will further their interests. Moreover, we might say that members of the public may believe that government should heed the opinions expressed by such an individual even though they may not be aware of many of the issues on which he expressed opinions, and even though they may sometimes disagree with him. Finally, we might say that members of the public could exercise some control over a spokesman of this sort, not by inducing him to adopt their opinions but by no longer acknowledging him as their spokesman if they believe that, on the whole, his opinions do not further their interests.

If we believe that democratic or popular government should be described in any or all the ways just outlined, it is possible to argue that the authors of attitude studies are wrong to claim that their findings have much significance for evaluating the American political system in terms of normative theories of democracy. We could argue this by saying they are wrong to suppose that the relationship between public opinion and government is an important consideration in those theories.

For a variety of reasons, therefore, the authors of attitude studies may have been wrong to focus most of their attention on the relationship between majority opinion and government if they did so because they believed this would enable them to determine whether America has a system of popular government and how that system operates. Rightly or wrongly, however, the authors of attitude studies may have focused on rule by public opinion because they regarded it as the *sine qua non* for a democratic political system. Even if they did not believe this, as I mentioned above, they might have believed that rule by public opinion has a special significance in terms of normative theories of politics in a second way. As pointed out in Chapter 1, there are reasons why theorists who advocate representative government, rather than majority rule, should regard findings about the influence of majority opinion on government provocative. Advocates of representative democracy often express some fondness for majority rule even if they do not believe it is the best possible political system, and they may consider it important to differentiate their ideas about government from majoritarian notions. As a result, theorists who advocate representative democracy may devote a great deal of attention to rule by public opinion because they are interested in discovering how a majoritarian system works and in showing how it differs from the systems they favor.

Both traditional theorists and the authors of attitude studies may have focused on rule by public opinion for the three reasons I have been discussing. In addition, the authors of attitude studies may have adopted that focus for one other reason: They may have wished to follow in the footsteps of traditional theorists. I have shown in this and preceding chapters that they adopt many ideas which were first articulated by Tocqueville, Bryce, and other nineteenth-century thinkers. Contemporary researchers may believe that carefully worked out traditional theories provide a good starting point for research which should not be rejected too quickly. As a result, they may have devoted a great deal of attention to rule by public opinion because of the prominent place which discussions of that process played in traditional theories. In addition, while operating within the broad framework provided by traditional theorists, the authors of attitude studies may have wished to determine whether certain specific traditional notions are correct. In particular, they may have wished to determine whether majority opinion does in fact influence government actions in the United States. In their investigations, however, they may have accepted that any correspondences they find between public views and government actions are probably due to rule by public opinion because this was the hypothesis traditional theorists advanced most often.

All the reasons for focusing on rule by public opinion that have been discussed are valid to some extent. Surely simplicity of explanation is desirable, and there are particularly good reasons for adopting a fairly simple explanation of the relationship between public opinion and government if it highlights important aspects of a major political system or if it can help answer questions that are important in terms of normative political theory. Moreover, one can accept that the authors of attitude studies should not be too hasty in departing from ideas which have been accepted by students of politics for many decades. In short, there are undoubtedly many good reasons why both contemporary and traditional students of politics should have taken a special interest in rule by public opinion.

However, it is one thing for researchers to take a special interest in rule by public opinion and quite another thing for them to focus on that process so narrowly that they neglect the possibility that other processes might link public views to government actions. Although, for the purposes of simplicity of explanation, it may be attractive to say that correlations between government actions and public opinion must be due to the influence of majority opinion on government, it is not possible to determine whether this conclusion is correct unless one considers the possibility that those correlations might be due to the influence of government and the elite on the public. Although discussions of rule by public opinion may be intended only as discussions of one among many processes linking the public to government, my argument suggests that investigations of whether or how rule by public opinion functions must be conducted within the context of an understanding of other processes. Although rule by public opinion may be important because of its implications for normative theories of democracy, empirical investigations of it must take into account other possible relationships between public opinion and government that may not be as interesting in terms of those theories. Finally, although it may be wrong to dismiss traditional theories too quickly, attempts to determine whether certain parts of those theories are correct or to expand on them can be hampered if their weaknesses are accepted uncritically.

In short, although there is nothing intrinsically wrong with taking a special interest in rule by public opinion, both traditional and contemporary studies of public opinion are flawed because they focus almost exclusively on this form of the relationship between public opinion and government. Seen as attempts to explain the nature of popular government in the United States, they adopt a focus which may be too narrow in that it may lead them to neglect many important characteristics of the political system. Seen as empirical studies of the relationship between public opinion and government, they may apply that focus too narrowly in that they do not consider adequately that many of their findings might be explained by processes other than rule by public opinion.

IV. Summary and Conclusions

In a well-known article published over 20 years ago, Berelson wrote that "there exists a long and elegant tradition . . . for dealing with opinion problems; and this . . . theory provides a helpful framework for the organization and conduct of opinion studies." He promised that "the closer collaboration of political theorists and opinion researchers should contribute new problems, new categories, and greater refinement and elaboration on both sides."[1] Berelson's article is an appeal for public opinion researchers to pay more attention to normative democratic theory. But the sentences quoted can also be read as a description of the relationship that has long existed between public opinion research and both the empirical and normative aspects of traditional theories of public opinion. I have shown that public opinion researchers are very much in the debt of such theorists as Tocqueville, J.S. Mill, and Bryce. Likewise, through the application of attitude psychology, contemporary scholars have added greatly to the tradition of public opinion studies. In short, the marriage between traditional theories of public opinion and modern social science research techniques that Berelson called for has been consummated. Therefore, we can draw some tentative conclusions about whether his optimism about it was justified.

Successes

In many respects the marriage of public opinion theory to social science research has undoubtedly been successful. As with most marriages, its success has been due in large part to some important, although different, contributions by both partners. In light of the generally critical tone of my comments in preceding chapters, it seems appropriate at this point to emphasize what the beneficial contributions have been.

Traditional theorists have made three major contributions to public opinion research. First, they have contributed the concept of "public opinion" itself and certain ideas about why it is significant. Second, they have contributed the notion that one important component of studies of public opinion should be empirical investigations of how it is related to the processes of government. Third, they have suggested at least two well-elaborated models—one dealing with the influence of public opinion on elections and the other dealing with its influence on government decision making—that might describe parts of the relationship between public opinion and government.

These three contributions have established the basic intellectual framework within which contemporary public opinion research has developed. The authors of contemporary studies have adopted the traditional notion of public opinion, and, like traditional theorists, they consider public opinion significant because they believe it may influence the course of public affairs in many modern political systems. Moreover, the authors of public opinion studies have devoted their energies primarily to discovering whether and how this influence is exerted. In doing so, they have focused their investigations on the influence of public opinion on elections and government decision making; they have also followed up many of the specific insights into these functions of public opinion provided by traditional theorists, such as the traditional model of rule by public opinion.

When described in these broad terms, the influence of traditional theories on contemporary public opinion research must be judged beneficial. Certainly it is valuable for students of politics to discuss the relationship of mass opinion to the state. This is a subject that was neglected by classical theorists, for what may have been good reasons. Nevertheless, it is a subject of great importance for contemporary students of politics because the course of events has thrust it into prominence, if for no other reason. In many countries today the views of the mass of citizens can powerfully affect the course of public affairs by affecting votes, and there is some reason to believe that, as a result, those views may have an effect on government decision making. If this is true, modern political systems cannot be understood fully without understanding the role of public opinion, and normative conclusions about certain aspects of those systems may depend on findings about public opinion. Thus traditional theorists have certainly performed a valuable service by directing the attention of students of politics to the significance of public opinion.

Certainly, too, they have performed a valuable service by suggesting that studies of public opinion should have strong empirical components. Unless we have a firm understanding of exactly what role public opinion plays in political systems, it is hard to know what role it should play in political thought. Is it a significant or trivial element in politics? Does it have effects that might be regarded as beneficial in terms of normative theories of politics, or are its effects harmful?

Finally, the two models of the relationship between public opinion and government that traditional theorists developed have certainly been valuable starting points for research on public opinion. They have identified some likely ways in which public opinion might have an impact on the political process and have suggested some important considerations to be taken into account in studying its impact.

Attitude psychology has also had many beneficial effects on public opinion research. Attitude psychologists have contributed a sophisticated body of theories and techniques that has made it possible to pursue empirical investigations of public opinion with a precision unknown to traditional theorists. This has been possible because, in many ways, attitude psychology complements traditional public opinion theory. To begin with, the concept of "attitude" is in many ways similar to the concept of "opinion" used by traditional theorists. Moreover, when they refer to "distributions of public attitudes," psychologists mean much the same thing that traditional theorists meant by "public opinion." Finally, attitude psychologists have the necessary tools to answer many of the questions about public opinion that traditional theorists considered important, even if they have not always used those tools to maximum advantage. For example, attitude psychology can be applied to record the distribution of public attitudes on particular matters, to analyze the motivations of large numbers of people, and to relate the political behavior of members of the public to various social and political influences. Because attitude psychology complements public opinion theory in these ways, attitude psychologists can argue convincingly that they have been able to provide the strong empirical component of opinion studies which traditional theorists could not provide.

By adopting the intellectual framework developed by traditional public opinion theorists, therefore, contemporary public opinion researchers have been able to raise questions of importance for political studies; by applying attitude psychology within that framework, they have been able to avail themselves of powerful tools for answering those questions. Because of the contributions of traditional theorists and attitude psychologists, the authors of contemporary public opinion studies have been able to produce many valuable findings. Their solid accomplishments over the last few decades are too numerous to list here, but a few examples can be mentioned. To begin with, we now have an understanding of the level of political information and participation of different sectors of the general public and of many of the factors that affect both. Moreover, we have come to understand many of the factors that cause nonvoting and to appreciate the importance of an individual's early life in the formation of political attitudes. Finally, the mandate theory of elections, in at least its crude form, has been laid to rest. All these are impressive accomplishments that have furthered an understanding not only of public opinion, but also of many other aspects of the political systems of modern states.

Failures

I have argued, however, that despite their successes public opinion researchers have failed in the two tasks to which they have devoted most of their attention: identifying motives for votes and explaining the relationship between public opinion and government decision making. This is distressing because, like traditional theorists, contemporary researchers believe that public opinion plays an important role in the political process mainly because it influences the outcomes of elections and affects government decisions through a process of rule by public opinion. To conduct meaningful investigations of these two functions of public opinion, however, it is necessary for contemporary researchers to determine which attitudes motivate voting choices and whether and how public attitudes influence government decisions.

These tasks are important in themselves because they can provide the answers to many of the major questions that traditional and modern students of politics have raised about public opinion. For example, if researchers can identify motives for votes, they can tell us whether policy differences between candidates affect the outcomes of elections; if they can show how public opinion is related to government decision making, they can tell us what role the political elite plays in at least one aspect of the political process. Moreover, these tasks are important because unless they can be accomplished, the significance for political studies of many other findings about political attitudes will be in doubt. For example, if we do not know whether issue attitudes influence the outcomes of elections or government decisions, what is the significance for political studies of findings that those attitudes are based on little information or are influenced by the press? If issue attitudes do have a bearing on politics, such findings have broad ramifications; if they do not, such findings may be of interest to psychologists and sociologists, but will be of less interest to political scientists.

By failing to identify the attitudes that motivate votes and by failing to show whether and how public opinion influences government decisions, therefore, the authors of attitude studies have been unable to illuminate the aspects of public opinion which they and traditional theorists have considered most significant for political studies. There are undoubtedly many reasons for this failure. Identifying the motivations of large numbers of people and tracing the process of rule by public opinion are more difficult tasks technically than many of the other tasks (e.g., identifying the level of public information about certain issues) that the authors of attitude studies have undertaken. Although the theories and techniques of attitude psychology are probably equal to the tasks of identifying motives for votes and tracing rule by public opinion, the research designs that those tasks require are extremely difficult to devise, and massive amounts of data would be needed to implement those designs. Because public opinion research is a fairly new field of scholarship having limited resources, it should not be surprising that opinion researchers have not yet mastered the most difficult problems facing them.

Aside from the technical difficulties, however, there are more fundamental problems with contemporary studies of motives for votes and of rule by public opinion. In the preceding chapters I have shown that studies of both sorts are primarily hampered not by a lack of technical virtuosity but, rather, by a theoretical focus which is too narrow. In the case of studies of motives for votes, most of the difficulties arise because the authors assume that mass opinion (distributions of individual opinions on subjects of concern to most members of the public) must be the major influence on the outcomes of elections. They neglect the possibility that elections might be decided by opinions on a variety of subjects, each of which is of particular interest to only a limited sector of society. In the case of studies of rule by public opinion, major difficulties arise because the authors fail to consider the possibility that the elite might play an active role in the influence process and that influence might flow from government and the elite to the general public as well as from the general public to government and the elite.

The authors of attitude studies neglect the various possibilities in that they fail to take them into account in designing hypotheses about motives for votes and rule by public opinion and in testing those hypotheses. As a result, in important cases they assume their data have substantiated certain hypotheses about public opinion and proceed to draw conclusions on the basis of that assumption, but, in fact, those data might be explained equally well by other hypotheses that would lead to other conclusions. For this reason I have said that the theoretical focus of attitude studies of public opinion is too narrow and that many of the studies' findings are inconclusive.

I have shown that the deficiencies in the theoretical focus of public opinion research can be traced partly to similar deficiencies in traditional theories of public opinion. Traditional theorists were, to say the least, confusing in their treatment of the points I have raised. Certainly they were aware that views on subjects of concern to limited sectors of society could influence the outcomes of elections, that the elite often plays an active role in the relationship between public opinion and government, and that influence can flow from government and the elite to the general public. They also believed, however, that mass opinion influences the outcomes of elections, that the elite generally transmits public views with reasonable accuracy, and that government is malleable in the face of public opinion. Traditional theorists did not distinguish clearly between these two sets of ideas, and both can be found in their work, often used interchangeably. For example, they sometimes referred to public opinion as mass opinion and sometimes as the opinions of limited sectors of society, and one is often not sure which kind of public opinion they were referring to when they said that the views of the public influence the outcomes of elections. On the whole, however, traditional theorists emphasized the notions that mass opinion influences the outcomes of elections and that the relationship between public opinion and government is one in which influence flows from the public through the elite to government. Most of their general theories about the relationship of public opinion to the political process were cast in these terms, and these are the characteristics of public opinion they most often discussed. There is apparently no valid reason for this narrowness of theoretical focus, but it is found in almost all discussions of public opinion by nineteenth- and twentieth-century theorists.

In addition to inheriting much that is of value from traditional public opinion theorists, therefore, the authors of attitude studies have inherited a theoretical framework which, even in light of many of the observations of those theorists, is too narrowly focused. This in itself would not be problematic if the authors of attitude studies had not assumed that this framework is correct. For example, if they had adopted the notion that mass opinion influences the outcomes of elections as a working hypothesis and tested it in light of other traditional ideas about how public opinion might influence elections, they would not have encountered many of the difficulties I have outlined. Instead, however, they have implicitly assumed that mass opinion must be the major influence on votes, and they have not adequately considered other possibilities. Thus, although they claim that one of their major contributions to discussions of public opinion is to subject the conclusions of traditional theorists to rigorous empirical testing, they have not tested some of the most fundamental and problematic conclusions which those theorists draw.

I have shown, therefore, that the failures of attitude studies of public opinion are in large part due to their uncritical acceptance of certain problematic notions advanced by traditional public opinion theorists. Just as the authors of attitude studies have benefited greatly from their loyalty to many of the ideas of traditional theorists, they have also suffered from their loyalty to other ideas. The difficulties which result from that loyalty are far more worrisome than technical difficulties. The authors of attitude studies are aware of the need for ever greater technical sophistication, and this encourages the hope that whatever technical difficulties there are will be overcome. Because the problematic assumptions I have outlined are fundamental to their thinking about public opinion, however, it may be that they are unaware of them and will not try to come to grips with them.

Lessons

All in all, the marriage of attitude psychology to traditional theories of public opinion has produced some promising results as well as some disappointments. If there is one general conclusion which emerges from this review of results to date, it is that the success of the marriage between two fields of scholarship depends on the contributions of both partners. All the technical expertise in the world will not produce findings of significance for political studies unless that expertise is channeled into the proper directions by a sufficiently comprehensive theoretical framework. I cannot claim that this conclusion is original or even striking, but I do believe it is applicable to attitude studies of public opinion. It is a failure to develop a broad enough theoretical framework that has led the authors of these studies into difficulties.

There is one hopeful aspect of these difficulties, however. By attempting to impose empirical rigor on traditional notions about public opinion and by encountering difficulties in doing so, contemporary investigators have at least highlighted the confusion surrounding those notions. The realization that confusion exists may be the starting point for a reformulation of public opinion theory that will be significant in itself and will pave the way for even more substantial contributions to the study of politics. Perhaps, therefore, the difficulties I have outlined are simply the growing pains of a new discipline. If this is true, we can look forward to the fulfillment of at least one of Berelson's prophecies about the relationship of social science research to political theory. Regarding the future of the marriage between these two fields, he writes that we can not only expect that "the theorists can suggest new concepts and hypotheses for the researcher"; we can also expect that "the researcher can force the theorists to sharpen and differentiate . . . their formulations."[2]

Notes

Chapter 1

1. Although most political theorists have been interested in what is here called "the public"—the mass of people who do not hold government office—it was not until the late eighteenth century that they devoted much attention to "public opinion" in the sense that I define it. The authors of most histories of the concept of public opinion seem to agree with this. They also seem to agree that before the late eighteenth century references to public opinion were infrequent and had little significance in the works of the theorists who made them. See, for example, Paul A. Palmer, "The Concept of Public Opinion in Political Theory," in *Essays in History and Political Theory in Honor of Charles Howard McIlwain* (Cambridge, Mass.: Harvard University Press, 1936), pp. 230–57; and Francis Graham Wilson, *A Theory of Public Opinion* (Chicago: Regnery, 1962), pp. 1–137. Bauer, however, treats all discussions of the public as, in some sense, discussions of public opinion, although, like other commentators on that concept, he devotes most of his attention to eighteenth- and nineteenth-century authors (Wilhelm Bauer, "Public Opinion," in *Encyclopaedia of Social Sciences* [New York: Macmillan, 1948], 12: 669–74).

2. Avery Leiserson, "Political Opinion," in *The International Encyclopaedia of Social Sciences* (London: Macmillan, 1968), 13: 197; Jeremy Bentham, "Securities against Misrule," in *The Works of Jeremy Bentham,* ed. John Bowring (1823; repr. New York: Russell & Russell, 1962), 8: 400; and Walter Lippmann, *Public Opinion* (New York: Macmillan, 1960), p. 400.

3. Alexis de Tocqueville, *Democracy in America* (1840; paperback ed. New York: Vintage Books, 1945), vols. 1 and 2 (Volume 1 is of most interest to me here, and all my future references are to it); James Bryce, *The American Commonwealth* (1888; paperback ed. New York: Capricorn Books, 1959), pp. 280–378; Lippman, *Public Opinion;* and Walter Lippmann, *The Phantom Public* (New York: Harcourt, Brace, 1925).

4. A.V. Dicey, *Law and Public Opinion in England* (London: Macmillan, 1963); Walter Bagehot, *The English Constitution* (1866; repr. London: Kegan Paul, Trench, Trubner, 1929), pp. 160–75; and Tocqueville, p. 129.

5. John Stuart Mill, "On Liberty," in *Utilitarianism, Liberty, and Representative Government* (1859; repr. New York: Dutton, 1951), pp. 152–200; the quoted matter is from p. 166.

6. Tocqueville, p. 276; and Bryce, pp. 298, 283.

7. Mill, p. 165; Bagehot, p. 166; and Mill, p. 165.

8. Emden argues that in early nineteenth-century England, many writers regarded "the public" in a somewhat different way than I have said Mill and Bagehot did. Emden says that the public usually consisted of those people who did not yet have the right to vote, but who got it in the next round of parliamentary reform. This still means that the public consisted of a large group of people, but it was a different group than Mill and Bagehot seem to have had in mind. Although Emden may be correct about the way popular political commentators regarded the public, most major theorists in the nineteenth century regarded it as either all the citizens of the state who did not hold government office or as all voters (Cecil E. Emden, *The People and the Constitution,* 2nd ed. [London: Oxford University Press, 1956]).

9. Mill, p. 92; and Bryce, p. 283.

10. Mill, p. 113.

11. Bryce, pp. 334–36.

12. Mill, p. 206.

13. Bryce, p. 283; and Mill, p. 118.

14. Lippmann, *Public Opinion,* pp. 16–24.

15. Bryce, pp. 281–83; Tocqueville, p. 276; and Dicey, p. 3.

16. Tocqueville, pp. 271–72; Edmund Burke, "Speech to the Electors of Bristol: November 3, 1774," in *The Works and Correspondence of Edmund Burke* (London: Francis & John Rivington, 1852), 3: 236–37; and Tocqueville, pp. 62–82.

17. For a discussion of the way in which Gabriel Tarde and Josef Christiansen understood public opinion, see Wilson, pp. 125–33, 135–37; A. Lawrence Lowell, *Public Opinion and Popular Government,* 2nd ed. (New York: Longman's, 1914), pp. 12–15; Arthur F. Bentley, *The Process of Government* (Evanston, Ill.: Principia Press of Illinois, 1949), pp. 136–53, 223–40; and David Truman, *The Governmental Process* (New York: Knopf, 1951), pp. 1–32.

18. William Albig, *Public Opinion* (New York: McGraw-Hill, 1939), p. 3.

19. Bryce, p. 283.

20. Tocqueville, pp. 180, 264–97; and Mill, pp. 85–102, 152–200.

21. The distinction between adopting a certain view as one's own and believing that government should act in accordance with it because it has won out over other views in an agreed on government decision-making process is an interesting one. It is not important for my purposes, however, whether this distinction is valid or how it should be made. For a discussion of the distinction see Brian Barry, *Political Argument* (London: Routledge & Kegan Paul, 1965), pp. 58–66.

22. Tocqueville, p. 180.

23. Mill, pp. 175, 174.

24. Bryce, p. 292.

25. Ibid., p. 299.

26. Tocqueville, p. 262; and Bryce, p. 370.

27. Bryce, pp. 270, 332, 334.

28. For general discussions of how public opinion is conveyed to government, see Bryce, pp. 335–40, and Tocqueville, pp. 180–205.

29. For general discussions of the advantages and disadvantages of rule by public opinion, see Bryce, pp. 359–78, and Tocqueville, pp. 246–80.

30. Bryce, p. 369.

31. Ibid., p. 369.

32. Ibid., p. 359.

33. Paul F. Lazarsfeld, "Public Opinion and the Classical Tradition," *Public Opinion Quarterly* 21, no. 1 (1957): 41.

34. Palmer, pp. 238–40.

35. These are familiar ideas about liberalism found in many commentaries on the history of political thought. See, for example, George H. Sabine, *A History of Political Theory,* 3rd ed. (New York: Holt, Rinehart & Winston, 1961), pp. 669–754.

36. John Stuart Mill, "Representative Government," in *Utilitarianism, Liberty, and Representative Government* (1861; repr. New York: Dutton, 1951), p. 278.

37. Ibid., pp. 279, 290–92.

38. Ibid., p. 479.

39. Ibid., pp. 271–92, 381–84.

40. Ibid., pp. 323, 421.

41. Ibid., p. 426.

42. Ibid., pp. 423–36.

43. G.W.F. Hegel, *Philosophy of Right,* trans. T.M. Knox (1821; translation published, London: Oxford University Press, 1952), pp. 204–5. Pages 236–37 of "Speech to the Electors of Bristol" contains one of the few passages in which Burke uses the phrase "public opinion." Although he is interested in the relationship between the public and government in many of his works, his discussions of that relationship usually deal with whether members of the public should be able to elect their sovereign or make changes in their constitution, rather than whether they should be able to influence legislation. See, for example, Edmund Burke, "Reflections on the Revolution in France and on the Proceedings in Certain Societies in London Relative to That Event," in *The Works and Correspondence of Edmund Burke* (London: Francis & John Rivington, 1852), 4: 153–355.Because I have suggested that public opinion is generally regarded as a collection of opinions about particular issues which are or might become the subject of legislation, and because Burke himself generally uses the term in this way, it is fair to say that he rarely refers to public opinion and that when he does, his references are brief.

44. Jean-Jacques Rousseau, "The Social Contract," in *The Social Contract and Dis-*

courses, trans. G.D.H. Cole (1762, translation published, New York: Dutton, 1950), p. 53. As far as I can tell, this is the only point at which Rousseau uses the phrase "l'opinion publique" in *The Social Contract.* For readers with other editions, this passage can be found in Book 2, Chapter 12.

45. Ibid., pp. 13–19, 23–37, 54–60, 89–92.
46. Ibid., pp. 17, 23–27; see, especially, p. 26.
47. Ibid., pp. 93–96.
48. Ibid., pp. 89–92.

Chapter 2

1. For an excellent history of the concept of "attitude," see Donald Fleming, "Attitude: The History of a Concept," in *Perspectives in American History,* ed. Donald Fleming and Bernard Bailyn (Cambridge, Mass.: Charles Warren Center for Studies in American History, 1967), 1: 287–365.Fleming's article is, to my mind, the best general history of attitude psychology. Other important surveys are Gordon W. Allport, "Attitudes," in *Handbook of Social Psychology,* ed. C.A. Murchison (Worcester, Mass.: Clark University Press, 1935), pp. 798–844; and Gordon W. Allport, "The Historical Background of Modern Social Psychology," in *Handbook of Social Psychology,* ed. Gardner Lindzey (Cambridge, Mass.: Addison-Wesley, 1954), p. 356.

2. It should be apparent from Figure 2.1 that most psychologists refer to attitudes as "dispositions." This word has been used in definitions of attitudes for over 50 years, and it is probably impossible to determine who first introduced it into the vocabulary of social psychologists. The notion that attitudes are comprised of cognitive, affective, and behavioral components is of more recent vintage. It was first formulated by Krech and Crutchfield in 1948, and it has since been incorporated into many general discussions of attitudes. See David Krech and Richard S. Crutchfield, *Theory and Problems of Social Psychology* (New York: McGraw-Hill, 1948); Paul F. Secord and Carl W. Backman, *Social Psychology* (New York: McGraw-Hill, 1964), p. 97; Daniel Katz and Ezra Stotland, "A Preliminary Statement of a Theory of Attitude Structure and Change," in *Psychology: A Study of a Science,* ed. Sigmund Koch (New York: McGraw-Hill, 1959), 3: 428–29; and James D. Halloran, *Attitude Formation and Change* (Leicester, England: Leicester University Press, 1967), p. 21.

3. Donald T. Campbell, "Acquired Behavioral Dispositions," in *Psychology: A Study of a Science,* ed. Sigmund Koch (New York: McGraw-Hill, 1963), 6: 97; Irving Sarnoff, "Social Attitudes and Resolution of Motivational Conflict," in *Attitudes,* ed. Marie Jahoda and Neil Warren (London: Penguin Books, 1966), p. 279; Arthur R. Cohen, "Attitudinal Consequences of Induced Discrepancies Between Cognitions and Behaviour," *Public Opinion Quarterly* 24, no. 2 (1960): 299; E.S. Bogardus, quoted in Otto Kleinberg, *Social Psychology* (New York: Henry Holt, 1940), p. 349; C.B. Osgood, G.J. Suci, and P.H. Tannenbaum, *The Measurement of Meaning* (Urbana: University of Illinois Press, 1957), p. 198; Muzafer Sherif and Hadley Cantril, *The Psychology of Ego-Involvements* (New York: Wiley, 1966), p. 17; Gordon W. Allport, "Attitudes," in *Handbook of Social Psychology,* ed. C.M. Murchison (Worcester, Mass.: Clark University Press, 1935), p. 45; Isidor Chein, "Behavior Theory and the Behavior of Attitudes," *Psychological Review* 55, no. 3 (1948): 117; M. Brewster Smith, "Attitude Change," in *The International Encyclopedia of Social Sciences* (New York: Macmillan, 1968), 1: 458; Theodore M. Newcomb, *Personality and Social Change* (New York: Holt, Rinehart & Winston, 1943), p. 18; Milton Rokeach, "Attitudes," in *International Encyclopedia of Social Sciences,* p. 450; Daniel Katz and Ezra Stotland, "A Preliminary Statement to a Theory of Attitude Structure and Change," in *Psychology: A Study of a Science,* ed. Sigmund Koch (New York: McGraw-Hill, 1959), 3: 428; E.E. Davis, *Attitude Change* (New York: UNESCO, 1965), p. 7; M. Brewster Smith, Jerome Bruner, and Robert W. White, *Opinions and Personality* (New York: Wiley, 1956), p. 7; David Krech, Richard S. Crutchfield, and Egerton L. Ballachey, *Individual in Society* (New York: McGraw-Hill, 1962), p. 139; Paul F. Secord and Carl W. Backman, *Social Psychology* (New York: McGraw-Hill, 1964), p. 97; Marie Jahoda, Mor-

ton Deutsch, and Stuart Cook, *Research Methods in Social Relations* (New York: Dryden Press, 1951), p. 112; L.L. Thurstone, "Attitudes Can Be Measured," *American Sociological Review* 33, no. 4 (1928): 531; and W.I. Thomas and Florian Znanecki, *The Polish Peasant in Europe and America* (Boston: Badger Publishing, 1918), p. 27.

4. Muzafer Sherif and Hadley Cantril, *The Psychology of Ego-Involvements* (New York: Wiley, 1947), p. 19.

5. See, for example, Secord and Backman, p. 98; and David Krech, Richard S. Crutchfield, and Egerton Ballachey, *Individual in Society* (New York: McGraw-Hill, 1962), p. 141.

6. See, for example, Krech, Crutchfield, and Ballachey, p. 140; and Sherif and Cantril, p. 25.

7. See, for example, Secord and Backman, p. 98; Sherif and Cantril, pp. 29–43; and Milton J. Rosenberg, "An Analysis of Affective-Cognitive Consistency," in *Attitude Organization and Change,* ed. Carl I. Hovland and Milton J. Rosenberg (New Haven, Conn.: Yale University Press, 1960), pp. 15–24.

8. See, for example, Krech, Crutchfield, and Ballachey, p. 140.

9. See, for example, ibid.; Secord and Backman, p. 98; and M. Brewster Smith, "Attitude Change," in *The International Encyclopedia of Social Sciences* (New York: Macmillan, 1968), 1: 458.

10. See, for example, Secord and Backman, p. 109; Krech, Crutchfield, and Ballachey, p. 142; and William J. McGuire, "The Nature of Attitudes and Attitude Change," in *The Handbook of Social Psychology,* ed. Gardner Lindzey and Elliot Aronson (Reading, Mass.: Addison-Wesley, 1968), p. 156.

11. See, for example, Secord and Backman, pp. 108–24; Krech, Crutchfield, and Ballachey, pp. 142–44; and Katz and Stotland, p. 444.

12. See, for example, McGuire, p. 156; and Secord and Backman, p. 98.

13. Some psychologists distinguish between descriptions of the affective component of an attitude and descriptions of the evaluative posture which all three components display, and they say that assignments of attitudes are descriptions of the latter sort (see, for example, Krech, Crutchfield, and Ballachey, p. 142). Other psychologists seem to believe this distinction is unnecessary and say that assignments of attitudes are descriptions of their affective components (see, for example, McGuire, p. 156). For my purposes, it is not important to determine which formulation is correct. I have chosen to say that assignments of attitudes are descriptions of their affective components primarily because this is a simpler formulation than saying they are descriptions of some characteristic of all three components.

14. See, for example, Allport, "Modern Social Psychology," p. 45; Sherif and Cantril, p. 21; and Krech, Crutchfield, and Ballachey, p. 146.

15. For example, Campbell writes that psychologists generally assign attitudes to an individual on the basis of evidence that his expressions of evaluation are stable and predictable (Donald T. Campbell, "Acquired Behavioral Dispositions," in *Psychology: A Study of a Science,* ed. Sigmund Koch [New York: McGraw-Hill, 1963], 6: 96).

16. Allport, "Modern Social Psychology," p. 45. Fleming traces the history of the notion that attitudes are "underlying" tendencies (Fleming, pp. 338–50).

17. The best-known discussion of these questions is found in Gilbert Ryle, *The Concept of Mind* (1949; repr. London: Penguin Books, 1966).

18. Discussions of the ideas of psychologists who have held this point of view can be found in McGuire, pp. 143–45, and Campbell, pp. 95–97.

19. Sherif and Cantril, pp. 1–28; and M. Brewster Smith, Jerome S. Bruner, and Robert W. White. *Opinions and Personality* (New York: Wiley, 1956), pp. 1–47.

20. Campbell, pp. 95–164.

21. Ibid.

22. Krech, Crutchfield, and Ballachey, pp. 216–19; Rosenberg, pp. 15–65; and William J. McGuire, "Cognitive Consistency and Attitude Change," *Journal of Abnormal and Social Psychology* 60, no. 2 (1960): 345–53.

23. For discussions of the relationship of action tendencies to other attitude components, see R.T. LaPierre, "Attitudes Versus Actions," *Social Forces* 14, no. 2 (1934):

230–37; Milton Rokeach, "Attitude Change and Behavioral Change," *Public Opinion Quarterly* 30, no. 4 (1966): 429–50; Raymond L. Gordon, "Interaction Between Attitude and the Definition of the Situation in the Expression of Opinion," in *Public Opinion and Propaganda,* ed. Daniel Katz (New York: Holt, Rinehart & Winston, 1965), pp. 425–34; Arthur R. Cohen, *Attitude Change and Social Influence* (New York: Basic Books, 1964), pp. 1–35; Carl I. Hovland, "Reconciling Conflicting Results Derived from Experimental and Survey Studies of Attitude Change," *American Psychologist* 14, no. 1 (1959): 8–17; Leon Festinger, "Behavioral Support for Opinion Change," *Public Opinion Quarterly* 28, no. 3 (1964): 404–17; Howard Schuman, "Attitudes vs. Actions *versus* Attitudes vs. Attitudes," *Public Opinion Quarterly* 36, no. 3 (1972): 347–54; and Alan G. Weinstein, "Predicting Behavior from Attitudes," *Public Opinion Quarterly* 36, no. 3 (1972): 455–60.

24. For a summary of findings about the kinds of attitude that most often have consistent behavioral components, see Irving Crespi, "What Kinds of Attitude Measures Are Predictive of Behavior?" *Public Opinion Quarterly* 35, no. 3 (1971): 327–34.

25. For reports of the classical forced compliance studies, see Secord and Backman, pp. 148–59; Krech, Crutchfield, and Ballachey, pp. 253–259; Arthur R. Cohen, "Attitudinal Consequences of Induced Discrepancies Between Cognitions and Behavior," *Public Opinion Quarterly* 24, no. 2 (1960): 297–318.

26. See, for example, Krech, Crutchfield, and Ballachey, pp. 226–231; Sherif and Cantril, pp. 45–50; and Smith, Bruner, and White, pp. 259–66.

27. See, for example, Sherif and Cantril, pp. 19–20; and Campbell, pp. 95–97.

28. See, for example, Sherif and Cantril, pp. 45–60; and Secord and Backman, pp. 200–205.

29. All the books and articles cited in note 23 contain discussions of this point.

30. For a summary of findings that individuals may form only one or two, rather than all three, attitude components, see, Katz and Stotland, pp. 430–35.

31. Most of the books and articles cited in note 23 contain discussions of this point.

32. Leon Festinger, *A Theory of Cognitive Dissonance* (London: Tavistock Publications, 1959); Fritz Heider, *The Psychology of Interpersonal Relations* (New York: Wiley, 1967); C.E. Osgood, G.J. Suci, and P.H. Tannenbaum, *The Measurement of Meaning* (Urbana: University of Illionois Press, 1957); Jack W. Brehm and Arthur R. Cohen, *Explorations in Cognitive Dissonance* (New York: Wiley, 1962); and Muzafer Sherif and Carl I. Hovland, *Social Judgment* (New Haven: Yale University Press, 1961). For a general discussion of the homeostatic principle, see Nathan Maccoby and Eleanor E. Maccoby, "Homeostatic Theory in Attitude Change," *Public Opinion Quarterly* 25, no. 4 (1961): 538–45.

33. Festinger, *Cognitive Dissonance*, p. 3.

34. Ibid.

35. Ibid., pp. 278–79.

36. Ibid., pp. 3–7, 260–80.

37. Festinger does not say exactly what he means by the "importance" of cognitions, but he apparently believes that one cognition may be more important than another for many reasons. For example, a cognition about my wife would be more important to me than a cognition about a stranger because I am more emotionally involved with my wife. A cognition that I have won $1,000,000 in a lottery would be more important to me than a cognition that I have won $1, because $1,000,000 will enable me to enjoy life more. Festinger discusses the "importance" of cognition on page seven of *Cognitive Dissonance.*

38. Heider, pp. 174–217.

39. Ibid., p. 180.

40. For general discussions of techniques for assigning attitudes, see Secord and Backman, pp. 97–126; Krech, Crutchfield, and Ballachey, pp. 150–69; Philip E. Vernon, *Personality Tests and Assessments* (London: Methuen, 1962); Alan L. Edwards, *Techniques of Attitude Scale Construction* (New York: Appleton-Century-Crofts, 1957); H.H. Remmers, *Introduction to Opinion and Attitude Measurement* (New York: Harper, 1954); Mildred B. Parten, *Surveys, Polls, and Samples* (New York: Harper, 1965), pp. 71–105; Marvin E. Shaw and Jack M. Wright, *Scales for the Measurement of Attitudes* (New York: McGraw-Hill, 1967), pp. 15–32; Warren F. Torgerson, *Theory and Methods of Scaling* (New York: Wiley, 1958); Paul Horst, *Psychological Measurement and Prediction*

(Belmont, Calif.: Wadsworth Publishing, 1966); and Hadley Cantril, *Gauging Public Opinion* (Princeton, N.J.: Princeton University Press, 1944).

41. L.L. Thurstone, "Attitudes Can Be Measured," *The American Journal of Sociology*, 33, no. 4 (1928): 532.

42. Ibid., pp. 533–534, 543.

43. Two other methods of assigning attitudes are often mentioned in standard works about attitude psychology: Likert scaling and Lazarsfeld's latent structure analysis. Neither of these is commonly used in attitude studies of public opinion, however. See Gardner Murphy and Rensis Likert, *Public Opinion and the Individual* (New York: Russell & Russell, 1967); and Paul F. Lazarsfeld, "The Logical and Mathematical Foundation of Latent Structure Analysis," in *Measurement and Prediction*, ed. Samuel A. Stouffer (Princeton, N.J.: Princeton University Press, 1950), pp. 362–412.

44. For explanations of the mechanics of Thurstone scaling and the assumptions on which this technique is based, see Thurstone, "Attitudes," pp. 529–53; L.L. Thurstone, "The Law of Comparative Judgment," *Psychological Review* 34, no. 1 (1927): 155–204; and L.L. Thurstone and E.J. Chave, *The Measurement of Attitudes* (Chicago: University of Chicago Press, 1929).

45. For an explanation of Guttman scaling, see Louis Guttman, "The Problem of Attitude and Opinion Measurement," "The Basis for Scalogram Analysis," "The Scalogram Board Technique for Scale Analysis," and "The Utility of Scalogram Analysis," in *Measurement and Prediction*, pp. 46–121.

46. Bernard Berelson, *Content Analysis in Communications Research* (Glencoe, Ill.: Free Press, 1952).

47. Smith, Bruner, and White, pp. 52–60; and T.W. Adorno, Else Frankel-Brunswik, David J. Levinson, and R. Nevitt Sanford, *The Authoritarian Personality* (New York: Harper, 1950), especially pp. 13–27.

48. See, for example, Krech, Crutchfield, and Ballachey, pp. 199–213; Secord and Backman, pp. 109–26; and Carl I. Hovland and Irving L. Janis, *Personality and Persuasibility* (New Haven, Conn.: Yale University Press, 1959).

49. V.O. Key, Jr., *Public Opinion and American Democracy* (New York: Knopf, 1961), p. 208.

50. Samuel A. Stouffer, "An Overview of the Contributions to Scaling and Scale Theory," in *Measurement and Prediction*, p. 5.

51. Ibid., p. 40.

52. Ibid., pp. 41–44.

53. See, for example, Edward A. Suchman, "The Intensity Component in Attitude and Opinion Research," in *Measurement and Prediction*, pp. 213–76.

Chapter 3

1. Angus Campbell, Philip E. Converse, Warren E. Miller, and Donald E. Stokes, *The American Voter* (New York: Wiley, 1960); Bernard R. Berelson, Paul F. Lazarsfeld, and William N. McPhee, *Voting* (Chicago: University of Chicago Press, 1954); V.O. Key, Jr., *Public Opinion and American Democracy* (New York: Knopf, 1961); and Robert E. Lane and David O. Sears, *Public Opinion* (Englewood Cliffs, N.J.: Prentice-Hall, 1965).

There are two editions of *The American Voter*. The first edition, which I have cited, was published in 1960, and an abridged edition was published in 1964 (Angus Campbell, Philip E. Converse, Warren E. Miller, and Donald E. Stokes, *The American Voter: An Abridgement* [New York: Wiley, 1964]). The two editions contain the same arguments presented in much the same way. I was in somewhat of a quandary about which edition to cite, however. On the one hand, the 1960 edition has been out of print for many years and the explanations in the 1964 edition are often more concise. On the other hand, the 1964 edition does not contain certain methodological explanations found in the 1960 edition. I decided in favor of the 1964 edition, primarily because of its availability. As a result, almost all my references will be to it; in those cases where a passage is found only in the

1960 edition, however, I will cite it. I refer to the two editions as Campbell et al., 1960, and Campbell et al., 1964.

2. Campbell et al., 1960, p. 33.

3. Campbell et al., 1964, p. 15.

4. Ibid., pp. 104–8.

5. Ibid., pp. 31–108; see especially pp. 31–33.

6. Ibid., pp. 36–48.

7. Ibid., pp. 69–72, 40–42.

8. Ibid., pp. 109–23.

9. Ibid., p. 110.

10. Ibid., pp. 124–44.

11. Ibid., p. 125. See M. Brewster Smith, Jerome S. Bruner, and Robert W. White, *Opinions and Personality* (New York: Wiley, 1956).

12. Campbell et al., 1964, pp. 33–48.

13. Ibid., pp. 27–29, 72–79.

14. Berelson et al., pp. 278–80.

15. Ibid., pp. 182–252.

16. Ibid., pp. 216, 230–32.

17. Ibid., pp. 182–234.

18. Key, pp. 62, 242.

19. Lane and Sears, pp. 17–72.

20. Campbell et al., 1964, pp. 13–64. The authors of *The American Voter* do not explain how they used content analysis in either the 1960 or 1964 editions of their book. In a separate article, however, they discuss this point thoroughly (Donald E. Stokes, Angus Campbell, and Warren E. Miller, "Components of Electoral Decision," *American Political Science Review* 52, no. 2 [1958]: 367–87).

21. Campbell et al., 1964, pp. 111–13.

22. Ibid., pp. 121–23. Herbert McClosky, "Conservatism and Personality," *American Political Science Review* 52, no. 1 (1958): 27–45.

23. Campbell et al., 1964, pp. 99–100.

24. Ibid., pp. 83–85.

25. Bernard Berelson, "Democratic Theory and Public Opinion," *Public Opinion Quarterly* 16, no. 3 (1952): 313–15, 329–330; and Paul F. Lazarsfeld, "Public Opinion and the Classical Tradition," *Public Opinion Quarterly* 21, no. 1 (1957): 39–40.

26. Berelson et al., pp. 348–62.

27. Ibid., pp. 368–80.

28. Ibid., pp. 348–62.

29. Key, pp. 21–25.

30. See, for example, Lane and Sears, pp. 31–35.

31. See, for example, David Krech, Richard S. Crutchfield, and Egerton L. Ballachey, *Individual in Society* (New York: McGraw-Hill, 1962), pp. 174–75, 210–11.

32. Campbell et al., 1964, p. 13; Berelson et al., p. 216; and Lane and Sears, p. 5.

33. Bernard Berelson, "The Study of Public Opinion," in *The State of the Social Sciences*, ed. L.D. White (Chicago: University of Chicago Press, 1956), pp. 86–102.

34. Key, pp. 3–15.

35. Berelson, "Democratic Theory and Public Opinion," pp. 329–30; and Lazarsfeld, pp. 39–41, 52–53.

36. Angus Campbell, Philip E. Converse, Warren E. Miller, and Donald E. Stokes, *Elections and the Political Order* (New York: Wiley, 1966), pp. 1–5.

37. James Bryce, *The American Commonwealth* (1888; paperback ed. New York: Capricorn Books, 1959), pp. 281–283; and Alexis de Tocqueville, *Democracy in America* (1840; paperback ed. New York: Vintage Books, 1945), 1: 365–80.

38. Survey Research Center, University of Michigan, *A Manual for Coders* (Ann Arbor: University of Michigan, Institute for Social Research, mimeographed, 1955), p. 8.

39. See, for example, Lane and Sears, pp. 43–56.

40. See, for example, Campbell et al., 1964, pp. 164–71, 184–209.

41. See, for example, Berelson et al., pp. 91–98.

42. Lane and Sears, p. 1.
43. Key, pp. 14, 409–531.
44. Lazarsfeld, p. 53.
45. Campbell et al., 1964, p. 281.
46. Ibid., pp. 3, 4.
47. See, for example, Key, p. 490.
48. See, for example, Key, pp. 500–531.
49. Campbell et al., 1964, pp. 32–33.
50. Ibid., p. 78.
51. Berelson, "Democratic Theory and Public Opinion," p. 330.

Chapter 4

1. Angus Campbell, Philip E. Converse, Warren E. Miller, and Donald E. Stokes, *The American Voter: An Abridgement* (New York: Wiley, 1964), pp. 26–33. I pointed out in footnote 1 of the preceding chapter that there are two editions of *The American Voter*. In this chapter, as in the preceding chapter, most of my references will be to the 1964 edition: the two editions will be cited as Campbell et al., 1960, and Campbell et al., 1964.
2. See, for example, Campbell et al., 1964, p. 32.
3. Campbell et al., 1960, pp. 24–33. There is no diagram of the funnel of causality in *The American Voter*. Figure 4.1 is my creation based on the discussion by Campbell et al.
4. Campbell et al., 1964, pp. 40–42.
5. Ibid., pp. 31–48, 67–108.
6. Ibid., pp. 40–43.
7. Ibid., pp. 26–33. For a discussion of how psychologists regard the differences between attitudes and the other psychological factors mentioned, see William J. McGuire, "The Nature of Attitudes and Attitude Change," in *The Handbook of Social Psychology*, ed. Gardner Lindzey and Elliot Aronson (Reading, Mass.: Addison-Wesley, 1968), pp. 150–53.
8. Campbell et al., 1964, pp. 32.
9. Ibid., p. 81.
10. Ibid., pp. 31–48. The authors of *The American Voter* do not explain exactly how they assigned and analyzed the six partisan attitudes in either the 1960 or 1964 editions of their book. They discuss both questions at length in a separate article, however (Donald E. Stokes, Angus Campbell, and Warren E. Miller, "Components of Electoral Decisions," *American Political Science Review* 52, no. 2 [1958]: 367–87).
11. Stokes et al., pp. 370–72.
12. Campbell et al., 1964, pp. 97–99.
13. Ibid., pp. 33–48.
14. Ibid., p. 38, n. 3.
15. Ibid., p. 32.
16. Ibid., p. 38, n. 3.
17. Ibid., p. 38.
18. Ibid., pp. 34–35; and Stokes et al., pp. 370–72.
19. Campbell et al., 1964, pp. 33–34.
20. Ibid., p. 34.
21. Ibid., pp. 42–48, 83–85.
22. Ibid., p. 46.
23. Ibid., pp. 36–37, 369–74; and Stokes et al., pp. 380–87.
24. For a general discussion of multiple regression analysis, see Hubert M. Blalock, *Social Statistics* (New York: McGraw-Hill, 1960), pp. 326–59. For a discussion of how Campbell et al. use multiple regression analysis, see Stokes et al., pp. 386–87.
25. Campbell et al., 1964, pp. 370–72.
26. Ibid., pp. 67–85.
27. Ibid., p. 68.
28. Ibid., pp. 80–81.

29. Ibid., p. 81.
30. Ibid., p. 78.
31. Ibid., pp. 72–85.
32. Ibid, p. 78.
33. Ibid., pp. 97–108.
34. These findings are reported in ibid., pp. 99–105.
35. These findings are reported in ibid., pp. 72–79, 105–7.
36. I have already shown that this is true of attitudes toward foreign and domestic issues and toward the group affiliations of parties and candidates. It is also true of attitudes toward the personal qualities of candidates and toward parties as managers of government. For example, an individual may be assigned a favorable attitude toward Eisenhower because he tends to approve of Eisenhower's military record, integrity, and speaking ability. Party preference can be considered a very broad or a very narrow attitude. It is assigned to an individual on the basis of his statement that he considers himself a member of a certain party, and it is not clear from this method of assignment how broad a range of consistent evaluations an individual who makes such a statement tends to make. Party preference might be a tendency to express only general statements of approval for a certain party. Campbell et al. claim, however, that party preference determines all the other evaluative tendencies which they study; as a result, they seem to regard all those tendencies as part of an individual's party preference. They seem to believe, therefore, that party preference is a very broad attitude.

Chapter 5

1. V.O. Key, Jr., *Public Opinion and American Democracy* (New York: Knopf, 1961), pp. 461–62.
2. Angus Campbell, Philip E. Converse, Warren E. Miller, and Donald E. Stokes, *The American Voter: An Abridgement* (New York: Wiley, 1964), p. 38.
3. Philip E. Converse, "The Nature of Belief Systems in Mass Publics," in *Ideology and Discontent,* ed. David E. Apter (New York: Free Press of Glencoe, 1964), pp. 245–46.
4. For reviews of some of the most famous findings about issue publics, see Key, pp. 121–52, 509–31; and Robert E. Lane, *Political Life* (New York: Free Press, 1965), pp. 195–203, 235–55. Discussions of issue publics are particularly important in pluralist theories of politics. For a statement of the pluralist position on issue publics, see Nelson W. Polsby, *Community Power and Political Theory* (New Haven, Conn.: Yale University Press, 1963), pp. 112–15.
5. Key, pp. 110–18, 509–31.
6. Ibid., 121–52, 509–31.
7. Lane, pp. 236–38, 251–55.
8. Campbell et al., 1964, pp. 161–82, 210–30. Campbell et al. argue that even though they find that the distribution of issue attitudes and voting choices is different in some economic and social groups than in the general public, it would be wrong to conclude that this is because members of these groups form issue attitudes which affect their voting choices. Rather, they conclude that these differences must be due to the fact that the distribution of long-standing party preferences in these groups is different than in the general public. They believe that these party preferences determine both issue attitudes and voting choices. The reasons for believing this which Campbell et al. present are the same as their general reasons for believing that party preference determines issue attitudes (see Chapter 6).
9. Campbell et al., 1964, pp. 36–40.
10. Ibid., p. 81.
11. In the pages that follow I neglect two other techniques which the authors of *The American Voter* use to investigate the relationship between attitudes and voting choices: analyzing the intensity of attitudes and studying their relationship to measures of political involvement. This is not because I think these two techniques are unimportant. Indeed, it is shown later that analyses of intensity are of great importance. At this point, however,

dealing with intensity and political involvement would simply lead to needless repetition. Most of what I have to say about the other parts of the argument of *The American Voter* can be extended easily to discussions of intensity and involvement, and I leave it to the reader to work out these fairly simple extensions if he wishes.

12. Campbell et al., 1964, pp. 18–26.

13. Ibid., pp. 42–48, 107.

14. Donald E. Stokes, Angus Campbell, and Warren E. Miller, "Components of Electoral Decisions," *American Political Science Review* 52, no. 2 (1958): 367–87.

15. Campbell et al., 1964, pp. 109–23.

16. Key, pp. 461–72.

17. David E. RePass, "Issue Salience and Party Choice," *American Political Science Review* 65, no. 2 (1971): 389–400. For a discussion of RePass's article, see Robert A. Brody and Benjamin I. Page, "The Assessment of Policy Voting," *American Political Science Review* 66, no. 2 (1972): 450–58.

18. RePass, p. 400.

19. Campbell et al., 1964, pp. 34–35. For reviews of some famous studies of the relationship of attitude intensity to behavior, see Muzafer Sherif and Hadley Cantril, *The Psychology of Ego-Involvements* (New York: Wiley, 1947), pp. 130–34; and Key, pp. 205–33.

20. For discussions of salience and associated concepts, see M. Brewster Smith, Jerome S. Bruner, and Robert W. White, *Opinions and Personality* (New York: Wiley, 1957), pp. 35, 259–79; Carl I. Hovland, Irving I. Janis, and Harold H. Kelly, *Communication and Persuasion* (New Haven, Conn.: Yale University Press, 1953), pp. 155–65; Sherif and Cantril, pp. 117–51; and M.L. DeFleur and F.R. Westie, "Verbal Attitudes and Overt Acts," in *Attitudes*, ed. Marie Jahoda and Neil Warren (London: Penguin Books, 1966), pp. 213–22.

21. Stokes et al., pp. 370–71.

22. Bernard R. Berelson, Paul F. Lazarsfeld, and William M. McPhee, *Voting* (Chicago: University of Chicago Press, 1954), pp. 200–202.

23. Key, pp. 173–74.

24. V.O. Key, Jr., *The Responsible Electorate* (New York: Vintage Books, 1968), p. 134.

25. Key does not actually say that almost 90% of the public who identified one problem as most important voted for the candidate who they believed could handle it best. The application of a little arithmetic to the Gallup data he reports shows this was the case, however.

26. See Hubert M. Blalock, *Social Statistics* (New York: McGraw-Hill, 1960), pp. 326–59.

27. RePass, pp. 393–394.

28. Ibid., p. 393.

29. Ibid., pp. 393–94, 400.

30. This view has recently been put strongly in Norman H. Nie, Sidney Verba, and John R. Petrocik, *The Changing American Voter* (Cambridge, Mass.: Harvard University Press, 1976).

Chapter 6

1. Angus Campbell, Philip E. Converse, Warren E. Miller, and Donald E. Stokes, *The American Voter: An Abridgement* (New York: Wiley, 1964), pp. 81, 70.

2. Ibid., pp. 88–96, 374–79; V.O. Key, Jr., *Public Opinion and American Democracy* (New York: Knopf, 1961), pp. 470–80; V.O. Key, Jr., *The Responsible Electorate* (New York: Vintage Books, 1968); and V.O. Key, Jr., "A Theory of Critical Elections," *Journal of Politics* 17, no. 1 (1955): 3–18.

3. Key, *Responsible Electorate*, pp. 34–35.

4. Campbell et al., 1964, p. 82.

5. Key, *Responsible Electorate*, pp. 43–59, 73–97, 125–46.

6. Bernard Berelson, Paul F. Lazarsfeld, and William N. McPhee, *Voting* (Chicago:

University of Chicago Press, 1954), pp. 54–75, 88–117; and Key, *Public Opinion*, pp. 121–52.

7. See, for example, Key, *Responsible Electorate*, pp. 1–8; Richard W. Boyd, "Popular Control of Public Policy: A Normal Vote Analysis of the 1968 Election," *American Political Science Review* 66, no. 2 (1972): 429–49; Philip E. Converse, "Information Flow and the Stability of Partisan Attitudes," in *Elections and the Political Order*, ed. Angus Campbell, Philip E. Converse, Warren E. Miller, and Donald E. Stokes (New York: Wiley, 1967), pp. 136–57.

8. The discussion in this paragraph is based on findings reported in Key, *Public Opinion*, pp. 432–57; V.O. Key, Jr., *Politics, Parties, and Pressure Groups* (New York: Thomas Y. Crowell, 1958); Douglass Cater, *Power in Washington* (New York: Vintage Books, 1964), pp. 179–99; Ernest S. Griffith, *The American System of Government* (London: Methuen, 1966), pp. 131–140; and Berelson et al., pp. 88–117.

9. Philip E. Converse, Warren E. Miller, Jerrold G. Rusk, and Arthur C. Wolfe, "Continuity and Change in American Politics: Parties and Issues in the 1968 Election," *American Political Science Review* 63, no. 4 (1969): 1085; and Key, *Public Opinion*, p. 509.

10. Converse et al., p. 1085; Key, *Public Opinion*, p. 523.

11. See, for example, Berelson et al., pp. 19–20, 129–32, 283–84; David Krech, Richard Crutchfield, and Egerton L. Ballachey, *Individual in Society* (New York: McGraw-Hill, 1962), pp. 495–96.

12. Robert E. Lane, *Political Life* (New York: Free Press, 1964), pp. 197–203.

13. Berelson et al., pp. 94–96, 128–32.

14. Ibid., pp. 102–15.

15. Ibid., pp. 94–102.

16. Ibid., pp. 234–52; and Key, *Public Opinion*, pp. 344–369.

17. Converse, pp. 139, 146.

18. Berelson et al., pp. 264–72.

19. One of the few studies of public perceptions of self-interest is reported in *The American Voter*. On the basis of an impressionistic analysis of answers to free-response questions, Campbell et al. conclude that perceptions of self-interest are of great importance in determining attitudes toward candidates and issues (Campbell et al., 1964, pp. 116–21).

20. For a review of studies of ideology, see Key, *Public Opinion*, pp. 151–81. See also Campbell et al., 1964, pp. 107–23; Philip E. Converse, "The Nature of Belief Systems in Mass Publics," in *Ideology and Discontent*, ed. David E. Apter (New York: Free Press, 1964), pp. 206–61; and Herbert McClosky, "Conservatism and Personality," *American Political Science Review* 52, no. 2 (1958): 27–45. For the most famous attempt to identify widely held personality traits and a critique of it, see T.W. Adorno, Else Frankel-Brunswik, David J. Levinson, and R. Nevitt Sanford, *The Authoritarian Personality* (New York: Harper, 1950); and Richard Christie and Marie Jahoda, eds., *Studies in the Scope and Method of "The Authoritarian Personality"* (Glencoe, Ill.: Free Press, 1954).

21. Robert E. Lane, *Political Ideology* (New York: Free Press, 1958); and M. Brewster Smith, Jerome S. Bruner, and Robert W. White, *Opinions and Personality* (New York: Wiley, 1956).

22. Campbell et al., 1964, pp. 105–8.

23. Ibid., p. 107.

24. Ibid., pp. 105–7.

25. Campbell et al., 1960, pp. 45–48. For the distinction between Campbell et al., 1960, and Campbell et al., 1964, see Chap. 3, n. 1.

26. After a comprehensive survey of the literature, McCombs concludes that the available evidence does not show whether the political beliefs of members of the public are often influenced by any of the selective processes I have mentioned (Maxwell E. McCombs, "Mass Communications in Political Campaigns: Information, Gratification, and Persuasion," in *Current Perspectives in Mass Communications Research*, ed. F. Gerald Kline and Philip J. Tichenor [Beverly Hills, Calif.: Sage Publications, 1972], pp. 169–94).

27. Campbell et al., 1964, pp. 76–79.

28. The only other evidence they present to support their argument about party prefer-

ence is, as pointed out previously, that degree of political involvement varies with intensity of party preference. This part of their argument has been omitted from my discussion for the sake of brevity. Findings about degree of political involvement are consistent with the alternative hypothesis I have elaborated, however. Studies have shown that both degree of involvement and intensity of party preference correlate highly with level of information. It is possible, therefore, that information flow may cause correlations between degree of involvement and intensity of party preference. See, for example, Lane, *Political Life*, pp. 192–97.

Chapter 7

1. This discussion of the American voter is based on Angus Campbell, Philip E. Converse, Warren E. Miller, and Donald E. Stokes, *The American Voter: An Abridgment* (New York: Wiley, 1964), pp. 269–90.

2. Ibid., pp. 184–209, 145–55.

3. For example, much of the American journalistic commentary on the results of the 1972 presidential election reflected the crude form of the mandate theory to some extent. See, for example, "Mr. Nixon's Victory," editorial, *New York Times*, 8 November 1972, p. 46.

4. Campbell et al., 1964, pp. 274–79. See also Philip E. Converse, "The Concept of a Normal Vote," Angus Campbell, "Surge and Decline: A Study of Electoral Change," Angus Campbell, "A Classification of the Presidential Elections," and Philip E. Converse, Angus Campbell, Warren E. Miller, and Donald E. Stokes, "Stability and Change in 1960: A Reinstating Election," in *Elections and the Political Order*, ed. Angus Campbell, Philip E. Converse, Warren E. Miller, and Donald E. Stokes (New York: Wiley, 1966), pp. 9–39, 40–62, 63–77, 78–95.

5. My statements in this and the preceding sentence are based on the articles from *Elections and the Political Order*, cited in note 4.

Chapter 8

1. See, for example, M. Brewster Smith, Jerome S. Bruner, and Robert W. White, *Opinions and Personality* (New York: Wiley, 1956); Robert E. Lane, *Political Ideology* (New York: Free Press, 1962); and Robert E. Lane and David O. Sears, *Public Opinion* (Englewood Cliffs, N.J.: Prentice-Hall, 1964), pp. 17–56.

2. Angus Campbell, Philip E. Converse, Warren E. Miller, and Donald E. Stokes, *The American Voter: An Abridgement* (New York: Wiley, 1964), pp. 34–38.

Part III

1. For Key's discussion of linkage, see V.O. Key, Jr., *Public Opinion and American Democracy* (New York: Knopf, 1961), pp. 411–531.

2. Ibid., p. 259.

Chapter 9

1. V.O. Key, Jr., *Public Opinion and American Democracy* (New York: Knopf, 1961), pp. 212–18, 428–31.

2. Ibid., p. 413.

3. Ibid., pp. 424, 212–18.

4. Ibid., p. 495.

5. Ibid., pp. 413–31, 500–531.

6. Ibid., pp. 420–22.

7. Ibid., pp. 428–31.

8. One may wonder whether members of government also use public opinion polls as an important source of information about the attitudes of their constituents. It is certainly arguable that polls provide more reliable accounts of the distribution of public issue attitudes than, for example, newspaper accounts and group leaders do. If politicians rely heavily on polls, therefore, we could be assured that they are fairly well informed about public opinion, or we could at least be assured that it is easy to identify the information they receive in particular cases. In fact, many students of government decision making report that members of government do often commission special polls and read the national polls reported in newspapers and elsewhere. After surveying the available literature about the use of polls, however, Key and Wilcox report that members of government generally mistrust them and use them only to supplement other sources of information they consider more reliable (Key, pp. 420–21; and Walter Wilcox, "The Congressional Poll—and Non-Poll," in *Political Opinion and Electoral Behavior*, ed. Edward C. Dreyer and Walter A. Rosenbaum [Belmont Calif.: Wadsworth Publishing, 1966], pp. 390–400). In addition, congressmen and other members of government who are primarily interested in the opinions of particular constituencies, rather than the entire American public, do not find most polls reported in newspapers to be useful. Moreover, they rarely have the resources to commission polls of the issue attitudes of their constituents. Most of their commissioned polls are surveys of candidate preferences at election time. As a result, for many members of government polls are not sources of information about the policy preferences of the constituencies that concern them.

Unfortunately, the studies of the use of polls that Wilcox reports are now almost 10 years old, and the studies which Key reports are older. We might, however, look at information about more modern campaign management techniques. These data are largely anecdotal, but they suggest that candidates and their managers do in fact rely on polls to a certain extent. Yet, for the most part, this reliance does not appear to be germane to the questions I am discussing. It seems that contemporary political consultants use polls for two primary purposes: to determine the popularity of their candidate and to identify issue attitudes held by members of the public so their candidate can adjust his stands on issues. The first use of polls obviously has no relationship to rule by public opinion. The second use is related to my concerns here only insofar as it is assumed that candidates will keep their campaign pledges, that those pledges cover a fairly broad spectrum of the issues they will have to address when elected, that the questions put by the polls are sufficiently specific to provide guidance to the candidate who obtains office, and that subsequent events do not change the merits of the issues at stake. All of these are highly questionable assumptions, and in light of our limited knowledge about this subject, we are not warranted in assuming that polling data have more than a marginal impact on candidates once elected. For an interesting discussion of the use of polls, see Joseph Napolitan, *The Election Game and How To Win It* (Garden City, N.Y.: Doubleday, 1972).

9. Key, pp. 421, 481–91, 535–58.

10. Ibid., p. 421.

11. See, for example, Carl J. Friedrich, *Constitutional Government and Democracy* (New York: Ginn, 1950), pp. 259–66.

12. Edmund Burke, "Speech to the Electors of Bristol: November 3, 1774," in *The Works and Correspondence of Edmund Burke* (London: Francis & John Rivington, 1852), 3: 236–37.

13. Key, pp. 438–80.

14. Another study in which it is assumed that the weak form of rule by public opinion is a process by which public issue attitudes influence government decisions is Warren E. Miller and Donald E. Stokes, "Constituency Influence in Congress," in *Elections and the Political Order*, ed. Angus Campbell, Philip E. Converse, Warren E. Miller, and Donald E. Stokes (New York: Wiley, 1966) pp. 351–72.

15. For a discussion of how elite leaders and members of the general public sometimes suggest policies to members of government, see Charles L. Clapp, *The Congressman* (Garden City, N.Y.: Anchor Books, 1963), pp. 88–89, 183–201.

16. Key, pp. 29–32, 75, 284–87.

17. Ibid., pp. 313–22.

18. Ibid., p. 423.

19. Ibid., pp. 500–531.

20. Ibid., pp. 390–95, 413–22.

21. John Johnstone, *Newsmen and Newswork* (Chicago: University of Illinois Press, 1976). For a review of other recent studies of the characteristics of journalists, see Percy H. Tannenbaum and Bradley S. Greenberg, "Mass Communication," in *Annual Review of Psychology* 19 (1968): 355–57.

22. Ben A. Bagdikian, "The Politics of American Newspapers," *Columbia Journalism Review* 10, no. 6 (1972): 8–13.

23. Walter Weiss, "Mass Communication," *Annual Review of Psychology* 22 (1971): 310–12.

24. Edith Efron, *The News Twisters* (New York: Manor Books, 1971); and Robert Cirino, *Don't Blame the People* (New York: Vintage Books, 1971). Efron's analysis has been criticized by some scholars, but no one has yet conducted a comprehensive investigation of television news that would refute her conclusions. For an analysis of limited scope that draws different conclusions, however, see Frank D. Russo, "A Study of Bias in TV Coverage of the Vietnam War: 1969 and 1970," *Public Opinion Quarterly* 35, no. 4 (1971): 539–43.

25. Key, pp. 524–31.

26. See, for example, Miller and Stokes: and Robert E. Lane and David O. Sears, *Public Opinion* (Englewood Cliffs, N.J.: Prentice-Hall, 1965), pp. 1–4.

27. Key, p. 14.

Chapter 10

1. Walter Weiss, "Mass Communication," in *Annual Review of Psychology* 22 (1971): 327.

2. Key reports a number of studies of the relationship between the views expressed by group leaders and the opinions of their constituents on particular issues: he also relates anecdotal information about how individual elite leaders did or did not accurately transmit their constituents' views in certain cases (V.O. Key, Jr., *Public Opinion and American Democracy* (New York: Knopf, 1961), pp. 508–31.

3. Probably the most famous contemporary study of the ways in which elite leaders influence mass opinion is Elihu Katz and Paul F. Lazarsfeld, *Personal Influence* (Glencoe, Ill.: Free Press, 1955). For a review of more recent studies of opinion leadership, see Weiss, pp. 323–24.

4. A number of contemporary studies suggest that the mass media may influence the broad political attitudes of the public and the frames of reference in terms of which members of the public consider political objects, but that the media do not have a great effect on popular attitudes toward particular issues or candidates. Four of the most important studies of this sort are Joseph T. Klapper, *The Effects of Mass Communications* (Glencoe, Ill.: Free Press, 1960); Kurt Lang and Gladys Engel Lang, *Politics and Television* (Chicago: Quadrangle Books, 1968); Jay G. Blumer and Denis McQuail, *Television in Politics* (Chicago: University of Chicago Press, 1969); and Maxwell E. McCombs and Donald L. Shaw, "The Agenda-Setting Function of Mass Media," *Public Opinion Quarterly* 36, no. 2 (1972): 176–87. For references to other studies of the political effects of the mass media, see Weiss, pp. 328–31, and Key, pp. 344–405.

5. Key, pp. 420–22.

6. See, for example, Charles L. Clapp, *The Congressman* (Garden City, N.Y.: Anchor Books, 1963), pp. 183–206; Douglass Cater, *Power in Washington* (New York: Vintage Books, 1964), pp. 199–253; and Douglass Cater, *The Fourth Branch of Government* (Boston: Houghton Mifflin, 1959).

7. Key, pp. 35–36, 278.

8. Warren E. Miller and Donald E. Stokes, "Constituency Influence in Congress," in

Angus Campbell, Philip E. Converse, Warren E. Miller, and Donald E. Stokes, *Elections and the Political Order* (New York: Wiley, 1966), pp. 351–72.

9. Ibid., p. 358, n. 10.

10. Ibid., p. 359.

11. Ibid., p. 360.

12. Ibid.

13. Ibid., p. 361.

14. Ibid.

15. Ibid., p. 362.

16. Ibid., p. 363.

17. Ibid.

18. Ibid., pp. 363–66.

19. Ibid., p. 364.

20. Ibid.

21. Ibid., pp. 365–66.

22. Ibid., p. 364.

23. Ibid.

24. Ibid., pp. 364–65, n. 14.

25. See, for example, *Survey of Broadcast Journalism: 1972,* ed. Marvin W. Barrett (New York: Columbia University Press, 1972), pp. 3–72.

26. For references to several studies that attempt to show whether public opinion influences government by correlating government action with constituency views, see Key, pp. 482–91. A study that uses the same techniques employed by Miller and Stokes is Charles F. Cnudde and Donald J. McCrone, "The Linkage Between Constituency Attitudes and Congressional Voting Behavior," *American Political Science Review* 60, no. 2 (1966): 66–72.

Chapter 11

1. Heinz Eulau, John G. Wahlke, William Buchanan, and LeRoy C. Ferguson, "The Rule of the Representative: Some Empirical Observations on the Theory of Edmund Burke," *American Political Science Review* 53, no. 3 (1959): 742–56; V.O. Key, Jr., *Public Opinion and American Democracy* (New York: Knopf, 1964).

2. Key, *Public Opinion,* pp. 27–39, 59–76, 85–93, 212–18, 228–33.

3. Angus Campbell, Philip E. Converse, Warren E. Miller, and Donald E. Stokes, *The American Voter: An Abridgement* (New York: Wiley, 1964), pp. 280–85.

4. See, for example, Charles L. Clapp, *The Congressman* (Garden City, N.Y.: Anchor Books, 1963), pp. 186–203; and Douglass Cater, *Power in Washington* (New York: Vintage Books, 1964), pp. 199–253.

5. I think this is what most political theorists mean by democratic or popular government when they refer to those kinds of political systems generically. They may differ, however, about precisely what controls members of the public do or should exercise over government and how those controls are or should be exercised when they describe operating democratic systems or prescribe what kinds of democratic systems should be established. However, I am not concerned here with differences between political theorists about what form democratic systems do or should take. I am concerned only with whether certain characteristics of political systems fit under the broad rubric of a generic definition of democracy; that is, I am concerned with whether *someone* might say that they are characteristics of a democratic system without greatly abusing the concept of democracy. Whether these characteristics of political systems might be considered characteristics of democratic government according to specific theories of politics is discussed later in this chapter.

6. James Bryce, *The American Commonwealth* (1888; paperback ed. New York: Capricorn Books, 1959), p. 298 (first two quotes) and p. 335.

7. Ibid., pp. 283, 359.

8. See, for example, Carl J. Friedrich, *Constitutional Government and Democracy*

(New York: Ginn, 1950), pp. 259–324; and Alfred DeGrazia, "Representation: Theory," in *The International Encyclopaedia of Social Sciences* (London: Macmillan, 1968), 13: 461–68.

Part IV

1. Bernard Berelson, "Democratic Theory and Public Opinion," *Public Opinion Quarterly* 16, no. 3 (1952): 313–14.
2. Ibid., p. 330.

Bibliography

Books

Adorno, T.W., Else Frenkel-Brunswik, Daniel J. Levinson, and R. Nevitt Sanford (in collaboration with Betty Aron, Maria Hertz Levinson, and William Morrow). *The Authoritarian Personality*. New York: Harper and Brothers, 1950.

Albig, William. *Public Opinion*. New York: McGraw-Hill, 1939.

Allport, Gordon W. *Personality: A Psychological Interpretation*. London: Constable and Co., 1949.

————, and Leo Postman. *The Psychology of Rumor*. New York: Russell and Russell, 1965.

Anastasi, Anne. *Psychological Testing*. 2nd ed. New York: Macmillan, 1961.

Angell, Norman. *The Public Mind: Its Disorders: Its Exploitation*. London: Unwin (Noel Douglas), 1926.

Asch, Solomon E. *Social Psychology*. New York: Prentice-Hall, 1952.

Bagehot, Walter. *The English Constitution*. 1866. Reprint. London: Kegan Paul, Trench, Trubner and Co., 1929.

Barrett, Marvin W., ed. *Survey of Broadcast Journalism: 1972*. New York: Columbia University Press, 1972.

Barry, Brian. *Political Argument*. London: Routledge and Kegan Paul, 1965.

Bentham, Jeremy. *Securities against Misrule, Adapted to a Mohammedan State*. In *The Works of Jeremy Bentham*, edited by John Bowring. Vol. 8. 1823. Reprint. New York: Russell and Russell, 1962.

Bentley, Arthur F. *The Process of Government*. Evanston: Principia Press of Illinois, 1949.

Berelson, Bernard. *Content Analysis in Communications Research*. Glencoe, Ill.: Free Press, 1952.

————,ed. *The Behavioral Sciences Today*. New York: Harper and Row, Harper Torchbooks, 1964.

————, and Morris Janowitz, eds. *Reader in Public Opinion and Communication*. Enlarged edition. Glencoe, Ill.: Free Press, 1953.

Berelson, Bernard, Paul F. Lazarsfeld, and William N. McPhee. *Voting: A Study of Opinion Formation in a Presidential Campaign*. Chicago: University of Chicago Press, 1954.

Birch, A.H. *Representative and Responsible Government: An Essay on the British Constitution*. London: Allen and Unwin, 1964.

Blalock, Hubert M. *Social Statistics*. New York: McGraw-Hill, 1960.

Blondel, Jean. *Voters, Parties and Leaders: The Social Fabric of British Politics*. 4th printing, revised. London: Penguin Books, 1967.

Blumer, Jay G. and Denis McQuail. *Television in Politics*. Chicago: University of Chicago Press, 1969.

Braithwaite, R.B. *Scientific Explanation: A Study of the Function of Theory, Probability and Law in Science*. 1st paperback edition. Cambridge, England: Cambridge University Press, 1968.

Brehm, Jack W., and Arthur R. Cohen. *Explorations in Cognitive Dissonance*. New York: John Wiley and Sons, 1962.

Brown, J.A.C. *Techniques of Persuasion: From Propaganda to Brainwashing*. London: Penguin Books, 1963.

Bryce, James. *Modern Democracies*. London: Macmillan, 1921.

———. *The American Commonwealth*, edited, abridged, and introduced by Louis M. Hacker. 2 volumes. 1888. Paperback edition. New York: Putnam, Capricorn Books, 1959.

Burdick, Eugene, and Arthur J. Brodbeck, eds. *American Voting Behavior*. Glencoe, Ill.: Free Press, 1959.

Campbell, Angus, Philip E. Converse, Warren E. Miller, and Donald E. Stokes. *The American Voter*. Survey Research Center, University of Michigan. New York: John Wiley and Sons, 1960.

———. *The American Voter: An Abridgement*. New York: John Wiley and Sons, 1964.

———. *Elections and the Political Order*. New York: John Wiley and Sons, 1966.

Cantril, Hadley. *The Psychology of Social Movements*. New York: John Wiley and Sons, 1941.

———. *Gauging Public Opinion*. Princeton, N.J.: Princeton University Press, 1944.

Cater, Douglass. *The Fourth Branch of Government*. Boston: Houghton Mifflin, 1959.

———. *Power in Washington*. New York: Vintage Books, 1964.

Cattell, Raymond B. *The Scientific Analysis of Personality*. London: Penguin Books, 1965.

Childs, Harwood L. *An Introduction to the Study of Public Opinion*. New York: John Wiley and Sons, 1940.

———. *Public Opinion: Nature, Formation and Role*. New York: Van Nostrand Reinhold, 1965.

Christie, Richard, and Marie Jahoda, eds. *Studies in the Scope and Method of "The Authoritarian Personality": Continuities in Social Research*. Glencoe, Ill.: Free Press, 1954.

Cirino, Robert. *Don't Blame the People*. New York: Random House, Vintage Books, 1971.

Clapp, Charles L. *The Congressman*. Garden City, N.Y.: Doubleday and Co., Anchor Books, 1963.

Cohen, Arthur R. *Attitude Change and Social Influences*. New York: Basic Books, 1964.

Coombs, Clyde H. "Scaling and Data Theory." Unpublished manuscript, University of Michigan, 1966.

Deutsch, J.A. *The Structural Basis of Behavior*. 2nd impression. Cambridge, England: Cambridge University Press, 1964.

Dewey, John. *The Public and Its Problems*. Denver: Alan Swallow, 1954.

Dicey, A.V. *Lectures on the Relation Between Law and Public Opinion in England During the Nineteenth Century*. London: Macmillan, 1963.

Doob, Leonard W. *Public Opinion and Propaganda*. New York: Holt and Co., 1948.

Dreyer, Edward C., and Walter A. Rosenbaum, eds. *Political Opinion and Electoral Behavior: Essays and Studies*. Belmont, Calif.: Wadsworth Publishing Co., 1966.

Duverger, Maurice. *Political Parties: Their Organization and Activity in the Modern State*, translated by Barbara North and Robert North. 2nd English edition revised. New York: John Wiley and Sons, 1963.

Edwards, Allen L. *Techniques of Attitude Scale Construction*. New York: Appleton-Century-Crofts, 1957.

Efron, Edith. *The News Twisters*. New York: Manor Books, 1971.

Emden, Cecil E. *The People and the Constitution*. 2nd ed. London: Oxford University Press, 1956.

Eulau, Heinz. *The Behavioral Persuasion in Politics*. New York: Random House, 1963.

————, Samuel J. Eldersveld, and Morris Janowitz. *Political Behavior: A Reader in Theory and Research.* Glencoe, Ill.: Free Press, 1956.

Eysenck, H.J. *The Psychology of Politics.* London: Routledge and Kegan Paul, 1954.

Festinger, Leon. *A Theory of Cognitive Dissonance.* London: Tavistock Publications, 1959.

Friedrich, Carl J. *Constitutional Government and Democracy.* New York: Ginn and Co., 1950.

————. *Man and His Government.* New York: McGraw-Hill, 1963.

Gallup, George, and Saul F. Rae. *The Pulse of Democracy: The Public Opinion Poll and How it Works.* New York: Simon and Schuster, 1940.

Griffith, Ernest S. *The American System of Government.* London: Methuen and Co., 1966.

Halloran, J.D. *Attitude Formation and Change.* Leicester, England: Leicester University Press, for the Television Research Committee, 1967.

Hampshire, Stuart. *Thought and Action.* 2nd impression. London: Chatto and Windus, 1960.

Hegel, G.W.F. *Philosophy of Right,* translated by T.M. Knox. 1821. Reprint. London: Oxford University Press, 1952; paperback, 1967.

Heider, Fritz. *The Psychology of Interpersonal Relations.* New York: John Wiley and Sons, 1967.

Hempel, Carl G. *Philosophy of Natural Science.* Englewood Cliffs, N.J.: Prentice-Hall, 1966.

Horst, Paul. *Psychological Measurement and Prediction.* Belmont, Calif.: Wadsworth Publishing Co., 1966.

Hovland, Carl I., and Irving L. Janis. *Personality and Persuasibility.* New Haven, Conn.: Yale University Press, 1959.

————, and Harold H. Kelley. *Communication and Persuasion: Psychological Studies of Opinion Change.* New Haven, Conn.: Yale University Press, 1953.

Jahoda, Marie, and Neil Warren, eds. *Attitudes: Selected Readings.* London: Penguin Books, 1966.

Johnstone, John. *Newsmen and Newswork.* Chicago: University of Illinois Press, 1976.

Katz, Daniel, Dorwin Cartwright, Samuel Eldersveld, and Alfred McClung Lee, eds. *Public Opinion and Propaganda: A Book of Readings Edited for the Psychological Study of Social Issues.* New York: Holt, Rinehart and Winston, 1965.

Katz, Elihu, and Paul F. Lazarsfeld. *Personal Influence.* Glencoe, Ill.: Free Press, 1955.

Key, V.O., Jr. *Politics, Parties and Pressure Groups.* New York: Thomas Y. Crowell, 1958.

————. *Public Opinion and American Democracy.* New York: Alfred A. Knopf, 1961.

————. *The Responsible Electorate: Rationality in Presidential Voting, 1956–1960.* New York: Random House, Vintage Books, 1968.

Klapper, Joseph T. *The Effects of Mass Communications.* Glencoe, Ill.: Free Press, 1960.

Klineberg, Otto. *Social Psychology.* New York: Henry Holt and Co., 1940.

Krech, David, and Egerton L. Ballachey. *Individual in Society: A Textbook of Social Psychology.* New York: McGraw-Hill, 1962.

Krech, David, and Richard S. Crutchfield. *Theory and Problems of Social Psychology.* New York: McGraw-Hill, 1948.

Lane, Robert E. *Political Ideology: Why the American Common Man Believes What He Does.* New York: Free Press of Glencoe; London and New York: Macmillan, 1962.

————. *Political Life: Why and How People Get Involved in Politics.* New York: Free Press, 1959; paperback, 1964.

————, and David O. Sears. *Public Opinion*. Englewood Cliffs, N.J.: Prentice-Hall, Foundations of Political Science Series, 1965.

Lang, Kurt, and Gladys Engel Lang. *Politics and Television*. Chicago: Quadrangle Books, 1968.

Lazarus, Richard S., and Edward M. Opton, Jr., eds. *Personality: Selected Readings*. London: Penguin Books, 1967.

Lippmann, Walter. *Public Opinion*. New York: Macmillan, 1922; paperback, 1960.

————. *The Phantom Public*. New York: Harcourt, Brace and Co., 1925.

Lipset, Seymour Martin. *Political Man*. New York: Doubleday and Co., Anchor Books, 1963.

Locke, John. *An Essay Concerning Human Understanding*. 1690. Reprint. New York: Dover Publications, 1959.

Lowell, A. Lawrence. *Public Opinion and Popular Government*. 2nd ed. New York: Longmans, 1914.

McPhee, William N., and William A. Glaser. *Public Opinion and Congressional Elections*. New York: Free Press of Glencoe, 1962.

A Manual for Coders. Survey Research Center, University of Michigan. Mimeographed. Ann Arbor: University of Michigan, Institute for Social Research, 1955.

Miller, George A. *Psychology: The Science of Mental Life*. London: Hutchinson, 1964.

Murphy, Gardner. *An Historical Introduction to Modern Psychology*. 4th ed., revised. London: Kegan Paul, Trench, Trubner and Co., 1938.

————, and Rensis Likert. *Public Opinion and the Individual: A Psychological Study of Student Attitudes on Public Questions, with a Retest Five Years Later*. New York: Russell and Russell, 1967.

Newcomb, Theodore M. *Personality and Social Change: Attitude Formation in a Student Community*. New York: Holt, Rinehart and Winston, 1943.

Nie, Norman H., Sidney Verba, and John R. Petrocik. *The Changing American Voter*. Cambridge, Mass.: Harvard University Press, 1976.

Osgood, C.E., G.J. Suci, and P.M. Tannenbaum. *The Measurement of Meaning*. Urbana: University of Illinois Press, 1957.

Parten, Mildred B. *Surveys, Polls and Samples*. New York: Harper and Row, 1965.

Polsby, Nelson W. *Community Power and Political Theory*. New Haven, Conn.: Yale University Press, 1963.

Remmers, H.H. *Introduction to Opinion and Attitude Measurement*. New York: Harper and Brothers, 1954.

Riker, William H. *Democracy in the United States*. 2nd ed. New York: Macmillan, 1965.

Robinson, John P., Jerrold G. Rusk, and Kendra B. Head. *Measures of Political Attitudes*. Ann Arbor, Michigan: Institute for Survey Research, 1968.

Rogers, Lindsay. *The Pollsters: Public Opinion, Politics, and Democratic Leadership*. New York: Alfred A. Knopf, 1949.

Rokeach, Milton. *The Open and Closed Mind: Investigations into the Nature of Belief Systems and Personality Systems*. New York: Basic Books, 1960.

Rosenau, James N. *Public Opinion and Foreign Policy: An Operational Formulation*. New York: Random House, 1961.

Rosenberg, Milton J., Carl I. Hovland, William J. McGuire, Robert P. Albelson, and Jack W. Brehm. *Attitude Organization and Change: An Analysis of Consistency Among Attitude Components*. New Haven, Conn.: Yale University Press, 1960.

Rousseau, Jean-Jacques. *Du Contrat Social: ou principes du droit politique (The Social*

Contract and Discourses), translated by G.D.H. Cole. 1762. Reprint. New York: E.P. Dutton and Co., 1950.

Rudner, Richard S. *Philosophy of Social Science.* Englewood Cliffs, N.J.: Prentice-Hall, 1966.

Ryle, Gilbert. *The Concept of Mind.* London: Penguin Books, 1966.

Sabine, George H. *A History of Political Theory.* 3rd ed. New York: Holt, Rinehart and Winston, 1961.

Secord, Paul F., and Carl W. Backman. *Social Psychology.* New York: McGraw-Hill, International Student Edition, 1964.

Shaw, Marvin E., and Jack M. Wright. *Scales for the Measurement of Attitudes.* New York: McGraw-Hill, 1967.

Sherif, Muzafer, and Hadley Cantril. *The Psychology of Ego-Involvements: Social Attitudes and Identifications.* New York: John Wiley and Sons, 1947.

————, and Carl I. Hovland. *Social Judgment: Assimilation and Contrast Effects in Communication and Attitude Change.* New Haven, Conn.: Yale University Press, 1961.

Smith, M. Brewster, Jerome S. Bruner, and Robert W. White. *Opinions and Personality.* New York: John Wiley and Sons, 1956.

Storing, Herbert J., ed. *Essays on the Scientific Study of Politics.* New York: Holt, Rinehart and Winston, 1962.

Stouffer, Samuel A., Louis Guttman, Edward A. Suchman, Paul F. Lazarsfeld, Shirley S. Star, and John A. Clausen, eds. *Measurement and Prediction.* Princeton, N.J.: Princeton University Press, 1950.

Thurstone, L.L., and E.J. Chave. *The Measurement of Attitudes.* Chicago: University of Chicago Press, 1929.

Tocqueville, Alexis de. *Democracy in America,* translated by Henry Reeve. 2 Vols. 1840. Reprint. New York: Random House, Vintage Books, 1945.

Tönnies, Ferdinand. *Community and Association (Gemeinschaft und Gesellschaft),* translated and supplemented by Charles P. Loomis. 1887. Reprint. London: Routledge and Kegan Paul, 1965.

Torgenson, Warren F. *Theory and Methods of Scaling.* New York: John Wiley and Sons, 1958.

Truman, David. *The Governmental Process.* New York: Alfred A. Knopf, 1951.

Vernon, Philip E. *Personality Tests and Assessments.* London: Methuen, 1962.

Wallas, Graham. *Human Nature in Politics.* 2nd ed. London: Constable, 1910.

————. *The Great Society: A Psychological Analysis.* New York: Macmillan, 1917.

Wilson, Francis Graham. *A Theory of Public Opinion.* Chicago: Henry Regnery Co., 1962.

Articles

Allport, Floyd. "Toward a Science of Public Opinion." *Public Opinion Quarterly* 1, no. 1 (1937):7–23.

Allport, G.W. "Attitudes." In *Handbook of Social Psychology,* edited by C.M. Murchison, pp. 798–844. Worcester, Mass.: Clarke University Press, 1935.

————. "The Historical Background of Modern Social Psychology." In *Handbook of Social Psychology,* edited by Gardner Lindzey, pp. 3–56. Cambridge, Mass.: Addison-Wesley, 1954.

Asch, Solomon E. "Perspective on Social Psychology." In *Psychology: A Study of a Science,* edited by Sigmund Koch. Formulations of the Person and the Social Context, Vol. 3, pp. 363–83. New York: McGraw-Hill, 1959.

Axelrod, Robert. "The Structure of Public Opinion on Policy Issues." *Public Opinion Quarterly* 31, no. 1 (1967):51–61.

Bagdikian, Ben A. "The Politics of American Newspapers." *Columbia Journalism Review* 10, no. 6 (1972):8–13.

Bauer, Wilhelm. "Public Opinion." In *Encyclopedia of the Social Sciences,* Vol. 12, pp. 669–74. New York: Macmillan, 1948.

Berelson, Bernard. "Democratic Theory and Public Opinion." *Public Opinion Quarterly* 16, no. 3 (1952):313–30.

———. "The Study of Public Opinion." In *The State of the Social Sciences,* edited by L.D. White, pp. 86–102. Chicago: University of Chicago Press, 1956.

Blumer, Herbert. "Public Opinion and Public Opinion Polling." *American Sociological Review,* 13 (1948):542–54.

Boyd, Richard W. "Popular Control of Public Policy: A Normal Vote Analysis of the 1968 Election." *American Political Science Review* 66, no. 2 (1972):429–49.

Brody, Robert A., and Benjamin I. Page. "The Assessment of Policy Voting." *American Political Science Review* 66, no. 2 (1972):450–58.

Brown, Roger. "Models of Attitude Change." In *New Directions in Psychology,* edited by T.M. Newcomb, pp. 56–89. New York: Henry Holt and Co., 1963.

Burke, Edmund. "Reflections on the Revolution in France and on the Proceedings in Certain Societies in London Relative to that Event." In *The Works and Correspondence of Edmund Burke,* Vol. 4, pp. 149–355. London: Francis and John Rivington, 1852.

———. "Speech to the Electors of Bristol: November 3rd, 1774." In *The Works and Correspondence of Edmund Burke,* Vol. 3, pp. 232–37. London: Francis and John Rivington, 1852.

Campbell, Angus. "A Classification of the Presidential Elections." In *Elections and the Political Order,* edited by Angus Campbell et al., pp. 63–77. New York: John Wiley and Sons, 1966.

———. "Surge and Decline: A Study of Electoral Change." In *Elections and the Political Order,* edited by Angus Campbell et al., pp. 40–62. New York: John Wiley and Sons, 1966.

Campbell, Donald T. "Acquired Behavioral Dispositions." In *Psychology: A Study of a Science,* edited by Sigmund Koch, Vol. 6, pp. 94–172. New York: McGraw-Hill, 1963.

Chein, Isidor. "Behavior Theory and the Behavior of Attitudes." *Psychological Review* 60, no. 3 (1948):175–87.

Cnudde, Charles F., and Donald J. McCrone. "The Linkage between Constituency Attitudes and Congressional Voting Behavior." *American Political Science Review* 60, no. 2 (1966):66–72.

Cohen, Arthur. "Attitudinal Consequences of Induced Discrepancies Between Cognitions and Behavior." *Public Opinion Quarterly* 24, no. 2 (1960):297–318.

Converse, Philip E. "The Nature of Belief Systems in Mass Publics." In *Ideology and Discontent,* edited by David E. Apter, pp. 206–61. New York: Free Press of Glencoe, 1964.

———. "The Concept of a Normal Vote." In *Elections and the Political Order,* edited by Angus Campbell et al., pp. 9–39. New York: John Wiley and Sons, 1966.

———. "Information Flow and the Stability of Partisan Attitudes." In *Elections and the Political Order,* edited by Angus Campbell et al., pp. 136–58. New York: John Wiley and Sons, 1966.

———, Angus Campbell, Warren E. Miller, and Donald E. Stokes. "Stability and Change in 1960: A Reinstating Election." In *Elections and the Political Order,* edited by Angus Campbell et al., pp. 78–95. New York: John Wiley and Sons, 1966.

————, Warren E. Miller, Jerrold G. Rusk, and Arthur C. Wolfe. "Continuity and Change in American Politics: Parties and Issues in the 1968 Election." *American Political Science Review* 63, no. 4 (1969):1083–1105.

Cooper, J.B., and J.L. McGaugh. "Attitudes and Related Concepts." In *Attitudes,* edited by Marie Jahoda and Neil Warren, pp. 26–31. London: Penguin Books, 1966.

Crespi, Irving. "What Kinds of Attitude Measures are Predictive of Behavior?" *Public Opinion Quarterly* 35, no. 3 (1972):327–34.

Davison, W. Philip. "The Public Opinion Process." *Public Opinion Quarterly* 22, no. 2 (1958): 91–106.

DeFleur, M.L., and F.R. Westie. "Verbal Attitudes and Overt Acts." In *Attitudes,* edited by Marie Jahoda and Neil Warren, pp. 213–22. London: Penguin Books, 1966.

DeGrazia, Alfred. "Representation: Theory." In *The International Encyclopaedia of Social Sciences,* Vol. 13, pp. 461–68. London: Macmillan, 1968.

Dollard, John. "Under What Conditions Do Opinions Predict Behavior?" *Public Opinion Quarterly* 12, no. 4 (1949):623–32.

Duncan, Graeme, and Steven Lukes. "The New Democracy." *Political Studies* 11, no. 2 (1963):156–77.

Eulau, Heinz, John G. Wahlke, William Buchanan, and Leroy C. Ferguson. "The Role of the Representative: Some Empirical Observations on the Theory of Edmund Burke." *American Political Science Review* 53, no. 3 (1959):742–56.

Festinger, Leon. "Behavioral Support for Opinion Change." *Public Opinion Quarterly* 28, no. 3 (1964):404–17.

Fleming, Donald. "Attitude: The History of a Concept." In *Perspectives in American History,* edited by Donald Fleming and Bernard Bailyn, Vol. 1, pp. 287–365. Cambridge, Mass.: Charles Warren Center for Studies in American History, 1967.

Glickman, Harvey. "Viewing Public Opinion in Politics: A Common Sense Approach." *Public Opinion Quarterly* 23, no. 4 (1959):495–506.

Gordon, Raymond L. "Interaction between Attitude and the Definition of the Situation in the Expression of Opinion." In *Public Opinion and Propaganda,* edited by Daniel Katz et al., pp. 425–34. New York: Holt, Rinehart and Winston, 1965.

Guttman, Louis. "The Basic for Scalogram Analysis." In *Measurement and Prediction,* edited by Samuel A. Stouffer et al., pp. 60–90. Princeton, N.J.: Princeton University Press, 1950.

————. "The Problem of Attitude and Opinion Measurement." In *Measurement and Prediction,* edited by Samuel A. Stouffer et al., pp. 46–59. Princeton, N.J.: Princeton University Press, 1950.

————. "The Scalogram Board Technique for Scale Analysis." In *Measurement and Prediction,* edited by Samuel A. Stouffer et al., pp. 91–121. Princeton, N.J.: Princeton University Press, 1950.

Hovland, Carl I. "Reconciling Conflicting Results Derived from Experimental and Survey Studies of Attitude Change." *Amercan Psychologist* 14, no. 1 (1959):8–17.

Hyman, Herbert. "Toward a Theory of Public Opinion." *Public Opinion Quarterly* 21, no. 1 (1957):54–60.

Katz, Daniel. "The Functional Approach to the Study of Attitudes." *Public Opinion Quarterly* 24, no. 2 (1960):180–87.

————, and Ezra Stotland. "A Preliminary Statement to a Theory of Attitude Structure and Change." In *Psychology: A Study of a Science,* edited by Sigmund Koch. Formulations of the Person and the Social Context, Vol. 3, pp. 423–75. New York: McGraw-Hill, 1959.

Kelman, H.C. "Processes of Opinion Change." *Public Opinion Quarterly* 25, no. 1 (1961): 57–78.

Key, V.O., Jr. "A Theory of Critical Elections." *Journal of Politics* 17, no. 1 (1955): 3–18.

———. "The Politically Relevant in Surveys." *Public Opinion Quarterly* 24, no. 1 (1960): 54–61.

———. "Public Opinion and the Decay of Democracy." In *Political Opinion and Electoral Behavior*, edited by Edward C. Dreyer and Walter A. Rosenbaum, pp. 412–20. Belmont, Calif.: Wadsworth Publishing Co., 1966.

Koch, Sigmund. "Some Trends of Study I (Vols. 1–3), Epilogue." In *Psychology: A Study of a Science*, edited by Sigmund Koch, Vol. 3, pp. 733–43. New York: McGraw-Hill, 1959.

LaPierre, R.T. "Attitudes vs. Actions." *Social Forces* 14, no. 2 (1934):230–37.

Lasswell, Harold, and Abraham Kaplan. "Publics, Public Opinion and General Interests." In *Public Opinion and Propaganda*, edited by Daniel Katz et al., pp. 66–70. New York: Holt, Rinehart and Winston, 1965.

Lazarsfeld, Paul F. "The Logical and Mathematical Foundation of Latent Structure Analysis." In *Measurement and Prediction*, edited by Samuel A. Stouffer et al., pp. 362–412. Princeton, N.J.: Princeton University Press, 1950.

———. "Interpretation of Statistical Relations as a Research Operation." In *The Language of Social Research*, edited by Paul F. Lazarsfeld and Morris Rosenberg, pp. 115–25. Glencoe, Ill.: Free Press, 1955.

———. "Public Opinion and the Classical Tradition." *Public Opinion Quarterly* 21, no. 1 (1957):39–53.

Leiserson, Avery. "Political Opinion." In *The International Encyclopaedia of Social Sciences*. Vol. 13, pp. 197–204. London: Macmillan, 1968.

McClosky, Herbert. "Conservatism and Personality." *American Political Science Review* 52, no. 1 (1958):27–45.

———, Paul J. Hoffman, and Rosemary O'Hara. "Issue Conflict and Consensus Among Party Leaders and Followers." *American Political Science Review* 54, no. 3 (1960): 406–27.

Maccoby, Nathan, and Eleanor E. Maccoby. "Homeostatic Theory in Attitude Change." *Public Opinion Quarterly* 25, no. 4 (1961):538–45.

McCombs, Maxwell E., and Donald L. Shaw. "The Agenda-Setting Function of Mass Media." *Public Opinion Quarterly* 36, no. 2 (1972):176–87.

McGuire, William J. "Cognitive Consistency and Attitude Change." *Journal of Abnormal and Social Psychology* 60, no. 2 (1960):345–53.

———. "The Nature of Attitudes and Attitude Change." In *The Handbook of Social Psychology*, edited by Gardner Lindzey and Elliot Aronson, pp. 136–314. Reading, Mass.: Addison-Wesley, 1968.

McPhee, William N., Bo Anderson, and Harry Milholland. "Attitude Consistency." In *Public Opinion and Congressional Elections*, edited by William N. McPhee and William A. Glaser, pp. 78–122. New York: Free Press of Glencoe, 1962.

Mill, John Stuart. "On Liberty." In *Utilitarianism, Liberty and Representative Government*, pp. 152–200. 1859. Reprint. New York: E.P. Dutton and Co, 1951.

———. "Representative Government." In *Utilitarianism, Liberty and Representative Government*, pp. 235–532. 1861. Reprint. New York: E.P. Dutton and Co., 1951.

Miller, Warren E., and Donald E. Stokes. "Constituency Influence in Congress." In *Elections and the Political Order*, edited by Angus Campbell et al., pp. 351–72. New York: John Wiley and Sons, 1966.

Palmer, Paul A. "The Concept of Public Opinion in Political Theory." In *Essays in History and Political Theory in Honor of Charles Howard McIlwain*, pp. 230–57. Cambridge, Mass.: Harvard University Press, 1936.

Plamenatz, John. "Electoral Studies and Democratic Theory: A British View." *Political Studies* 6, no. 1 (1958):1–15.

Protho, James W., and Charles M. Grigg. "Fundamental Principles of Democracy: Bases of Agreement and Disagreement." *Journal of Politics* 22, no. 2 (1960):276–94.

RePass, David E. "Issue Salience and Party Choice." *American Political Science Review* 65, no. 2 (1971):389–400.

Rokeach, Milton. "Attitude Change and Behavioral Change." *Public Opinion Quarterly,* 30, no. 4 (1966):429–50.

Rosenberg, Milton J. "An Analysis of Affective-Cognitive Consistency." In *Attitude Organization and Change,* edited by Carl I. Hovland and Milton J. Rosenberg, pp. 15–65. New Haven, Conn.: Yale University Press, 1960.

———, and Robert P. Abelson. "An Analysis of Cognitive Balancing." In *Attitude Organization and Change,* edited by Carl I. Hovland and Milton J. Rosenberg, pp. 112–63. New Haven, Conn.: Yale University Press, 1960.

Russo, Frank D. "A Study of Bias in TV Coverage of the Vietnam War: 1969 and 1970." *Public Opinion Quarterly* 35, no. 4 (1971):539–43.

Sartori, Giovanni. "Representational Systems." In *International Encyclopedia of Social Sciences,* Vol. 13, pp. 465–73. London: Macmillan, 1968.

Schuman, Howard. "Attitudes vs. Actions *versus* Attitudes vs. Attitudes." *Public Opinion Quarterly* 36, no. 3 (1972):347–54.

Smith, M. Brewster. "Attitude Change." In *International Encyclopedia of Social Sciences,* Vol. 1, pp. 458–67. New York: Macmillan, 1968.

Speier, Hans. "The Historical Development of Public Opinion." In *Social Order and the Risks of War,* by Hans Speier, pp. 323–38. New York: George Stewart, 1952.

Stokes, Donald E., Angus Campbell, and Warren E. Miller. "Components of Electoral Decisions." *American Political Science Review* 52, no. 2 (1958):367–87.

Stouffer, Samuel A. "An Overview of the Contributions to Scaling and Scale Theory." In *Measurement and Prediction,* edited by Samuel A. Stouffer et al., pp. 3–45. Princeton, N.J.: Princeton University Press, 1950.

Suchman, Edward A. "The Intensity Component in Attitude and Opinion Research." In *Measurement and Prediction,* edited by Samuel A. Stouffer et al., pp. 213–76. Princeton, N.J.: Princeton University Press, 1950.

———. "The Utility of Scalogram Analysis." In *Measurement and Prediction,* edited by Samuel A. Stouffer et al., pp. 22–171. Princeton, N.J.: Princeton University Press, 1950.

Tannenbaum, Percy H., and Bradley S. Greenberg. "Mass Communication." *Annual Review of Psychology* 19 (1968):351–86.

Thurstone, L.L. "A Law of Comparative Judgement." *Psychological Review* 34, no. 1 (1927):273–86.

———. "Attitudes Can Be Measured." *American Journal of Sociology* 33, no. 4 (1928): 529–54.

Turner, Henry A. "Woodrow Wilson and Public Opinion." *Public Opinion Quarterly* 21, no. 4 (1957):505–20.

Vernon, Philip E. "The Concept of Validity in Personality Study." In *Personality Assessment,* edited by Boris Semenoff, pp. 407–24. London: Penguin Books, 1966.

Watt, D.C. "Public Opinion." In *A Dictionary of the Social Sciences,* pp. 563–64. London: Tavistock, 1964.

Weinstein, Alan G. "Predicting Behavior from Attitudes." *Public Opinion Quarterly* 36, no. 3 (1972):355–60.

Weiss, Walter. "Mass Communication." *Annual Review of Psychology* 22 (1971):309–36.

Young, Kimball. "Comments on the Nature of 'Public' and 'Public Opinion.' " In *Public Opinion and Propaganda,* edited by Daniel Katz et al., pp. 62–66. New York: Holt, Rinehart and Winston, 1965.

Zajonc, Robert B. "Balance, Congruity, Dissonance." In *Attitudes,* edited by Marie Jahoda and Neil Warren, pp. 261–78. London: Penguin Books, 1966.

Index